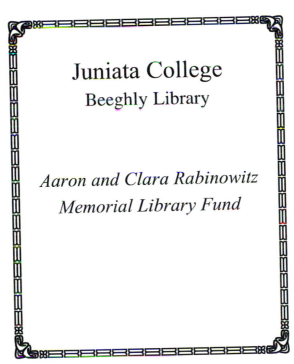

Modern Critical Views

Modern Critical Views

JEAN-PAUL SARTRE

Edited and with an introduction by
Harold Bloom
Sterling Professor of the Humanities
Yale University

CHELSEA HOUSE
P U B L I S H E R S
An imprint of Infobase Publishing

Bloom's Modern Critical Views: Jean-Paul Sartre

Copyright © 2001 by Infobase Publishing
Introduction © 2001 by Harold Bloom.

Chelsea House
An imprint of Infobase Publishing
132 West 31st Street
New York NY 10001

Library of Congress Cataloging-in-Publication Data

Jean-Paul Sartre / editor, Harold Bloom.
       p.   cm.   — (Modern critical views)
     Includes bibliographic references and index.
     ISBN 0-7910-5917-0 (alk. paper)
      1. Sartre, Jean Paul, 1905–1980—Criticism and interpretation.
      I. Bloom, Harold.   II. Series.

     PQ2637.A82 Z752 2000
     848'.91409—dc21   00-064440

Contributing Editor: Tenley Williams

Produced by: Robert Gerson Publisher's Services, Santa Barbara, CA

Printed in the United States of America

IBT 10 9 8 7 6 5 4 3 2

This book is printed on acid-free paper.

Contents

Editor's Note

My Introduction concludes that Sartre will ultimately be remembered for his literary biographies and autobiographical writings, rather than for his novels and plays.

The French philosopher-critic Robert Champigny applies the philosophy of being to *Le Diable et le bon Dieu*, after which Fredric Jameson comments on Sartre's methods of handling time in his works. Gary Woodle reviews the short story *Erostrate* as a prelude to *La Nausée* (*Nausea*), and Dominick LaCapra argues that a knowledge of Sartre's early theoretical studies is necessary to understand later works such as *Being and Nothingness*.

Sartre's "concept of the self" is examined by Hazel E. Barnes, after which S. Beynon John expounds on the unfinished tetralogy *Les Chemins de la liberté*, and Catherine Savage Brosman finds in Kean a self-portrait of Sartre, closely aligned with his concurrent work on *The Words*.

After Thomas B. Spademan explains how Sartre, in his *Notebooks for an Ethics*, expands on Marx's theory of rights in a capitalist society, Brian Seitz discusses Sartre and Nietzsche.

Walter Redfern looks into Sartre's "Le Mur," after which Marie McGinn provides her interpretation of *Nausea* and Robert Pickering applies the Resistance concept of *témoignage* to Sartre's writings during the Second World War. Sharon Ghamari-Tabrizi's comments on feminine substance in *Being and Nothingness* conclude this volume.

Introduction

Sartre's achievement began in 1938, with his early novel *La Nausée*. Now, in 2000, what survives of Sartre? Fashions go by, and Existentialism is mostly a blurred memory. The novels of Sartre, with the possible exception of *La Nausée*, are no longer read. A better dramatist than he was a narrator, Sartre still has some life in the theater: *No Exit* continues to be revived, with some success. As political sage and as moralist, Sartre once had enormous currency, yet that eminence also has receded. Was he, after all, a grand period piece, triumphant in the 1950s and earlier 1960s, and then rendered largely irrelevant by the advent of the Counterculture in 1967–70?

Rather than relying only upon my own perspectives in regard to Sartre, I choose to invoke the late novelist-philosopher Iris Murdoch, who published a lucid short book, *Sartre: Romantic Rationalist*, in 1953, when Sartre's influence was most prevalent.

It could be argued that Sartre's largest achievements came after Murdoch's study: *Saint Genet, The Words, The Family Idiot: Gustave Flaubert*. But Murdoch, the author of such superb novels as *The Good Apprentice* and *Bruno's Dream*, can be judged to have anticipated Sartre's final phase as biographer and autobiographer, after she demonstrated so clearly his limits as philosopher, novelist, and moral psychologist:

> But Sartre's special talent is social diagnosis and psychoanalysis; he is at his most brilliant when he dissects some deformed life and lays it out for our inspection.

Sartre, analyzing Flaubert, Genet, and himself, indeed manifests brilliance, whereas his fiction generally reduces to "intellectually pleasing schemes and patterns" (Murdoch). Not much in Sartre's narratives can survive a comparison with Dostoevsky or Conrad or Faulkner. Sartre always knows too well what he thinks he is doing, and his characters never break

1

away from him. In this he is like Camus, his friend and rival, who wrote moral essays and called them fiction. A few pages of Proust, read almost at random, suffice to obliterate the ideograms that Sartre and Camus vainly wish to establish as persons.

Murdoch, writing in the early 1950s, praised Sartre because "he has the style of the age." But when that age passes, what abides? Sartre's vision of Genet interests me rather more than Genet does, but that scarcely can be said of Sartre's Flaubert. Yet who could expect otherwise? The single book by Sartre I tend to reread is *The Words*, because it is a marvelous account of the gestation of a consciousness. Murdoch shrewdly sums up Sartre's obsession with consciousness:

> For him the psyche is coextensive with consciousness. Whereas for Freud the deepest human impulse is sexual, for Sartre it is the urge toward "self-coincidence" which is the key to our being.

One cannot make Sartre into Molière or Racine; he was not a great dramatist. Perhaps he should have turned earlier to literary biography and autobiography, but he wished too strongly to alter the lives of his readers. His will be a partial survival only, yet *The Words* alone would be enough for him to be remembered as we go on into another era.

ROBERT CHAMPIGNY

Comedian and Martyr

> "Maybe we cannot do otherwise; maybe
> we have to choose to be nothing or play
> what we are. It would be dreadful, he
> thought; we would be fakes by nature."
> —Sartre, *Les Chemins de la liberté*.

Le Diable et le bon Dieu is divided into three acts and eleven tableaux. In Act I (first tableau) the archbishop of Worms learns of the victory of his troops over the troops of Conrad, a revolted vassal, who has been killed. The scene shifts to Worms, which has also rebelled against the archbishop. It is besieged by the troops of Goetz, the illegitimate brother of Conrad. Goetz has betrayed Conrad and allied himself with the archbishop. Inside Worms, Nasty, the leader of the poor, tries to counteract the effect of the news of Conrad's defeat. The scene shifts back to the archbishop's palace. The archbishop and a banker discuss how Goetz can be persuaded to spare Worms, in whose prosperity both the archbishop and the banker are interested. In the famished city, Heinrich, a priest, tries to fight Nasty's influence over the people. The bishop (not to be confused with the archbishop, who is not in Worms) is besieged by the people within the city itself. He reminds Heinrich that he has to choose between the people and his allegiance to the church. The bishop addresses the people of Worms. Nasty

From *Stages on Sartre's Way, 1938–52.* © 1959 by the Indiana University Press.

3

persuades the people that the bishop is concealing reserves of grain. Riot. Before dying, the bishop entrusts Heinrich with the key to an underground passage which will admit Goetz's troops. Heinrich is to surrender Worms to Goetz on condition that the latter spare the priests.

Second tableau, Goetz's camp. Goetz takes pleasure in tormenting Heinrich, who cannot bring himself to reveal the secret entrance. Goetz points out to Heinrich the similarity of their positions: they are both outcasts. He advises Heinrich to imitate him: "Choose evil." Goetz learns of Conrad's death. Heinrich then perceives that Goetz loathes himself; he gives the key to Goetz. Now it is Goetz's responsibility.

Third tableau, Goetz's tent. Catherine, Goetz's mistress, discovers an officer who has been lying in ambush for Goetz. Catherine hides him in the tent: she will give him the signal to kill Goetz if she chooses. Goetz arrives. He tells Catherine that he is going to receive Conrad's estate and that he will taker her with him. The banker arrives. He tries to persuade Goetz to spare Worms. Goetz refuses his bribes—Conrad's lands and money. The banker is taken away. Goetz has changed his mind; he will abandon Catherine. She gives the signal to the hidden officer, but changes her mind at once and warns Goetz. The officer is disarmed and taken away. Nasty arrives. He had left Worms to raise a peasant army, but, upon learning that Worms had been betrayed, he has surrendered to Goetz's soldiers. He offers Goetz the generalship of the poor. Goetz refuses this new temptation of "the good." He has Heinrich brought in so that the latter may confess his arch-enemy, Nasty. Heinrich and Nasty insult each other. Meanwhile, Goetz is getting ready to invade the city. As for Catherine, she will be "married" to the soldiers. But Heinrich finally succeeds where the banker, Catherine, and Nasty have failed. He does not tempt Goetz with the good, but tells him that everyone does evil, as does Goetz, since to do the good is impossible. Goetz's Luciferian pride is hurt. He wagers against Heinrich that the good can be done. He subordinates his decision between good and evil to a dice throw, but cheats in order that the dice may "order" him to do the good. He decides to spare Worms and Catherine. He will meet Heinrich in one year in order that the latter may decide whether Goetz has won his bet or not.

Act II, fourth tableau. The scene is laid in Conrad's estate, Heidenstamm, which has been given to Goetz. Goetz is practising Christian love and charity. Not only the barons, but also Nasty, try in vain to persuade him not to distribute his lands to the peasants. This action will entice the peasants to revolt everywhere. And Nasty thinks that these spontaneous uprisings will be premature.

Fifth tableau. In Heidenstamm the peasants themselves do not respond to Goetz's gesture as he had expected. They think within the framework of the old order. Tetzel, the seller of indulgences, provides Goetz with a lesson in popular psychology. Heinrich, who now imagines that a devil dogs his steps and pretends to be possessed, tells Goetz that Catherine is in Heidenstamm, dying. Goetz leaves in search of Catherine. To Nasty Heinrich proposes a scheme to prevent premature uprisings in the whole country: the priests will leave their parishes and abscond, thus paralyzing with fear the myth-ridden minds of the peasants. A realist, Nasty accepts.

Sixth tableau. The peasants have taken refuge in a church in the absence of their priest. Heinrich's device has succeeded. Goetz arrives. He has learned that Catherine is dying in this church. Hilda is presented. The daughter of a rich miller, she devotes her life to the poor. She has been taking care of the dying Catherine. The latter, a prey to infernal visions, implores Goetz to save her. Goetz asks God to make him a scapegoat for Catherine's sins. As no sign descends from heaven, he pierces his hands and presents his wounds as divine stigmata to Catherine, who dies in peace, and to the peasants who accept him as a prophet.

Act III, seventh tableau. Goetz has established a perfect Christian community. The peasants are taught universal love and nonviolence. Hilda feels that she has been robbed by Goetz's success. Meanwhile, in other parts of the country, the peasants have started a revolt against the lords. Nasty asks Goetz to take command of the peasant army.

Eighth and ninth tableaux, the camp of Nasty's army. Goetz advises the peasants not to fight—their chances are too small. In order to persuade them, he takes advantage of his reputation as a prophet. But Karl, his former servant, who hates him, beats Goetz at his own game. Goetz leaves the camp and decides to forget about saving men. During his absence, a troop of peasants, incensed by the refusal of Goetz's people to join them in their revolt, have killed everyone in sight. Hilda is the only survivor. Goetz is confirmed in his decision to become a masochistic hermit.

Tenth tableau, one year after the beginning of the play. Heinrich arrives, accompanied by his devil, in order to judge whether Goetz has won his bet. But instead of playing the role of the Pharisee, as Heinrich had expected, Goetz plays the role of the Publican—and even the role of the prosecutor when Heinrich is not equal to the task. The exchange between the two characters exposes the comedy which they have been playing. Goetz does not believe in his god any more than Heinrich believes in his devil. Heinrich cannot tolerate this disclosure of metaphysical emptiness. The two men fight. Heinrich is killed.

Eleventh tableau, the camp of Nasty's army. Despite his repugnance, Nasty lets a witch give confidence to his men: the application of a magic talisman is supposed to make them invulnerable. Goetz arrives. He would like to enlist as a soldier, so as to avoid responsibility. But Nasty needs a general, not soldiers. Goetz accepts. He lets the witch minister to him, too. He accepts the responsibility of a general: he kills an officer who has challenged his authority. He accepts a situation which he did not choose: "There is a war to make and I will make it."

According to Sartre, "having, doing and being are the fundamental categories of human reality." On the same page of *L'Etre et le néant* the author intimates that a moral choice has to give precedence to one of these categories: "Is the supreme value of human activity doing or being? And, whichever solution may be adopted, what becomes of having? Ontology should give us some information on this problem; it is, as a matter of fact, one of its essential tasks, if man is a being defined by action."

Sartre's ontological analysis not only informs but at the same time orients a moral choice, since we are told that man is defined by action. The motto of Sartrean morals would probably not be action for the sake of action, but rather action for the sake of liberation. What is certain at least is that the criticism of the morals of being is the unifying theme of his production from 1938 to 1952.

We have encountered this theme in *La Nausée* and *Les Mouches*. It is also present in *Le Diable et le bon Dieu*. But as we advance from *La Nausée* to *Le Diable et le bon Dieu*, the situations become more complex and varied. To the criticism of the morals of being, *Les Mouches* adds a criticism of its reflection—the morals of non-being—and an emphasis on action. *Le Diable et le bon Dieu* deals with the same themes, but in a more complex manner. "Having," the expression of which was sacrificed in *Les Mouches*, comes to the fore, though it does not constitute an independent category. Mainly, however, the difference between the two plays lies in the treatment of moral action. Orestes abandons the morals of justification but accepts the reduction of his action to a mythical, theatrical gesture. In *Le Diable et le bon Dieu*, we find an attempt to go beyond the realm of gesture.

If man tries to *be* instead of to do, value is absorbed by fact, body becomes flesh. Man tries to be, but since by himself, he *is* not, he becomes what he has. The activity of the verb is gradually "clogged" by the substantiality of the substantive. It is this plenitude of the substantive which stirs nausea in the Sartrean man.

Since his being tends to coincide with his having, the man of property relies on other people in order that what has, hence what he is, may be given value and meaning. Through another's glance, the man of property is possessed by his possession.

This was the case with the cosmos of Jupiter and the order of Aegisthus in *Les Mouches*. At the beginning of *Le Diable et le bon Dieu*, the archbishop identifies himself with his currency: "Lord, the thumbs of my subjects have worn away my effigy on my gold coins. . . . What use can you have, Lord, for a transparent servant?" The subjects of the archbishop have become his subjectivity. In Hegelian terms, the slave gives meaning to the master.

When the philosophy of being-having is clothed in ethical language, being (through having) becomes the good; non-being (through not having) becomes evil. In theological terms, the Lord, the one who is, needs a devil in order to become the "good" Lord. Sartre's dialectical games with Good and Evil may seem obsolete. But the society in which Sartre lives *is* obsolete. The ethical principles of the French bourgeoisie are based on being through having, and since the bourgeoisie is still the ruling class, its ideology must be taken into account. It must, as a matter of fact, be used as a starting point, for its molds the social situation.

Thus, if the philosophy of being through having does not directly apply to the main characters in *Le Diable et le bon Dieu*, who are "have-nots," and consequently of the devil's party, the philosophy serves at least as a background. Instead of turning at the start to a philosophy of doing, these have-nots linger in the roles which have been devised for them by the "haves." This applies to Goetz until his "conversion" at the end of the play and to Heinrich, the priest who has espoused the cause of the poor (in modern terms, the worker-priest), but who does so *as* a priest, as a man whose role has been determined by the haves (the high prelates). The bishop of Worms asks Heinrich: "Who fed you? Who brought you up? Who taught you to read? Who gave you your knowledge? Who made you a priest?"; and Heinrich is obliged to answer: "The Church, my holy mother."

Less simple is the case of Nasty, the leader of the popular revolt (in modern terms, the Communist leader). His aim is to change the social situation; thus he has broken the spell of the philosophy of the haves. But he has to bow to the ideology of the sacred which has been instilled in the have-nots, that is, in his troops. And he himself seems to need the drug of the sacred. He wants to believe that God (in modern terms, historical determinism) is backing his enterprise: thus he knows that he is right *and* that he cannot fail.

Our study of the play will be mainly concerned with the evolution of Goetz. The other protagonists (Nasty, Catherine, Hilda) are rather stagnant and dull. It is on Goetz, and to a lesser extent on Heinrich, his alter ego, that the play relies for its appeal. *Saint Genet comédien et martyr*, an introduction to Genet's work, was published at about the same time as the play and can be used as a commentary. It is to *Le Diable et le bon Dieu* what *L'Existentialisme est un humanisme* is to *Les Mouches*. In both *Saint Genet* and *Le Diable et le bon Dieu*, Sartre describes what may happen when a lively and resolute have-not clings to the hieratic philosophy of the haves. Either work could be considered as a dialectical ballet, a game of hide-and-seek, a farce of travesty and metamorphoses, between the dancer (Genet or Goetz) and two elusive monsters: Good and Evil.

"We are nothing and we have nothing." Goetz, the illegitimate son of a noblewoman, likens his situation to that of Heinrich, the priest torn between his allegiance to the Church and his duty to the people. Goetz does not try to change his situation: he refuses the temptation offered by the banker. Goetz's situation has been imposed on him by society; now he wills it and thus tries to make it his own, to appropriate and justify it: "We are not inside the world. We are outside! Refuse this world which rejects you. Choose Evil!"

Not only does Goetz accept the social order which made him an outcast, he also claims the hieratic morals that go with it. Goetz *has* not, hence *is* not, hence is evil. In the optimistic theological scheme which is adopted by the ruling classes, evil can but be a lack and the good, plenitude. Evil is deprived of creative power and identified with non-being. Value tends to coincide with fact and law since fact and law are favorable.

It is consequently toward those whose existence has not been "clotted" with having that Sartre turns in order to keep alive the questions about value. These anxious souls experience the nothingness to which *L'Etre et le néant* gives such importance. They could be called *naturaliter sartrianae*. Goetz is a social outcast; the Sartrean man is a metaphysical outcast. Goetz's condition and problems are exemplary. He will be a "comedian and martyr" in the same way as Sartre's Genet. They are martyrs because they are scapegoats and witnesses. They are more fundamentally comedians than other men because of their alienated social situation. Caught in a philosophy of being which identifies being with having, their existence is but a reflection.

Like Genet, the abandoned child, Goetz, the illegitimate child, is branded by the ruling ideology with an original sin; he is made to feel his existence as stolen. Goetz's proud choice, his justification, consists in turning constraint into will. What is said of Genet can be applied to Goetz:

"He assumes and projects before him the curse which, from the depths of his past, from the past of his mother, rises to the present: It will be his future. It was imposed on him: He turns it into a mission. . . . He needed rules, precepts, advice; he loved the constraint of the Good: He will build a black system of ethics with precepts and rules, with uncompromising restraints, a Jansenism of Evil. But he will not reject, for all that, the crude theological morals of men of property: It is on this concept of morals that his system of values will be grafted and will grow like a cancer."

Unlike the morals of the Good, which are based on human and divine law, the morals of Evil are not stereotyped, even though they are a shadow of the morals of the Good. The Good is the invention of God, but Evil has to be invented by man. Goetz's mistress has to assure him, time and again, that he keeps deserving her hatred: "What I like in you is the horror you feel for me." Looking for the worst, which, according to Claudel, is difficult to find, Goetz is led to betray his half-brother, Conrad. The action has a symbolic sparkle which delights Goetz: "Of course bastards are traitors, what else could they be? I am a double agent by birth; my mother gave herself to a peasant and I am made up of two halves which do not fit." But by betraying his brother, Goetz has not only played his role, he has gone beyond what was expected, he has made the role his own by overplaying it: "I have created myself. I was a bastard by birth, but it is to myself that I owe the fair title of fratricide." As Sartre notes on the subject of Genet, the historian may rehabilitate a murderer, but his task will be more difficult with a traitor.

Although the morals of evil may be called inventive, they are not creative, since Evil is conceived as a mere negation of the Good. In productive ethics, negation is a necessary prelude to construction. But Goetz is fascinated by his negative situation. He appropriates reality through destruction. He is a soldier, not an artist. His pride is Luciferian, not Promethean.

His concept of morals is thus an alliance of hieratics and histrionics. At this stage, he bears some analogy to Electra in *Les Mouches*. He has not written the text; he prides himself on the way he interprets it. He is not an agent, but an actor, half-possessed by his role, half-inventing his role. His actions are gestures. Here again it is relevant to quote what Sartre says of Genet:

"He wants action. But he falls back at once into his obsession: He wants to do in order to be, to steal in order to be the evil-doer. . . . An action which is accomplished in order to *be*, is no longer an action, but a gesture. . . . Thus Evil is not the absolute end of his projects, it is the means which he has chosen to represent his 'nature' to himself. But if he does not *do* evil, he *is* not an evil-doer; he plays the role of the evil-doer."

Like the life of Sartre's Genet, Goetz's life has become imaginary: "This life of the evil-doer, which strives toward activity, lucidity, efficacy, has been transformed into a waking dream." No wonder, since Evil has been identified from the start with the mere negation of the Good.

Of course, objectivity, Goetz's destructions are real enough. So he is slightly jarred when Nasty tells him that far from destroying, he is a conservative: "You bring about disorder and disorder is the best servant of established order." But he recovers at once. For his concept of Evil is not social, or physical, but metaphysical. It is not men that he wants as victims, spectators, and judges, but God.

An actor, he needs a spectator as well as an author. He is but a passage between text and meaning. Catherine knows it: "What would you do without an audience?" It is not the physical reality of his destructions that interest him (in fact he loathes it), nor their social meaning: it is their metaphysical aura. His Luciferian pride consists in making God (the principle of the Good, or the Good itself) "bleed." The efficacy of Evil has to be proved metaphysically, not physically, not socially. Heinrich fancies that he has been "chosen": "An elect is a man who has been nailed to the wall by the finger of God." Likewise, Goetz turns his social situation into a divine "election." He has been chosen by God to play the role of the villain, and he prides himself on turning the villain into the hero.

This reaction may be labeled "infantile," but the term is equally applicable to the kind of ideology which has imposed on Goetz the situation to which he reacts. Is not what magazine psychologists (in Sartre's play, the banker) call "infantile" a revealing reflection of what they call "mature"?

Goetz has been cast out—he wants to be *the* Outcast: "Useless to men. But what do I care about men? God hears me. . . . He is the only enemy worthy of me. There is God, myself, and the rest is ghosts. It is God that I shall crucify tonight, through you and through twenty thousand men, because his suffering is infinite and it makes infinite the one who makes him suffer. . . . Then, I shall know that I am a monster of perfect purity."

So it if Heinrich, not Nasty, who shatters Goetz's pose at the end of the first act, Heinrich who, thanks to his own experience, is best qualified to understand and expose Goetz's game (while concealing his own). Heinrich derides Goetz's Luciferian *hybris*: Goetz is but a buffoon of the devil; does he believe that he will be the only one to be damned? Besides, is he even sure to be damned? God could play the trick of forgiveness on him, thus effacing the meaning which Goetz wants his actions to have in the eyes of God.

Goetz wanted to be exceptional and efficacious. But since, in his own scheme, God, not men, not Goetz, is supposed to be the judge of Goetz, he has to recognize that God is his invention (he is not yet ready for that), or that the meaning that God will give to Goetz's life may be far different from his assumptions. Goetz may appear to God as a banal sinner. Alienated at the start in his social situation, Goetz is alienated at the end in the meaning of his gestures.

It is then that the first metamorphosis occurs. Goetz had wanted to be the hero of Evil, but in so for as it possible for man to add something to the world, every man in the hero of Evil, since only Evil can be added to the perfection of the divine creation. Goetz had wanted to *do* Evil, but Evil cannot be taken as an end in a theological type of morals, since God can always turn it into good: the ways of God are beyond our understanding, and He can forgive whomever He pleases.

Heinrich has just contended that "to do the good" was impossible. Goetz accepts the challenge of his alter ego. The brutal metamorphosis of the character raises a question of psychological likelihood to which we shall return later. Let us note for the moment that the metamorphosis of soldier onto saint has historical precedents: "Saint Martin, Saint George, Saint Ignatius, in our time Father de Foucauld, who will probably be canonized, show how easily one can pass from the military condition to sainthood."

If the Good can really be *done*, its realization involves a change on the social structure: "The Good is love: all right; but the fact is that men do not love one another; what prevents them? Inequality of condition, servitude and poverty." It seems that, by giving his lands, Goetz has taken an active initiative, that he is no longer a half-possessed, half-calculating actor, but an agent.

Unfortunately, if he seems to escape metaphysical alienation, the meaning and value of his action remain alienated from him in an inescapable fashion. Sartre's analysis of bad faith in *L'Etre et le néant* points out a category of possession, of alienation through possession, which can be avoided. It affects the man who cuts himself in two, thus creating an imaginary Other, both convenient and dangerous, to whom the name of God (or the devil: see Heinrich's devil in the play) is sometimes given. There is, however, a category of alienation which cannot be avoided by man as man: it is the alienation imposed on man by the presence of other men. In so far as we *are*, it is other people as well as ourselves who decide on what we are.

In *L'Etre et le néant* and in the short essay *Visages* the appearance of the other is given a magic quality. In *Esquisse d'une théorie des émotions*, one could already read: "Man is always a sorcerer for man and the social world is first of all magic." The self of the Sartrean man is intimately haunted by the other. It is this eminently theatrical atmosphere which is the subject of *Huis clos*, the basis of the often misinterpreted aphorism: "Hell is the others." This fundamental experience indicates one of the limits within which morals have to be thought and lived. It contributes to making morals a perpetually renewed question instead of a set of wise formulas.

Goetz is not prepared to cope with this kind of alienation. When the peasants to whom he gives his lands prove unable or unwilling to interpret this action in the light in which Goetz likes to see it, the latter exclaims: "The Good will be done against all."

Goetz wants to be "the one who does the good at once." But his charitable gesture, his "good" *gesture* can become a good *action* only if the peasants take advantage of it. Man cannot coincide with being, he can but play at "being." Goetz is still an actor who needs spectators to assure him of the reality, meaning, and value of his role. His spectator had been God, but now that he wants to be the hero of the good, he is obliged to commit himself with reference to other men. His good has somehow to be recognized as good by the peasants: "No one can choose the good of others for them."

Thus, to his dismay, Goetz discovers ethical reciprocity. He is rejected by the peasants as he was rejected by the ruling classes. He is not one of the poor, but a former rich man. He tries to do good through charity, but fraternal love is the sanction of a good action, and as a giver, Goetz cannot be fraternally loved. The class-consciousness which frustrates Goetz's intention is an obvious allusion to the contemporary French situation. The answer to the social problem, in Sartre's opinion, is not charitable gestures, but revolutionary action.

Goetz's difficulty is reminiscent of that of Orestes at the beginning of *Les Mouches*. They are both emerging from the morals of non-being: esthetic wisdom in the case of Orestes, evil in the case of Goetz. But the situation is far more intricate this time, and Sartre will not let Goetz off as easily as Orestes. He will make his character enter two blind alleys before he is allowed to "find his way." The difference between the difficulties of Goetz and the difficulties of Orestes reflects to a certain extent the difference between the France of 1942 and the France of 1950.

The act of giving has not established satisfactory relations between Goetz and the peasants. Goetz might perhaps become a peasant himself, but then he would not be the-one-who-does-good. He is not thinking of a solidarity through work, of a solidarity based on reality; he is longing for a fraternity through love, for a fraternity based on magic. Tetzel, the seller of indulgences, is loved by the peasants through religious magic. And the only person who has ever loved Goetz, who still loves him, is the dying Catherine. Goetz has been loved through fleshly magic, not as a brother but as a master.

He takes advantage of these two lessons: he pierces his hands and presents his wounds to the peasants as divine stigmata. The directly narcissistic aspect of this gesture has been commented upon. By inflicting a wound on his own flesh, Goetz's tries to appropriate symbolically his existence and cancel its contingency. But Goetz's intention is first of all to incarnate himself in the eyes of others, through the ultimate goal remains to possess himself and the others through his sacred incarnation.

Incarnation, not embodiment. It seems relevant at this point to recall the distinction which has been made between flesh and body. Embodiment implies realization. It is the necessary instrument of the morals of doing. Incarnation permits exhibition, a certain category of gestures: those of the priest, of the actor.

It is therefore not surprising that Goetz chooses incarnation. By wounding himself, Goetz not only chooses his incarnation, but through his theatrical gesture, he fascinates the peasants: "At last! They are mine!" Goetz can now play the role of the prophet.

He has apparently reached his goal: he is loved. Doing was but the means: to be was the end. He may even think that he has "recuperated" his being. He has become an idol, he has given away his lands—but in order to possess the souls and hearts of the peasants.

Let us compare the situation which has been reached in *Le Diable et le bon Dieu* with the situation at the end of *Les Mouches*. The denouement of the latter is a question: How will the Argives react to Orestes' speech? Orestes' project has been conceived in the light of freedom: he has assumed his responsibility, he has chosen his good, and his action has been meant to help the Argives assume their moral freedom. But a more probable result is that the Argives will turn Orestes into a scapegoat, reduce his action to a gesture. And in his speech Orestes himself encourages this interpretation.

But he leaves, the play ends, and we are left with a question. In *Le Diable et le bon Dieu*, Goetz's desire "to do the Good" does not take moral freedom either as a basis or as an end. Unlike Orestes, Goetz is caught in the web of theological morals. With him, we have no hesitation: he deliberately assumes the role of scapegoat and prophet.

Yet *Le Diable et le bon Dieu* will take us farther than *Les Mouches*. For Goetz will not be permitted to leave. He will remain to the end caught in a social context. *Les Mouches* tells us what the reaction of the Argives will probably be after the speech and departure of Orestes; it tells us what the reaction of most French people *was* to the myth of the Resistance, once the occupation was over. Goetz's conversion to the morals of doing for the sake of freedom is not so quick as Orestes' conversion. But it involves a more realistic commitment.

Goetz's triumph brings about his downfall. The play illustrates the tragic irony which is already present in the description of the magic dialectics of love in *L'Etre et le néant*.

First of all, Goetz has sacrificed the means to the end. In order to make the peasants recognize his good as their good, he has assumed the role of the prophet. As far as he is concerned, he has abandoned the morals of purity, since his gesture is designed to deceive, to fascinate, to subjugate.

Moreover, the end attained by Goetz does not justify the means. At the beginning of Act III, the spectator witnesses an example of mass-education which might more aptly be called catechism, propaganda, or "brain-washing." In Goetz's village, the peasants are taught to love all men and practice nonviolence. A certain abstract concept of the good has been set up as an absolute, without consideration for the actual situation, and all that man has to do is to learn the recipes by heart and apply them mechanically.

Goetz's reign of sweet tyranny could perhaps be defended from the point of view of sedate wisdom: at least, the peasants enjoy a life of material and psychological peace, or slumber. But Sartre soon denies even this matter-of-fact success. A group of armed peasants, angered by the refusal of Goetz's people to join them in their struggle, destroy the village and slaughter its peaceful inhabitants.

Here again the allusion to the modern situation is obvious: no group of men can now achieve material happiness and spiritual peace, or sleep, in complete isolation from the rest of mankind. However intended it may be, the policy of the ostrich becomes every day less effective and less innocent. Humanity is no longer an abstract or sentimental, literary or scientific, myth; humanity has become, so to speak, a human concern. Sartre, always anxious to think in relation to his time, rather than *sub specie aeternitatis*, has pointed out this advent of the human age. It bolsters, on the objective side, the subjective statement that "in choosing myself, I choose man." In *L'Etre et le néant*, the stress was laid on the "I" and on the "you." Now the "we" receives an equal emphasis. Unlike Gabriel Marcel, whose point of view on morals is somewhat obsolete, Sartre focuses his attention on the collectivity rather than on private relations (e.g., the couple, the family, the local community).

The destruction of Goetz's paradise on earth, the refusal of Nasty's army to listen to Goetz when he urges them not to fight, make the hero abandon the role of prophet and paternalistic tyrant. By now, the actor has acquired enough suppleness and resiliency to snap into the new role which the relentless dramatist has kept in store for him: that of the masochistic hermit.

Goetz's dialogue with men has proved a failure, either through the perversity of circumstances, or through the actor's unwillingness to let anyone steal the show from him. Goetz returns to his old ways: a dialogue with God. God is a much more agreeable interlocutor. He remains absent from the stage, and one can make Him say whatever one wishes Him to:

"There we are, Lord: We are face to face again, as in the good old days when I was doing evil. Ah! I should never have meddled with them: They are a nuisance. They are the brushwood one must push aside in order to come to you. I am coming to you, Lord, I am coming; I am walking in your night; lend me your hand. Tell me: the night, it is you, isn't it? Night, the harrowing absence of everything! For you are the one who is present in universal absence, the one who is heard when all is silence. . . ."

Goetz explicitly returns to the sterile dialectics of being and non-being, of being and having, which in fact, as has been pointed out, he has never been able to outgrow: "Until I possess everything, I shall possess nothing. Until I am everything, I shall be nothing."

In *Saint Genet*, Sartre comments on what Genet calls "the eternal couple of the criminal and the saint." In *Le Diable et le bon Dieu* the author stresses the theoretical similarity between Goetz's first role and his new role, that of the masochistic hermit. In both cases, the apparent goal is *not* to *be* through *not* having. But this time, God is supposed not to condemn, but to reward. Goetz had been against God and man. Now he sides with God against man

Since he is a man, he must punish himself: "I asked you, Lord, and you answered me. Blessed be Thou for Thou hast revealed to me the wickedness of men. I shall punish their sins through my own flesh. I shall torment this body. . . ."

After playing the Pharisee (of evil, then of the good), Goetz has turned his talent to the role of the Publican. The Publican cuts himself in two: he is the breast which is beaten, but he is also the hand which beats the breast. Goetz still plays the scapegoat and the prophet. But he now tries to play these roles to himself. He thus avoids the alienation imposed by other men. Goetz tries to recuperate his being by tormenting his flesh, and at the same time to posses the whole of mankind symbolically through his flesh.

The Publican presents himself as a sinner: he *has* a body, he *is* a sinner. But in so far as it is he who presents himself as a sinner, he is not a sinner. His passive flesh is but a symbol of man and of his wickedness. Thus, though this thought remains lost in a smoke-screen of bad faith, the Publican ceases to be a sinner and becomes a judge. Yet, since God, and no man, can be the judge, the Publican can but *play* the role of the judge.

The Publican and the masochist try to transform the ambiguity of human condition into a duality: sinner and judge, breast and hand. But it is the others who hold the key to our objectivity:

"I need someone to judge me. Every day, every hour, I condemn myself, but I cannot manage to convince myself because I know myself too well to trust myself. I do not see my soul because it is right under my nose. I need someone who would lend me his eyes."

By means of this projection, Goetz could perhaps manage to play both roles with a good conscience. But Hilda refuses to enter this theatrical scheme, she refuses "to play the game." Then comes Heinrich, who has wagered against Goetz that the good can not be done. His hatred for Goetz seems to guarantee a satisfactory duo between judge and sinner.

Unfortunately, Heinrich is still Goetz's alter ego. Hilda has refused to play the role of judge as Goetz would have liked, and Heinrich, as a judge, resembles Goetz too closely for the comfort of bad faith.

Goetz pretends to be conversing with God (a god who reveals himself only through silence); for Heinrich, he has managed to pretend to himself that a devil is his constant companion, without, however, being quite able to believe in the existence of this devil.

Under these conditions, the judgment scene achieves a result contrary to Goetz's apparent purpose. Heinrich, embarrassed by Goetz's exhibitionism, which so closely resembles his own, forgets his lines, so that Goetz is obliged to prompt him and himself assume the role of the judge. The dialogue becomes a monologue. This brings about the "conversion" of Goetz, in terms which remind us of Orestes' conversion:

"I wondered at every moment what I could *be* in the eyes of God. Now I know the answer: nothing. God does not hear me, God does not know me. . . . God is the solitude of men. There was only myself: I alone decided on evil; I alone invented the good. . . ."

The spectator is meant to understand that Goetz has ceased to play hide and seek with himself, has ceased to set up screens—God, the devil, evil, the good, being, nothingness.

The judgment scene has the effect of an exorcism. The travestied monsters disappear from the ballet. The presence of Heinrich does not act as a screen, but as a mirror, with a cathartic result: Goetz kills Heinrich, the symbol of his theatrical possession, proclaims the death of God.

The naïve enthusiasm of Goetz as he awakes from self-hypnosis and announces to Hilda that "God is dead" should not be construed as indicative of the author's mood. A more adequate echo of this mood may be found in Hilda's answer: "Dead or alive, what do I care? I have not bothered about Him for a long time." In other words, the metaphysical question of the existence of a divinity is irrelevant to the moral problem: "Even if God existed, it would not change anything." The believer is responsible for his god. It is not the metaphysical problem of the existence of a divinity that concerns Sartre, it is the psychological and ethical implications of a hieratic way of thinking.

Besides a subjective denouement, the play provides an objective denouement which gives to Goetz a place in a collective enterprise. From this point of view, *Le Diable et le bon Dieu* takes us farther than *Les Mouches* and, unlike the latter but like the *Oresteia* of Aeschylus, includes the theme of reconciliation.

This reconciliation, however, must be carefully distinguished from a religious communion or a sentimental unanimism, from the kind of "human myth" which brought tears to the eyes of the "self-taught man" in *La Nausée*, from the kind of human myth which made Shelley exclaim at the end of *Prometheus Unbound*: "Man, oh! Not men."

The denouement of *Le Diable et le bon Dieu* includes a criticism of this concept of reconciliation. The criticism is both realistic and idealistic. It is realistic in so far as the actual situation is concerned; it is both realistic and idealistic from a broader philosophical point of view.

On awaking from his self-hypnotic game, Goetz tries to forsake solitude and participate in a common human enterprise. In a speech which can be taken as expressing the author's views, Goetz shows the results of his Sartrean conversion:

"The men of today are born criminals. I have to claim my share of their crimes if I want to share their love and their virtues. I used to long for pure love: This was absurd; to love is to hate the same enemy: I shall share your hatred. I wanted the good; this was absurd. On this earth and at this time, good and evil are inseparable. . . ."

This realistic criticism is directed against the myth of universal love. To love all men is to love none. It is easy to be a unanimist in words, but any ethical enterprise draws its unanimistic atmosphere and its efficacy from its hostility to other men. It is against men that man can be practically reconciled with men.

Though, in theory, Sartre accepts the Kantian imperative which advises us to treat men as ends, not as means, he points out that, in practice, ethical action entails the treatment of men as means.

Even inside the group which is united by a common enterprise, reconciliation is partial. "Leaders are alone." The leader has to treat his men as means. Goetz has to kill an officer who has challenged his authority. He will have to sacrifice certain men: in war, quantitative considerations, which are immoral, must intervene. The atmosphere is not that of a class in philosophy. The situation does not permit a leisurely education of the masses. The leader cannot achieve with his men the kind of spiritual comradeship which is supposed to have graced the relations between Socrates and his disciples. Nasty and Goetz have even to pretend to share the belief of their men in magic: a witch is supposed to make them invulnerable. The leader is reconciled with his men through lies.

Thus, in the eyes of Sartre, the morals of liberation are not an idyllic solution, but they do make possible a proper formulation of the ethical problem. In any case, violence is inescapable. When Goetz, as a self-styled prophet, tried to appropriate the minds of the peasants, he was already using violence. But in this case, the means was mistaken for the end, or the end was unauthentic. The advantage of the morals of liberation is that the end is authentic. But it cannot claim purity of means. It is in this sense that, with reference to the present situation, Sartre has recognized that authentic morals are "impossible":

"Any morality which does not present itself explicitly as *impossible today* contributes to the mystification and alienation of man. The moral 'problem' arises from the fact that morals are *for us* both unavoidable and impossible. Action must give itself its ethical norms in this climate of unsurmountable impossibility. It is in this light, for example, that one should consider the problem of violence or that of the relation between the means and the end."

And he reiterates this statement as a corrective to his criticism of Christian morals: "I do not present these contradictions to condemn Christian morals: I am too deeply convinced that *any* morals are both impossible and necessary." Sartre's main objection to the more authentic brands of Christian morality is that today they provide an inadequate statement of the ethical problem and can serve only as a mask for irresponsibility.

The reconciliation of Goetz with some of his fellow-men bears some analogy to the reconciliation which occurs at the end of the *Oresteia*. There is nothing idyllic about the Aeschylean reconciliation. And it is far from being universal, since the reconciliation between Athenians and the alliance with Argos are urged for a practical enterprise which is war. The difference, of course, is that in the *Oresteia* we are dealing with a war between states, whereas in Sartre's play we are dealing with a war between classes.

It is tempting to consider the situations depicted in *Le Diable et le bon Dieu*, particularly the denouement, in the light of the present situation in France. From this point of view, however, an important difference must be noted between the fiction and the reality. The denouement—Goetz's choice—has no application to the present situation in France. The situation is revolutionary, but a revolution is impossible. This is one of the reasons why Sartre considers that morals *today* are both necessary and impossible. Even though the denouement is far from idyllic, it appears to be wishful thinking when viewed against the background of contemporary France.

More broadly examined, the question of reconciliation does seem to be resolved on one level of action in *Le Diable et le bon Dieu*. If the actual situation at the end of the play does not permit a communion between oppressor and oppressed, or even between leader and men, there is at least communion among the soldiers. It is as an ordinary soldier that Goetz wants to enlist: "I want men everywhere—around me, above me, so that they may hide the sky from me. Nasty, allow me to be a nobody."

This time, the criticism of the myth of communion is both realistic and idealistic. What tempts Goetz now is no longer the desire to be a hero (of evil or good), but to become a nobody, a thing, an innocent, irresponsible instrument. But one does not return to innocence. In so far as soldiers are men, even a soldier cannot become a pure thing, cannot completely dissolve his subjectivity into the collective myth.

Moreover, if perfect communion is practically impossible, it should not be set up as an ideal, either. Sartre does not stress communion, but solidarity. Goetz says to Hilda: "We shall be alone together." This formula can be taken not only as a statement of fact but as a judgment of value. Sartre stresses both solidarity and aloneness, for they imply each other. It is through the subjectivity of others that our autonomous subjectivity, our aloneness, is revealed to us. It is because Sartre wants his philosophy to be a humanism, it is because he wants his "myth" to be human—not animal, not divine—that he stresses aloneness and solidarity, not communion. A reconciliation between men will be ethically valid if they are reconciled within themselves and with each other to the principle of aloneness and reciprocity, to the principle that there can be no valid ethics for the man who has not assumed his aloneness. The rest belongs to sentimental and mystical literature, to totalitarianism or pseudoscience.

For Blake, too, the chief enemy was alienation: he had to fight it in his own religious mind. *The Marriage of Heaven and Hell* might be a better introduction to *Le Diable et le bon Dieu* than Nietzsche's *Beyond Good and Evil*. Like Shelley, Blake strives toward an integration of the divine, but, unlike Shelley, he does not intend to set up a sentimental concept of mankind as a substitute idol. Blake stresses subjectivity. His ideal city is not a city of stultifying peace and drugged communion, it is the place of endless "spiritual strife." In the same way, Sartre does not imagine any order as the ideal. An order can be only a relative end; it must be conceived as a means for further negations and projects, as opening more opportunities for freedom. But Blake is a poet; he realizes his city symbolically for himself. Sartre stresses solidarity and thinks in relation to the social situation. Goetz's last words are: "There is a war to make and I will make it." But one does not make a war as one *makes* an epic poem.

And a play is not an epic poem. The theatre is the best medium for a philosophy of ambiguity, of clashes between freedoms (between freedom and itself), of aloneness and reciprocity.

In the really creative and poetic aspect of the morals of doing man is not placed face to face with man, but with things. There is no alienation there, for things have no subjectivity. There is no clash between freedoms, but a clash between freedom and nature.

The theatre cannot deal with the really positive aspect of the morals of doing, it cannot deal with making. For things are absent. The character exists only in relation to the other characters. His subjectivity is revealed negatively rather than creatively. He has only the other characters to work on, and he cannot create them: their freedom means his failure. Failure is experienced when he tries to possess the others and conversely when the others try to possess him. His subjectivity is revealed through these failures.

In so far as we *are* (this or that), it is the others as well as ourselves who decide on what we are. This point of view is pure theatre. And it is pure theatre that is implied in this formula: "As a successor to the theatre of *caractère*, we want to have a theatre of situations."

The word *caractère* refers to a certain tradition of French literary psychology. The English word "character" does not quite translate it. The play of *caractère* uses events and situations to bring out certain characteristics, in the same way that, by clever lighting, one brings out the interesting qualities of a statue. The play of *caractère* could also be compared to a lesson in anatomy.

The play of situations as it were throws the character outside himself. The character does not come into the play as a certain object to be gradually revealed. The character will have to interpret what he "is" from what the other characters tell him he is. His being is perpetually in question. He has to choose himself, he will be what the other characters make him and what his reactions to this attempt at possession will be.

Of course, there is nothing particularly new about this conception of the theatre. What Sartre brings to this conception is greater awareness. It must also be noted that there can be no pure play either of *caractère* or of situations. In *Le Diable et le bon Dieu*, the character is not a pure ghost when he enters the stage. The character has a certain past. But Sartre tries not to present this past as an "eternal nature."

First of all, we are meant to understand that this past is a choice, an "original choice." This choice, implicitly made by the child, is not authentically ethical, since the child is unaware of responsibility and reciprocity. It is a choice to be (or not to be). Thus Goetz enters the stage as a project not to be, through not having, or as a plan to be the evildoer.

This original choice, since it is conceived as a choice, must be distinguished from a nature established once and for all. *Le Diable et le bon Dieu* shows us that two things may happen: metamorphoses and an ethical conversion. Metamorphoses, as we have noted in the case of Goetz, bring about changes which the psychology of *caractère* might not allow: Molière and Balzac did not permit Harpagon and Grandet to become spendthrifts. Sartre tries to make these metamorphoses credible by the use of situations which rock the character to his foundations. Yet, as we have also noted, these metamorphoses do not effect a radical change in the original choice. Throughout his metamorphoses, Goetz's morals remain the morals of being.

He rings the changes, so to speak, on the ontological failure, on the failure to *be*.

The radical change is supposed to some with his conversion. The character breaks with his original choice and abandons the sterile pursuit of being. It is this possibility of conversion which makes Sartre's moral philosophy more optimistic than the psychology of *caractère*, or traditional psychoanalysis. It indicates Sarte's faith in man. Faith, not belief; for the endless variety of metamorphoses shows how difficult it may be to break the vicious circle of the original choice, the circle of the comedian and martyr.

In any case, either through metamorphoses or conversion, Sartre's play of situations tries to make us feel that anything may happen to the character. His being is at the mercy of the other characters and of himself; it depends on situation and action. *Le Diable et le bon Dieu* is made up of perpetual clashes between freedoms: Goetz and Heinrich, Heinrich and Nasty, Goetz and Nasty, Goetz and Hilda, Goetz and the peasants, ect. In Racine's tragedies the character was permitted to compose his soul leisurely through the use of a confidant. Sartre eliminates the confidants, or rather he turns the confidants into enemies.

These clashes between freedoms reflect the characters' attempts to possess each other. One character hopes to recuperate his precious being from another. But as this attempt fails again and again, illumination may come at last. The character may abandon the sterile pursuit of his being and turn to the morals of freedom.

A theatre can be "moral" in two opposite ways. The hero may be presented as a model, as an idol, or he may be presented as a telltale mirror.

In the first case, the theatre is the servant of the morals of being, and we are dealing with a moralizing, rather than a moral, theatre. The hero glorifies the natural attitude, the desire to *be*, and our own "original choice" may be flattered and countenanced through a metamorphosis: the desire to be like the hero.

Sartre tries to use the theatre not as a drug but as a purgation. *Le Diable et le bon Dieu* provides an even better illustration of this practice than *Les Mouches*. The moralizing theatre glorifies the original choice, the morals of being. This is what Sartre's play tries to determine. In "real" life, the thickness of things, temporal screens, the routine of daily occupations permit us sluggishly or drunkenly to lull our desire to be. But the theatre makes freedom clash against freedom, it presents a perpetual attempt at reciprocal possession. On stage the reverberation of the symbolic gesture, or word, is immediate. And in Sartre's theatre the use of "extreme" situations produces a brutal illumination. The original choice with which the character coincided when he entered the stage suddenly appears as a theatrical mask. The current of bad faith does not find any resistance in which to spend itself; bad faith is, as it were, short-circuited.

What Sartre says of Genet's theatre is, in this respect, applicable to his own plays, more especially to *Les Mouches*, *Huis clos*, and *Le Diable et le bon Dieu*: "Genet *betrays* his characters, he unmasks them, and the comedian whose imposture is exposed finds himself in the situation of the wicked man dispossessed of his weapons."

Through a hero, the moralizing theatre glorifies our desire to be. *Le Diable et le bon Dieu* exposes the spectator's spirit of seriousness and bad faith by turning the hero into a comedian and martyr (i.e., a witness). The play is not supposed to act as a drug on the spectator, but as a homeopathic treatment.

FREDRIC JAMESON

The Rhythm of Time

The writers with the most striking, most nakedly accessible sense of time are those who use long sentences: the exaggeration of the rhythms of normal breathing yields a kind of time whose texture is gross and easily perceived. And among these sentences long enough to let us listen to the beat of time, short sentences, expletives, recover some of their original shock, enjoy new and jarring force. But sentences of more ordinary length can function within some larger unity that controls their cumulative effect: the rhythms Flaubert made his paragraph divisions yield are well-known. Such forms, in which the individual sentences, beaten into solidity, are set together piece by piece into a whole that gives them their meaning, suggest an idea of the work of art as a craft, like handiwork in silver, an idea which hardly survives at all in the universe of mass merchandise contemporary artists inhabit.

The time of Sartre's world is regulated by an instrument in appearance more extrinsic to literature than any of these schemes. Once more, it is a question of the ways sentences are connected together, but it is as if the sentences themselves counted for little in the process, possessed little intrinsic weight or effect upon it, like the bits of valueless material which modern sculptors join together into a form that rises above the cheap or ephemeral nature of its contents. The pace at which this world unfolds is supervised by punctuation.

From *Sartre: The Origins of a Style.* © 1961 by Yale University Press.

Of course punctuation has always performed this function. But it has become so standardized that writers who use it as the schools or newspapers direct have no alternatives to choose from at the moments when they are obliged to punctuate. And where there is no possibility of doing something in different ways, there is no possibility of a style. We know this so well as readers that ordinarily we hardly even notice the punctuation at all: we do not have to, the convention is fixed, in a given case a given symbol will make its appearance. Limiting the writer's freedom in this matter even further are more curious restrictions: the colon, for example, is almost never seen in narration; some misfortune, possibly in its appearance, prevents it from ever straying out of the humdrum circle of expository prose.

The freedom with which Sartre uses these inherited symbols recovers for us some of their original freshness; he disposes of at least four different ways of linking sentences together, and his chaos begins to take on some appearance of order if we keep in mind that the marks are in his hands fairly precise symbols of different possible relationships between the complete sentences they separate:

> Daniel s'emplit d'une eau vaseuse et fade: lui-même; l'eau de la Seine, fade et vaseuse, emplira le panier, ils vont se déchirer avec leurs griffes. Un grand dégoût l'envahit, il pensa: "C'est un acte gratuit." Il s'était arrêté, il avait posé le panier par terre: "S'emmerder a travers le mal qu'on fait aux autres. On ne peut jamais s'atteindre directement."

> [Daniel filled up with muddy and insipid water: himself; the water of the Seine, insipid and muddy, will fill the basket, they'll tear each other apart with their claws. A strong revulsion came over him, he thought: "It's a gratuitous act." He had stopped, he had set the basket on the ground: "You've got to hurt other people to make yourself feel it. You can never get at yourself directly."]

The mingling of thought and objectivity in this passage is characteristic of the third person narration of the later novels, and obviously has something to do with the blinking rapidity with which the punctuation varies and succeeds itself. The rhythm of this paragraph is controlled by three instruments, each one marking a pause longer and more absolute than the others: the comma, the semicolon, and the period. The period comes as a deep silence, a consequential gap; it has something of the force of the past definite tense: after each one new areas are uncovered or new things happen.

It is uncertain just how distinct the opaque watery feeling Daniel experiences is from the sudden revulsion which also "fills" him, but in any case the revulsion is the accession of this feeling to a new plane; it has been named, and through the name the vaguer feeling takes on new shape and new intensity. The separation is even more striking after the next period. The sentence which follows it is a skip backward in time; its events, described in the pluperfect, have already happened, but have happened on such a different level from the feelings and thoughts that were going on simultaneously that they have had to be cleanly divided from them, there was no room for them in the earlier sentences. The mind, busy with its unpleasant sensations, did not notice the pause and the setting down of the basket until after it had already taken place.

This silence latent in the period is by no means intrinsic to it through some kind of "nature" that it might possess: its meaning is a function of its use, and the shock, the sudden break it causes, becomes easier to sense when we realize that the normal connection in this special world between straightforward sentences describing concrete actions is not the period at all but the comma. It is because we grow, over pages and pages, accustomed to this privilege of the comma, trained to it, that the period comes to strike us with the force it does. And it is certain that in a consecutive reading, attentive to the continuity of the narration, we have no trouble passing across the distance the period leaves between two sentences, and that the selection of small passages, their isolation and the slower reading they profit from, all exaggerate the effect of this punctuation far beyond what it is in a normal reading. But the magnifying and exaggeration of a phenomenon simply permits us to register more clearly what had to be there in the first place.

When the period is frequently used in a paragraph, the past definite is called into play and the effect is that of a jerky moving forward in time:

> Les chats miaulèrent comme si on les avait ébouillantés et Daniel sentit qu'il perdait la tête. Il posa le cageot par terre et y donna deux violents coups de pied. Il se fit un grand remue-ménage à l'intérieur, et puis les chats se turent. Daniel resta un moment immobile avec un drôle de frisson en aigrette derrière les oreilles. Des ouvriers sortirent d'un entrepôt et Daniel reprit sa marche. C'était là.

> [The cats shrieked as if they had been scalded and Daniel felt himself going out of his mind. He sat the cage on the ground and gave it a couple of violent kicks. There was a tremendous rumpus within and then the cats were silent. Daniel remained motionless

for a moment with a strange electric sensation suddenly shooting through the back of his head. Two workers came out of a warehouse and Daniel began walking again. The place was here.]

Each of these sentences is a complete event; the past definite hermetically closes off each of the verbs. We pause at each period and it takes a little effort to leap into the next sentence. And the frequency of *and*'s in this passage indicates a will to connect in some way the small units which threaten to fall apart; the *and*'s attempt to weaken the divisive period-time, and the pressure of this time is so great that at one point one connective has to be intensified to *and then* in order to hold things together.

This abnormal strength of the period accounts for the very frequent use of the semicolon: it is as if the period were so strong it had to be used with care, reserved for the most significant moments, so as not to wear it out and for fear it prove too powerful for the structure it is supposed to hold together:

C'était une place populeuse avec des bistros; un groupe d'ouvriers et de femmes s'était formé autour d'une voiture à bras. Des femmes le regardèrent avec surprise.

[It was a bustling square with bars along it; a group of workers and women had gathered around a pushcart. A few women stared at him with surprise.]

The group around the pushcart is part of the scene described in the first sentence; it develops the description of the square, but it is too leisurely, too contemplative, to warrant the sudden rush of motion which the comma would call up between the scenic framework and the detail. But the two sentences are static, descriptive; neither of them has enough autonomous energy to stand alone, bounded by a period, without falling flat. The semicolon offers a kind of neutral pause, and the real break is saved for the next sentence, so that when the women look at Daniel it will come with the shock of a completely new occurrence.

Let us recall for a moment some of Roquentin's ideas about narration. His criticism struck at the anecdote and only indirectly at the novel. The anecdote is a kind of primitive stage of the novel, distinguished from it above all by its length; the anecdote is short enough so that its beginning and its end can both be held together within the mind without much trouble, whereas the novel (even if it tells a story which can be converted into an anecdote) represents a enormous amount of time that passes in front of the mind and then is lost to view, never wholly existing in the present, always part memory or part anticipation. Roquentin shows how sentences like: "It was dark, the street was empty." are secretly charged with their energy from the impending climax of the story. We know that something is about to happen, and soon, and that these details are only apparently unimportant, that they must have meaning and are to be watched attentively. The end of a novel, much further away, does not exercise this power of gravity over the innumerable sentences that precede it. Only toward the last pages, and at the very beginning, of the novel, is time obviously distorted and stylized in the way Roquentin described; and this distortion can in the hands of a self-conscious artist turn into a bravura piece, a kind of exhibitionistic gesture to show his shaping power over what he narrates before effacing himself. Here (and in the weaker reflections of these moments which are the beginnings and endings of chapters) he can lead us into his story with the most breath-taking details, the most startling perspectives, and break it off at similar points, in the grand manner. For beginnings and ends are artificial, they are not "in nature."

The sentence is not in nature either. Sentences must also begin and end, and as long as our attention is directed to their succession, to the continuity of their subject matter, we are not aware of any violence done to time. But when we examine them more closely, focusing on small areas and attending to the manner in which they are linked together, we find that the time of the novelist, taken for granted, flowing on smoothly before, threatens to fall apart, to leave a ruin of separate moments and separate events, with no way of getting from one to another except by fiat, through a solution by violence.

This possibility of a breakdown in the continuity of sentences is the reflection on an aesthetic level of a technical philosophical problem: that of a theory of time. The conflict between the unity of time, its continuity, and the divisibility and multiplicity of the individual moments, a conflict out of which such things as Zeno's paradoxes arise, does not offer a choice between irreconcilable alternatives but a formulation of two requirements, two simple and incontrovertible facts about time which the new description will have to take into account. Sartre unites these opposites in conceiving time as a "unity which multiplies itself," a relationship within being, and within a being split against itself. Time is therefore not a *thing*, the nature of which we can describe. It is not somewhere *inside* the world, it is the way we live the world; we are temporal in the structure of our being and time is one of the negations that we bring to the pure simple being of the world by surging in its midst. We *are* time, are its privileged place of existence.

This has immediate implications for the literary problem we just described. Since we are our time, it is up to us whether it turns toward us the face of continuity or that of divisibility. There are nor real beginnings, and yet our time is full of beginnings and endings. We constantly interrupt a time continuity to do something else, our time sense expands and contracts like an accordion: fast or slow, continuous, absorbed, or jerky. It is on this possibility of variations in the quality of time that the variations we have discovered in Sartre's narration are founded, and the effect of the period, in particular, is inconceivable without some possibility of a kind of absolute break in time which it could echo.

This absolute break is the moment or instant: but the break must somehow take place within time, or time would cease altogether. It cannot take place within the unity of action, of a project, otherwise it would slip back into a continuity. The only moment free enough from a continuity of time already past and from the ceaseless rush into the future to qualify as moments, are those which are in themselves both the end of something and the beginning of a new thing. The moment is no longer strongly attached to the dying continuity, and the new one has not yet taken on enough life to catch the moment up in its motion. Yet these instants are in their turn merely the reflection of a more basic reality and happen on the basis of a more fundamental possibility. These partial beginnings can happen only because beginnings are somehow possible, or at least a certain type of beginning is: that of the original choice of our being, the unjustifiable choice that gives meaning to our smallest attitudes and acts, that accounts for our tastes, our ambitions, our habits. All of these are themes within a unity, parallel expressions of an underlying reality. The description of this original choice takes the form of a kind of myth, as the "look" did: it is the abstract structure which all later choices carry within themselves like a meaning, and insofar as it is the structure of an act, it cannot be reduced completely to an abstract idea but preserves the act's shape. Yet in another sense, since it precedes our time itself and is itself the basis of the quality of the time we live, it can never be localized in a moment of our personal history: we are not born grown-up, and there is never a full dress moment in which we can be said to have chosen ourselves, and yet everything happens as though we had. In certain cases, as with the childhood trauma of Genet, the original choice can even crystallize into a drama which can be temporally represented, whether in fact it happened all at once or not. The "myth" of the original choice is therefore an instrument of analysis that risks perpetuating itself as a concrete image.

There are nonetheless certain specialized moments of our personal history that seem to stand in a more privileged relationship to this moment of original choice than do the ordinary contents of daily living, moments that have a feeling of beginning about them stronger than most, that we think of as change, as absolute dates. Such are those rare moments, in which in our freedom, the original choice is abandoned for some new choice of being. There are no "reasons" for such conversions, as Sartre calls them; the idea of a reason for doing something, a motive behind a project, has meaning only *within* a global choice; and very often a will to change completely, the passionate desire to alter from top to bottom that choice which is ourselves, is a kind of rationalization, a struggle against ourselves which is part and parcel of our original choice and not in any sense set against it. Yet these sudden conversions show our freedom at its most absolute, freedom exercising an ultimate power over all reasons and all values, and they have for us therefore a very special fascination, an excitement which the tone of the following passage betrays:

> At every moment I am aware that this initial choice is contingent and unjustifiable. . . . Hence my anxiety, my fear of being suddenly exorcized, of suddenly becoming radically other; hence also the frequent coming into being of these conversions which wholly transform my initial project. . . . Think for example of the *instant* in which the Philoctetes of Gide suddenly abandons everything, his hatred, his fundamental project, his reason for being and even being itself; think of the *instant* in which Raskolnikov decides to give himself up. These extraordinary, marvelous instants, in which the older project collapses into the past in the light of a new project which rises on its ruins and which has hardly even taken full shape yet, these instants in which humiliation, anxiety, joy, hope are all inextricably united, in which we let go of everything in order to seize something new, in which we seize the new in order to abandon everything, such instants have often seemed to furnish the clearest and most touching image of our freedom. But they are only one manifestation of it among others.

In other words, if we are free are all, we cannot be "more" free at certain moments than at others; freedom is not a quality that we possess degrees of; so that in spite of everything, from the point of view of the idea of freedom, these conversions are not more privileged than any other moments of our lives.

Yet from the point of view of the notion of an original choice, the conversions are in a sense the *only* real moments in our lives, the only real events. This curious difference in perspectives, where an idea suggests more than it really means, suggests something radically different from what it is supposed to mean, is perhaps attributable to the "myth"-like nature of the

notion of choice. We will see later on also how certain notions, above and
beyond their purely thought content, because their formulations are very
close to images, tend to have this double development, in which from their
images consequences can be drawn, secretly, implicitly, mistakenly, which
range far beyond anything the pure thought of the notion ever intended to
convey. In the case of the original choice, in terms of which every detail of a
life can be interpreted (an interpretation and a method which Sartre has
called "existential psychoanalysis"), the unique individual force of the events
of a life seems to fade, the events become mere expressions, simply
manifestations of the ever-present single choice. So that we approach the
strange image of a world in which nothing happens, in which the same thing
repeats itself over and over in different forms, in which only one real solid
event—the choice itself—has ever taken place and in which only one new
event can take place: the conversion, the sudden reversal of values at any time
possible. That these extensions and suggestions latent in the notion of choice
do not really do justice to Sartre's practice as a novelist is apparent from the
impression of a richness of action which his books leave with us. There is
little overt effort made to show on some manner an original choice
operating behind each of his characters—such an effort would have resulted
in a kind of personification, a kind of world of "humors," of character-ideas
in action rather than real people. And yet the moment of conversion, so
dependent on this whole complex of ideas, occupies a place of great
importance in this work. The conversion can seem a waking up, as it does
in the consul's office in Indochina, where Mercier urges Roquentin to
accept a place in the new expedition:

> Je fixais une petite statuette khmère, sur un tapis vert, à côté
> d'un appareil téléphonique. Ii me semblait que jétais rempli de
> lymphe ou de lait tiède. Mercier me disait, avec une patience
> angélique qui voilait un peu d'irritation: "N'est-ce pas, j'ai
> besoin d'être fixé officiellement. Je sais que vous finirez par dire
> oui: il vaudrait mieux accepter tout de suite." Il a une barbe
> d'un noir roux, très parfumée. A chaque mouvement de sa tête,
> je respirais une bouffée de parfum. Et puis, tout d'un coup, je
> me réveillai d'un sommeil de six ans. La statue me parut
> désagréable et stupide et je sentis que je m'ennuyais
> profondément. Je ne parvenais pas à comprendre pourquoi
> j'étais en Indochine. Qu'est-ce que je faisais là? Pourquoi
> parlais-je avec ces gens? Pourquoi étais-je si drôlement habillé?
> Ma passion était morte. Elle m'avait submergé et roulé pendant
> des années; à présent, je me sentais vide.

[I was staring at a little Khmer statuette, on a green cover, next to the telephone. I felt as if I were filled with lymph or with tepid milk. Mercier was saying, with angelic patience that concealed some irritation: "As you are well aware, I have to receive an official appointment. I know that sooner or later you will say yes: it would be better to do so at once."

He had a reddish black beard, highly scented. Every time he moved his head I got a whiff of the perfume. And then, all of a sudden, I woke up out of a sleep six years long.

The statue looked disagreeable and stupid and I realized that I was profoundly bored. I couldn't manage to understand why I was in Indochina at all. What was I doing there? Why was I talking with these people? What was I dressed so oddly for? My passion was dead. I had been submerged in it, swept along by it, for years; now I felt empty.]

Here is a moment in which freedom suddenly stirs convulsively, shatters the crust of habits that had seemed to be forming around it, emerges without any connections at all, without any obligations, into a world which had gradually forgotten it was there. And yet the astonishing thing is that this sudden self-assertion of freedom is presented in terms of its opposite: it is something that happens to Roquentin, he himself does nothing, seems hardly responsible for it. He seems merely the passive locus of a wholly impersonal event, like a sudden bodily reaction. He merely "wakes up," and wakes up after it is all over. His passion does not die, he realizes that it is dead. The moment, the leap in time from one world-choice to another, is so sudden and so radical that it apparently eludes the instruments which were supposed to register it. It is deduced after the fact, from its consequences. For this moment is in the beginning wholly negative: the new passions, new interests, new thoughts, which will gradually fill this void have not yet appeared; the astonished mind is alone for the time being with the trophies of its former enthusiasm. That is why the image of death is the privileged expression of this change: the image of the loss of everything familiar, everything to which we are passionately attached, of the pain of the organism acceding to a new condition—so that the emptiness, the abandonment of the consciousness is its first sensation.

The most shocking, polemic statement of this event is the death of love: such moments take on their significance when opposed to the heavy burden of works composed from the very beginnings of literature to glorify love as a divine, irresistible, irrational force—one which begins with the inevitability of a chemical process, mastering the soul and setting it under very real slavery. It is not the reality of these feelings which is denied; but the test of a literature of freedom is the presentation of just such a passion—showing it as it is, with all the passivity it involves, the feeling that it seizes us without our consent, and showing at the same time that it is freely assumed, and that we somehow put ourselves into a passional state, that we make ourselves passive to be "enslaved" by our own freely chosen passions. Yet the direct description of the passion is somehow insufficient. Love, like the passions of Roquentin, is a value, and each value tends toward self-sufficiency, to toward absorbing the whole world into itself at the exclusion of everything else. It denies its existence as "a" value and insists on being Value pure and simple. The value is moreover a kind of absence: it is that which consciousness lacks, that path by which consciousness hopes eventually to arrive at its own special form of being: a lack which propels consciousness forward in time, and which all of the acts of consciousness are designed to fill. So that very often the value itself escapes detection, and people even deny they have any: only their acts, often performed under motives which their doers attempt to conceal from themselves, show secretly the ever-present influence of this absent center of gravity. Yet in the moment of the death of a value, the eye manages to register it directly; suddenly it becomes aware of what was there now that it is gone; and in the place where the value used to be it seizes it as the outline of an absence.

Thus the real meaning of love as freely chosen, a meaning obscured during its existence by the passive nature of the feeling which is lived as being submitted to, suddenly emerges when love dies. Like the other moments, the death of love happens abruptly and without transition: the person merely wakes up into a world from which his love is gone, he remembers the former gestures inspired by it without any longer understanding them. This sudden absence is not *caused*, is wholly gratuitous. Yet it can happen against the background of a world so unexpectedly and radically altered that the older value, persisting a moment in its new surroundings, becomes incomprehensible, and then vanishes altogether. This is what happens in *Dead without Burial*, after Lucie has been tortured and her world sealed off by the imminence of death, when her love for Jean, a kind of peacetime love nourished by the idea of a continuing future, suddenly proves to be at cross-purposes with the passion in which she wants to live her coming extinction. Love has nothing to offer her in such a world; it is a toy she drops without regret.

Yet we should not make any mistake about the tone of these sequences. They have no trace of any sadness at the evanescence of human passions or emotions; they are painful, "humiliation, anxiety, joy, hope" all mingled together, but they have no built-in effect. The very same moment, which in

Dead without Burial had some of the somberness of approaching death, becomes in *Kean* pure comedy, in the astonishing scene in which the passion shared by Kean and Elena suddenly gives way beneath them and drops them from Alexandre Dumas into a play of a different nature altogether. If there is any dominant tone in such moments at all, it is more likely to be excitement, which does not have to be wholly free from anxiety: a kind of relief of the consciousness at finding itself once more naked and without any ties, left with absolutely nothing. There is in it some of the exhilaration of all negativity, all destruction.

It is the ever-present possibility of such moments of radical change, the constant threat that time will collapse into one of these moments and then reissue wholly altered, that lends the world of Sartre that jerkiness we have discovered behind the use of the period. It is as if time might suddenly begin to divide itself into infinitesimal separate units and as if this process, like a chain reaction, once begun could never be arrested. And against this threat a host of smaller mannerisms stand guard: verbs of unusual violence, especially in the philosophic works where milder ones might have been used, keep things moving explosively forward: such verbs as "die," "surge," "seize," "invade," and so on. But such verbs have ambiguous effects: they do keep things going but at the same time they separate the new thing bursting into being somewhat irrevocably from all that has preceded it, as if it had been separated by the enormous gap of one of those instants. And the constant series of *and*'s and *then*'s and *afterward*'s push the minute separate events forward, both linking and dividing them. On every page we find adverbs of violence attempting to bring new events to birth: "suddenly," "brusquely," "all at once"—all these lend a kind of abruptness to this world which occasionally looks like the jerky, over-rapid and sectional movement of the early movies:

> Elle verse sans répondre; tout d'un coup il retire prestement le doigt de son nez et pose les deux mains à plat sur la table. Il a rejeté la tête en arrière et ses yeux brillent. Il dit d'une voix froide: "La pauvre fille."

> [She pours without replying; all of a sudden nimbly he withdraws his finger from his nose and spreads both hands out on the table. He has his head tossed back and his eyes are shining. Coldly he says: "Poor girl."]

The new gesture is so rapid that it will not all fit into the sentence which was supposed to circumscribe it and leaves some trailing, static now that the gesture is over, into the next ("He has his head tossed back"). There are long waits, unexpected things suddenly happen, time slows again and stops and then moves.

That jerkiness does not become intolerable because it is not the only kind of movement in this prose. In the silences of the period, time shows its possibility of being discontinuous, fragmented; the requirements of a sentence seemed to image faithfully this starting and stopping of time. Time's continuity is in some ways harder to fix. The basis for it could not be in the sentences themselves unless they were highly unusual like Faulkner's, but in the continuity of our reading, which provides the solidity with which the impression is filled out.

Sometimes the continuity is illusory: such is the movement which the colon provokes, a mere flash which quickly abolishes itself: "Daniel filled up with muddy and insipid water: himself." The colon here is a little pause, a slight catching of the breath before the last word is uttered which permits the sentence to fall, finished. It signifies equivalence between the two parts, an identity so great that the two sections seem to be held apart artificially and by force only. Once the colon is bridged, once the mirror-sentence on the other side of it has joined its predecessor, the two seem to merge into one like a rubber band stretched and snapping back, and they glide as a single unit into the past. The separation can be as slight as the distance between looking and seeing, between seeing and identification:

> De petits monsters mous rampant à terre et regardent le gai troupeau de leurs yeux sans prunelles: des masques à gaz.

> [Limp little monsters crawl on the ground alongside and stare at the joyous troop through the empty sockets of their eyes: gasmasks.]

The colon permits not an abstract description of the process of seeing something and then realizing what it is, a description that would use weak and faded words like "realize" and "it occurred to him suddenly," but a concrete presentation of the event in which we participate ourselves. We are suddenly lifted out of the realistic world of the rest of the novel, lifted higher and higher into fantasy the length of the whole sentence, until suddenly the single withheld word is released and the world immediately settles back to normal again. The sentence no longer displays a merely static meaning; it imitates with its own small drama the drama of its subject matter. And yet the drama caused by the colon is partly an artificial one: the colon assures us that there is no difference at all between the one and the other sentences it separates and yet it separates them. The colon unity throws up beyond itself the presence of the thing as it really is, the unified thing of which the two sentences are merely aspects, and then against this, the sentence which attempts to seize the solidly settled object through motion, through the illusory, snapping motion of the two temporarily separated parts rejoining. The sentence, the subjectivity, creates an illusion of separation, a mirage of dynamism and of happening, in order to convey a basically static reality. The colon here is therefore a kind of symbol of the events in which "nothing" really happened . . . ; it is also a privileged form through which certain objects in this world find their expression.

Such use of the colon permits a characteristic solution to one of the most serious problems in modern narration, that of the "thought." There is no "natural" solution to this problem. The interior monologue of Joyce is not less artificial than indirect discourse; it has merely the virtue of a conquest, of the new. The problem exists because of the relationship between thoughts and words. If thoughts were immediately equivalent to, immediately assimilable to words, there would be merely the ordinary problem of finding the exact words, there would be no question but that words were the perfect and privileged manifestation of thoughts. But the words pronounced inside the mind can be in direct contradiction to the mind's secret awareness, they can be an attempt of the mind to fool itself. Or the real thinking can be done through acts. We can sometimes think directly with the things we handle and use, so that the full dress "thought" is only a much later entity, a kind of reflection of an immediate reality. So unless a little violence is done to the traditional methods of presenting thoughts, the old worn-out notions of personalities and of the nature of thinking and of action will perpetuate themselves.

Sartre's renovation of this state of affairs is along the line of least effort, hardly perceptible: he preserves everything, the equivalence between thought and sentence, even to the quotation marks that give us the impression that the thought-sentence has been lifted bodily from someone's mind and set unchanged upon the paper. But this traditional arrangement is secretly subverted: the colon in itself would not be enough to install any real novelty into this form; its use in direct quotation before a sentence in quotation marks is in fact one of the rare applications of this symbol which is not rejected from French narrative prose; but the colon is the locus of this subtle change: "A strong revulsion came over him, he thought: 'It's a gratuitous act.'" The effect of this "thought" has been prepared by its context, by the kind of sentence that precedes it. The comma separating the two narrative sentences lends the second, carrying within itself the burden of the thought, the same weight as the first, more linear one. This forced

equation of two unequal lengths would of course be present even with
different kinds of separating punctuations:

> Il but. Il pensa: "Elle est enceinte. C'est marrant; je n'ai pas
> l'impression que c'est vrai."

> [He drank. He thought: "She's pregnant. It's funny: I can't
> believe it."]

Even here, where the "thought" section is far more complicated than the two
words it is dependent on, it has nonetheless been reduced to the status of a
mere clause by the influence and the parallel of the preceding small sentence.
What the period does here however is to alter the quality of the movement:
in the first passage the length of the beginning sentence and the rush ahead
caused by the comma help to complete the "he thought" effortlessly with the
substance of the thought. In the second group there is an abrupt stopping
short that caused the thought to tumble forward under the acquired
momentum in a kind of stumbling over its own feet; but in both cases the
"thought" has been solidified, turned into an entity, by the parallel with the
preceding sentence. What stands between the quotation marks is now no
longer language of the same quality as the sentences outside them: it is
unitary, and when it happens, it has to be at least as tangible an event as the
drink the man takes or the sudden wave of revulsion that comes over him.
The shortness of the "he thought:" is essential in lending the vague
subjective event the value of a precise gesture, and after it the colon comes as
relief, it points forward, indicating an empty space which the thought quickly
flows into and fills up; it holds the door open at the end of an incomplete
sentence and the completion arrives almost instantaneously. Thus the
thought, when it happens to the incomplete announcement preceding it, has
now all the force of an act, and the quotation marks, which were supposed to
indicate naïvely that we think in words, are forced to assist in conveying the
impression of a gesture of consciousness just a real and as solid as a gesture
of the hand. The "words" of the thought are now a kind of illusion: the
thought-sentences indicate the sudden decisive seizing of consciousness on
things; they are not any longer supposed to give faithfully "word for word'
what the consciousness "thought." The words of these sentences no longer
stand for the words of the thoughts in question; they stand directly for the
thoughts themselves, just as ordinary narrative sentences "stand for" the
wordless realities they describe.

The movement which the colon generated was ephemeral and
immediately abolished itself, a mere illusion of movement created to be as

quickly laid to rest: an instant only, since it could bind only two sentences, could represent nothing more substantial than an exchange of energy between two points alone. The comma, on other hand, has the seeds of perpetual motion within it: it connects complete sentences, lets them pile up one after another, and suggests no superior structure which would cause a period to happen at any given point, which would of itself set an end to the fissioning development.

But although the sentences it links are grammatically complete, the comma insists on their secret incompleteness, it urges us forward, assures us that everything has not yet been said: "He had stopped, he had set the basket on the ground: 'You've got to hurt other people to make yourself feel it.'" The center of gravity in this unit is in the thought, the other sentences slide down the incline toward it although they in no way duplicate it. The comma is precisely this slant at which complete sentences are leaned and which robs them of their autonomy. But the incompleteness is not a precise one, to be filled and satisfied by a single detail, a single subsequent sentence: it spreads out on all sides and the period that finally puts an end to it is arbitrary and dependent on the angle of vision, like a window frame that shuts off the view at an accidental point. For the comma generates a movement which whirls loose wider and wider. The colon was bounded, centripetal, moving in upon itself to vanish at a given moment; the comma has no natural term; the form which it governs is open, full of loose ends. In a sense the master image of this special kind of movement is the entire novel *The Reprieve*, in some ways nothing but a vast whirl of things linked by commas and which at its most concentrated moments shrinks to precisely the form we are describing:

> Des étoffes rouges et roses et mauves, des robes mauves, des robes blanches, des gorges nues, de beaux seins sous des mouchoirs, des flaques de soleil sur les tables, des mains, des liquids poisseux et dorés, encore des mains, des cuisses jaillissant des shorts, des voix gaies, des robes rouges et roses et blanches, des voix gaies qui tournaient dans l'air, des cuisses, la de la *Veuve Joyeuse*, l'odeur des pins, du sable chaud, l'odeur vanillée du grand large, toutes les îles du monde invisibles et présentes dans le soleil, l'île sous le Vent, l'île de Pâques, les îles Sandwiches, des boutiques de luxe le long de la mer, l'imperméable de dame à trois mille francs, les clips, les fleurs rouges et roses et blanches, les mains, les cuisses, "la musique vient par ici," les voix gaies qui tournaient dans l'air, Suzanne et ton régime? Ah! Tant pis, pour une fois. Les voiles sur la mer et les skieurs sautant, bras tendus, de vague en vague, l'odeur des pins, par bouffées, la paix. La paix à Juan-les-Pins.

[Red and pink and mauve fabrics, mauve dresses, white dresses, uncovered bosoms, beautiful breasts beneath handkerchiefs, pools of sunlight on tables, hands, sticky and golden liquids, more hands, thighs bursting out of shorts, gay voices, red and pink and white dresses, gay voices spinning in the open air, thighs, the *Merry Widow* waltz, the smell of pinetrees, of warm sand, the vanilla odor of the open sea, all the islands in the world invisible and present in the sunlight, the Leeward Islands, Easter Island, the Sandwich Islands, the luxury shops along the seashore, the lady's raincoat at three thousand francs, the costume jewelry, red and pink and white flowers, hands, thighs, "this is where the music is coming from," gay voices whirling in the air, what about your diet, Suzanne? Oh, just this once. Sails on the sea and the skiers leaping their arms stretched forward, from wave to wave, the smell of the pines in whiffs, peace. Peace at Juan-les-Pins.]

This cascade of sensations is pure of any individual minds; the people leave their separate identities along with their jobs and their winter clothing and merge into a common set of feelings, into a common world. The holiday world directs them, not the other way around: it proposes a series of well-traveled paths which they follow through their summer. For a time at least this collective world is the only living entity, the only reality. Yet take this resort as the widest frame of reference, expand its hints and fragments, let the bodies which are attached to the hands and thighs begin to appear, and let the situations attached to the disembodied voices little by little be guessed at, and the form of *The Reprieve* is unmistakably present before you. This form, which attempts to convey both the minute position we occupy in a world filled with history and the fragmentary nature of our awareness of that world, is supposed to be full of loose ends, open, fragmentary, in order to avoid the god's eye view of the world which some novels that do not remain within a single point of view suggest.

Yet in spite of its difference from the colon form, the comma also suggests a single central reality which the sentences do violence to; but this central reality, instead of being somehow separated in two only to be immediately reunited again, is infinitely divided, infinitely divisible. Time, in order to move forward, must change from moment to moment, but it must also, to be continuous, remain somehow the same. The most striking changes turn out to be grammatical fictions and necessities, the apparently separate events imperceptibly fade into what preceded them and into what will follow. Like the thoughts, the revulsion, the setting down of the basket, they are all distinct because they happen on different levels and have to be separated in their presentation, and yet somehow they are all simultaneous, form part of a single large reality which we sense after we have read all of them.

This movement forward which is also a kind of repetition is a form of generosity: a fear that the event, the reality, has not been sufficiently presented, a turning around it to strike it again and again from new sides and at new angles, so that no single formulation which might have caught your mind more immediately then others, will go unsaid. This sort of repetition is familiar to readers of Sarte's philosophic works; and since these are practical expository works, it is there unashamed and unconcealed. But in narration any real repetition is generally checked by the real movement forward of time, the necessity that very shortly things be in some real sense different from what has preceded them. Nonetheless sometimes this flow forward is slowed down as much as it can be, sometimes time marks time, and little pools of repetition gather:

> Mais il aurait fallu parler: Boris sentait qu'il ne pouvait pas parler. Lola était à côté de lui, lasse et toute chaude et Boris ne pouvait pas s'arracher le moindre mot, sa voix était morte. Je serais comme ça si j'étais muet. C'etait voluptueux, sa voix flottait au fond de sa gorge, douce comme du cotton et elle ne pouvait plus sortir, elle était morte.

> [But he would have had to say something: Boris felt himself unable to speak. Lola was beside him, tired and all warm and Boris couldn't tear the slightest word loose, his voice was dead. I would be like this if I were a mute. It was voluptuous, his voice floated deep down in his throat, soft as cotton and it couldn't get out, it was dead.]

This repetition, the describing in different ways of the same phenomenon, is not exactly circular: with each phrasing it rises to a new level, and the image of the "dead" voice, colorless and figurative at first, becomes real by the end of the passage. The mere abstract feeling of not being able (not wanting) to talk has become the awareness of a part of his body, and organ actually gone lifeless. Such a sudden unfolding of development, the quick rushing into being of variations on a single motif, is the characteristic form of a kind of Sartrean poetry. The passages begin with a single central datum or conceit: in this case the voice not working, the idea of the voice as a thing which operates like an organ of the body; and then this central "inspiration" is systematically exploited, used in as many different ways as possible, developed as exhaustively as possible, until a kind of feeling of completion is reached, the thing is there before us, and the continuous movement of narration sets in again.

In its most characteristic use, therefore, the comma ceases to be simply the rhythm at which events unfold, and turns into a kind of momentary departure from the narration, a form that develops above the line of the narration like a pause. There is a point here beyond which our analysis cannot pass: the coming into being of the "idea," the central image, the motif itself, the "inspiration"; this surges out of nothingness, the *Einfall* is a kind of irreducible. And yet there is a quality about all of this Sartrean rhetoric, or poetry, which can be formulated: we feel a kind of contortionism in it, a straining which nonetheless remains graceful, lands back on its feet. The motif surges in a kind of receptive tension in the author's mind; at points in the steady continuity he strains his imagination for a certain kind of perception and suddenly, out of nowhere, the right thing comes. But this pressure of the imagination does not exist in a void: it is not content it seeks, but a special way of treating content which is already given in the story line. It is as if the things of the narration were constantly being stared at to yield up a kind of poetry, as if the things were being constantly forced to take the shape of a subjectivity, to take on some of the grace and the autonomous movement of a kind of thought. But what it is that happens to these things, what can happen to them, what this specialized attention directed on them means, we will only find out by leaving behind us the forms into which this content organizes itself, and interrogating the content itself directly.

GARY WOODLE

Erostrate: *Sartre's Paranoid*

Although the collection of short stories under the title *Le Mur* contains some of Sartre's finest work, it has been almost ignored by criticism, which tends to focus on his theater and on his philosophy proper, even at the expense of *La Nausée*. The third story, *Erostrate*, was completed in 1936 but seems to belong to a slightly earlier period; it makes specific references to the sensational murder by the Papin sisters of their mistresses, which occurred in February, 1933. *Erostrate* is playful and amusing, and simply told, with none of the labored phenomenological performances which mar so much of his last novels. It provides an accessible, perhaps indispensable introduction not only to *La Nausée*, which it anticipates in many ways, but to Sartre's work in general.

Paul Hilbert, the narrator and semi-hero, has isolated himself on the seventh floor of a hotel in Montparnasse, not far from the bustle of the great Boulevard, with, in those days, its railroad station and its cluster of celebrated cafés. He leaves his room only when absolutely necessary, to eat and to go to work, anxious to avoid contact with the "enemy," his fellow man. Things get better for him, he says, after he buys a revolver. From time to time he fondles the heavy object; knowing that it is loaded and ready to explode at any time gives him a new sense of power, and he no longer fears strolling the crowded Paris streets. He is aware that the gun in his pocket must make him walk like a man with a constant erection.

From *Review of Existential Psychology and Psychiatry* 13, no. 1 (1974): 30–41. © 1974 by Humanities Press, Inc.

On the first Saturday of every month Hilbert takes a prostitute, Léa, to a hotel room where he manages sexual gratification of sorts by watching her undress. Once, unable to find the willing Léa, he uses his new revolver to force a reluctant surrogate to strip and parade and humiliate herself before him; he realizes that his pleasure increases in proportion to the helplessness of the victim. She is no longer young, and her very maturity makes her seem more "nude" to him and thus more vulnerable. The gun, of course, makes her totally defenseless and him absolutely powerful. Later he recalls her terrified eyes and regrets not having shot her in the stomach; he soon dreams of bullet holes grouped around a navel and begins to imagine the pleasure he would take firing point-blank at his fellow men. Having horrified a prostitute (which, he claims, is not easy), Hilbert hatches a plan to astound the world by the gratuitous murder of a random selection of people in the street, to be followed by that ultimate refusal of the Human, his own suicide. He prepares his publicity in advance by mailing an explanatory letter to 102 French Humanist writers, the benevolent shepherds of the Human Race who imagine they perform great works dispensing to the masses the false comfort of Universal Brotherhood. Eventually he stops going to the office, loses his job, and spends the last of his savings. When his food is gone he goes down to the rue d'Odessa, fires his revolver at a man, finds himself pursued by a mob and finally run to ground in the toilet of a café.

Hazel Barnes suggested once that *Erostrate* might be read as the work of a traditional Freudian, and then, in her latest study, that a follower of Adler might have written it. There is no question that Hilbert is a pathological case, and getting worse. Broadly speaking a paranoid, he exhibits an array of related symptoms around a basic sexual inadequacy. He has never slept with a woman and is convinced, from what he has heard, that she gets more from it than the man. At best he would need a pious and frigid woman who would submit with disgust. He claims that he wants nothing from anyone and wants to give nothing (having nothing to give, of course, given his rigidity and flattened sensibilities). Clinically speaking, he fears loss of control; by his sadistic manipulation of the whore he turns the tables on his own passivity and takes revenge against some lost authority figure. Sartre would add that he captures the free subjectivity of the Other, dangerous to his own, by making it as far as possible an object for his mute gaze. The most serious of his evident problems are, in no particular order, his sadism, his voyeurism, his fear of crowds and of being touched, and of course his sense of moral superiority and growing megalomania, the exaggerated response of the paranoid to the increasing debilitation of the Ego. Repetitions conforming to the calendar, a fastidious attention to detail in his planning, and a ritual hand-washing before leaving his room at the end might also counts as symptoms. Prior to his crime he experiences visual hyperacuity and hallucinations. Conspicuous by its absence is any indication of the latent homosexuality (or even fear of it, or confusion of sexual identity) intrinsic to Freud's formulation of paranoiogenesis. A paranoid without homosexuality may be as disturbingly anti-Freudian as Sartre's later portrayal of the homosexual Genet, especially in light of the fact that the obvious model for the gun-toting paranoid was a friend of his who was indeed a homosexual. Suffice it to say here that any final assessment of Sartre's system will have to come to grips with his radical anti-Freudian interpretation of Genet's homosexuality.

It is impossible now to say whether Sartre had read Freud's analysis of Dr. Schreber. Simone de Beauvoir says that by around 1930 he had read the *Interpretation of Dreams* and the *Psychopathology of Everyday Life*. We also know that by then he had read Adler's *Neurotic Constitution* and preferred it to Freud because it gave less importance to sexuality. In general, Sartre was suspicious of psychoanalysis, put off by what he saw as dogmatic symbolism, mechanistic explanation, a preponderant role for the unconscious and sexuality, and an analytic method dividing the personality into hermetic components rather than attempting to comprehend it both in its singularity and, synthetically, as an indivisible totality. Beauvoir grants that at the time their knowledge of psychoanalysis was superficial and that they confused readily the serious analysts and their amateur counterparts. A serious study of it, she says, could have tempered their exaggerated notion of human freedom, according to which the lucid, "normal" individual could triumph over complexes, trauma, influences, and memories. They were ready to admit, however, that the psychoses, neuroses, and their symptoms have meaning, and that the meaning refers to the infancy of the subject.

Hilbert makes much of his physical deficiencies and of certain unspecified frustrated ambitions, which might prompt an Adlerian, rather than Freudian approach. He claims that the police, after his arrest, worked him over for two hours, breaking his lorgnon and repeatedly kicking his rear while he groped helplessly on the floor. This did not surprise him, however, because "they," the big guys, had been waiting for years to take advantage of his weakness and inability to defend himself. Bullies in the streets, after all, had long been bumping into him for laughs. Just before the shooting a passer-by clicks his tongue at him. These kinds of outrages are clearly imaginary, and his physical weakness itself must be exaggerated for at one point he brags of his hard, wiry body and his ability to climb more than four flights of stairs, in spite of his paunch, without breathing hard. It doesn't much matter, in any case, whether his paranoia and over-compensating megalomania are due to an unhappy infantile sexual experience with self-hatred and guilt projected outside or represent a response to real or imagined inferiority and thwarted ambitions, since Sartre would set up a case for psychoanalysis only in order to break it down and use it to the ends of his own psychology.

Traditional complexes are important in Sartre's scheme but remain merely "secondary" structures which only partially explain behaviour. We cannot reduce Hilbert simply to a paranoid whose grandiosity has become dangerously anti-social. A psychoanalytic interpretation doesn't exhaust the meaning of his act any more than a reduction to complexes exhausts, in Sartre's view, human reality. The inferiority complex, for example, is a way we freely choose our relation with others. Inferiority as felt and lived is the instrument we choose, in shame and anger, to make ourselves as much as we can like things, objects for others. The recognition of a fundamental inferiority is not unconscious, it is free choice and flight from freedom. Hilbert's poor eyesight, his potbelly are real enough, but he seems to have largely invented his physical weakness for the cause, that is, to guarantee the superiority of his enemies and his own inferiority in their eyes as if they were looking. Hilbert, besides being a subject for therapy, is a study in Sartrean "bad faith." Since this concept is supposed to replace the Freudian unconscious, *Erostrate* has to be seen as at least a partial repudiation of psychoanalysis.

We may approach the story by viewing Hilbert first from the outside, as he might be seen by the newspapers or in a case-study, then from the inside, as he "lives" his crime and the events leading to it. Sartre has managed with remarkable skill and consistency to wed at every point in the narrative this "psychoanalytic" Hilbert—a bundle of neurotic symptoms the gradual deterioration of which leads to acute paranoid turmoil and a potentially tragic anti-social act—with the "Sartrean" Hilbert—a free consciousness making its way toward the crime according to Sartrean categories, "faisant pour se faire et se faisant pour etre" ("doing in order to make itself and making itself in order to *be*") against an objective background which includes those "secondary" structures, the pathological symptoms. One might be tempted, from the outside, to account for all of Hilbert's behaviour in psychoanalytic terms, in which case the various contents of his ravings would appear as simple rationalizations. His doctrinaire anti-Humanism, given a certain culture and the relatively high intelligence usually associated with the paranoid, would express conceptually his neurotic fear and aggression and above all the special irritation provoked by the purveyors of Brotherhood, the Humanists of whatever stamp, irritating enough to set most to raving, but the particular enemy of the paranoid temperament. His hatred of emotional promiscuity would be a simple extension of his fears of losing control and of being touched and crowded. The moral superiority he claims for himself would serve to rationalize his megalomania, in turn the last-ditch effort of the inferior Ego to save itself. His desire to astonish the world would be an extension of his sadistic joy, "comme un enfant," in horrifying the prostitute. The projected crime itself would be classed as the acting out of his problem in a mode characteristic of the paranoid—assassination to gain attention. The crime as projected doesn't come off at all but its failure is perfectly consistent with Hilbert's role both as Sartrean example and as paranoid type. When he first contrives the plan, Hilbert makes no decision to carry it through but chooses to act as if he has, preoccupying himself with the necessary details—practicing his marksmanship at the shooting gallery and attending to his advance publicity by elaborating his notion of the "black hero" to his colleagues at the office. He never does not make the decision and "wakes up" one day to find himself in a no-longer recognizable street, as he really is, stripped of his delusional system, "horriblement seul et petit." Mechanically, he follows a man down the rue d'Odessa. When the man turns and sees his gun, Hilbert asks when the rue de la Gaîté, of all places, is. Fearful of humiliating himself by screaming in the middle of the street, retaining a minimal sense of "dignity" by refusing to lose control in that way, yet needing to relieve the intolerable pressure, he fires. He tries to manufacture some emotion to accompany the shots by shouting "salaud" at the man, then runs down the street towards the crowded Boulevard du Montparnasse. He fires a second time because he feels a hand on his shoulder and fears "suffocation" by the crowd. His act is a failure not because he lacks the courage of his conviction, as Philip Thody has suggested, but because he never had conviction in the first place.

But Hilbert is more than a crystallized paranoid type; he is an anti-Christ (a comic Sartrean version of the religious paranoid) and a study in bad faith. That Sartre is playing with the Christ-figure is obvious: Hilbert is thirty-three years old and spends his last three days locked in a dark room, with food placed before his door. Unlike Christ and Dr. Schreber, however, whose missions were to redeem Mankind and restore a lost state of bliss, Hilbert's mission is to redeem his fallen Ego, for himself alone and against Mankind, not only because the redemption of the "I" is the constant passion of the depressed, or inferior, or depersonalized neurotic, but because in Sartre's system it is the principal of all of us most of the time. Hilbert has already attempted to refortify his lost sexual "I" by carrying the symbolic revolver-penis, but there is a crucial moment in the narrative when this no longer suffices, when the "Sartrean" hero takes over, as it were, and consciousness "overflows" the secondary, sexual structures to begin to work on the imaginative construction of an acceptably powerful and respectable

"I" in the image of Erostratus, who burned the temple of Ephesus to achieve immortal notoriety: "Quand je descendais dans le rue, je sentais en mon corps une puissance étrange. J'avais sur moi mon revolver, cette chose qui éclate et qui fait du bruit. Mais ce n'était plus de lui que je tirais mon assurance, c'étais de moi: j'étais un être de l'espèce des révolvers, des pétards at des bombes." ("When I would go down to the street, I would feel in my body a strange power. I had my revolver on me, that thing which explodes and makes noise. But it was no longer from it that I was getting my confidence, it was from me: I was a being in the nature of revolvers, firecrackers and bombs.")

The figure of Erostratus, supplied by one of his colleagues at the office, is timely; it encourages him to begin seeing himself not as a lonely, petty-bourgeois clerk, but as a "destiny," short and tragic and atrocious to be sure, but celebrated and immortal. Hilbert's imagination, which is considerable, works hard to create his new self-image. He repeatedly visualizes himself firing at a crowd. He attempts to convince himself that his very physiognomy is changing little by little (a frequent paranoid delusion), the eyes growing bigger and more beautiful, resembling those of an artist or assassin. Towards the end he desperately tries to maintain his fragile image as assassin by describing himself from the outside as terrified humanity must see him, a monster crouched in his dark room without food, awaiting only his moment to go down to the street to kill. His effort is to "become" the Assassin so completely that the decision to murder will not have to be made freely but will in some way follow necessarily from the nature of the beast. He thinks that a crime will change him even more than it did the Papin sisters, whose prim rectitude and comforting family resemblances disappeared from their photos. By their murderous act they achieved a certain individuality, each now representing in its own way the common crime. Hilbert wants more, an individuality that will cut him off from the Human Family altogether. He plans for an hour of freedom in his room to feel the "weight" of his crime and to savor his new identity, a futile hope given Sartre's theory of consciousness.

Consciousness, for Sartre, is empty, impersonal, and contingent, but it would rather be full (like his other term, Being-in-Itself), individualized, and necessary. It has no Ego behind it from which the content of its behavior might emanate and no Human Nature further back which would stand as everyman's permanent definition, securing for all time the individual's inclusion in the species, his "dignity" and his ascendance over beasts—to whom we feel superior, as Hilbert reminds us scornfully, because they walk on four legs and can't look us in the eye. The Ego as permanent and personalized Self, and Human Nature as guarantor of a permanent and privileged Creature represent together a lost paradise and state of bliss which the free consciousness, foot-loose and frightened, is perpetually trying to regain (pointing to an even more fundamental drive, to become God or the *ens causa sui*). Consciousness faces the constant temptation to create out of whole cloth a convincing Ego, as if substantized, which would endure as permanent explanation for and justification of any and all conduct. Consciousness undefined, existing as flux and utter potentiality (within a concrete situation), strives to save itself from the burden of perpetually choosing values, tentative and risky ones at that, as it goes along in Time, or, if you wish, *as* Time. The easiest way is to build an Ego around the expectations of others. Hilbert's choice of a permanent Being is neither the established norm of good conduct and values rationalized in morals, liberal politics, and idealistic philosophies (as in the *esprit de sérieux*), nor the desire to be loved, like Jesus, or to be virtuous—a disguise for rigidity and bigotry—like Dr. Schreber; he chooses to set himself against that establishment, radically, as Public Enemy Number One. Hilbert will go one step further by attempting, like Erostratus, to secure his identity for all time in the minds and hearts of his enemies. His effort is to bring about, if only for an instant, the coincidence or fusion of the Hero with his Act; of consciousness with the Self, of Existence with Being, and to present this fusion to his pseudocommunity, posterity, in a splendid baroque *tableau vivant*, featuring the anti-Christ, in a desperate attempt to pin down his "nature" as unique and superior, murdering his fellow creatures. The attempt is doomed to failure because consciousness constantly "overflows" the precarious "I" that it has created, and the only way to stop the action and guarantee the coincidence is to take one's life, so that Eternity can change you into Yourself, and who wants to do that? Certainly not Hilbert, who can't bring himself to commit suicide and surrenders meekly to the police. The surviving consciousness is condemned to go freely on its way where it will find, inexhaustibly, new worlds to organize, deal with, and escape from. Left behind, Hilbert's Act will supposedly divide his life in two and remain like a "glittering mineral" to shore up forever the newly-created Ego and prevent any backsliding. Instead it goes unrecognized, as if committed by somebody else. Hilbert hears the cries of "assassin" behind him as he runs but cannot identify with the criminal being chased. Even death is no guarantee of success, since posterity doesn't always see you as you want to be seen, in your Sunday best, or, in this case, worst. In this letter to the Humanists Hilbert is careful to point out that the tabloids will undoubtedly betray his purpose by making him out a raving maniac; he wants to make it absolutely clear that he killed in perfect calm and that he had sound objective reasons for his act (his doctrinaire anti-Humanism).

A further way for posterity to betray Hilbert's intentions is to treat him as a political anarchist, as an example, by Sartre, of misguided revolutionary zeal. Readers familiar with the period will notice at once that Hilbert, by firing indiscriminately at people in the street, performs the "simplest surrealist act" as proclaimed by Breton in the *Second Manifesto* of 1930; one might presume a sly attack by a Leftist on Surrealist revolutionary pretensions. Breton had anticipated and tried to answer in advance the inevitable criticism of the text in question. An attack of this kind would be consistent enough with Sartre's later politics and conceivable even in 1936, for although he was politically inactive before the War, not bothering to vote even for the Popular Front, he was not politically neutral by any means. His hatred of middle-class rectitude and hypocrisy, as well as its ideology and the fact of its dominance, is well-known, so that a corollary sympathy with the factory worker and the artisan is not surprising. Though Simone de Beauvoir tells us that as late as the early thirties they hadn't as yet any opinion about peasants. Even in 1936 Sartre would surely have held that, from the point of view of real revolutionary activity, Hilbert's act is individualistic, counter-revolutionary, and sick, a futile and self-defeating gesture acting out a romantic posture best associated with middle-class sons in revolt against their temporal and eternal fathers, an anarchist's *propagande du geste* coming, not from outside the power structure but from within the closed bourgeois world, therein muffled, absorbed and forgotten, a pop-gun explosion that destroys nothing, except a few lives, and doesn't even frighten. After the War Sartre did undertake (in *Qu'est-ce que la littérature*), from the polemical point of view of "committed" literature, a serious analysis of Surrealist revolutionary claims. It would be a mistake, however, to view the story from a narrow political point of view, not only because internal evidence is against it, but because it would prevent the understanding of an important element in Sartre's development, predominant in the early thirties, but which to a certain extent has never been abandoned. Although he would not have confused Hubert's act with genuine revolutionary activity, Sartre would have surely agreed with Breton that the purely negative act has a certain validity in itself, and this would in no way run counter to his later political thought, one of whose principal tenets is to maintain the free, critical, or "negative" moment at the heart of Marxist philosophy and Socialist practice. Simone de Beauvoir writes that in the thirties Sartre was interested only in the negative side of Socialist revolution. His broad negativity in general, his radical refusal of any restraint from the outside, and his deep hatred of the established order, its culture, its ideology, and its very language is consistent with the climate of the time and with the mood of the Surrealist movement that dominated it. Though his hostility towards bourgeois culture, spoon-fed to him by his grandfather Schweitzer, can be partly understood on the level of psychology, it would draw later on attitudes which came to a head in the Surrealist explosion. According to Beauvoir, the movement itself, although they were outside it by virtue of their age and university background, had been at least indirectly very important in their lives. Sartre would diverge from the Surrealist current in that he would demand, not the death of intelligibility, communication, and language itself, but the creation of a new kind of intelligibility, a use of all language for communication (and communication for change).

Hilbert goes to some lengths to establish the non-political character of his act. He elaborates to his co-workers at the office his ideal of the "black hero," who would definitely not be an anarchist because in his own way the anarchist, too, loves Mankind. He makes it clear that through his act he will attempt to do something *against* humanity. Later, in his letter to the Humanists, he reiterates: they will be all the more scandalized by the murders *because* they are non-political. Hubert's act, rather than representing an attack on Breton and the political failure of impatient anarchist violence as against true revolutionary patience, must be seen as positive, in Sartre's view, at least in its inspiration. Although Hubert's solution, which attempts to prolong the "abstract, negative moment of freedom," not only as long as he lives, as in Sartre's version of Genet, but forever, is negative from the point of view of "authentic" moral commitment, it is positive and admirable in so far as it represents the naked explosion of a human freedom. As such, it takes its place alongside Mathieu's broken vase in *L'Age de raison* and the black pilot who steals the plane in *L'Etre et le néant*, and, in real life, with increasing social and political content, it takes its place alongside the Papin sisters, Tito's defection, and the "events" of May, 1968. Its source can be traced to Sartre's uncompromising cult of freedom of the early thirties. He refused categorically any definition of man that would extend to him personally, and any definition of himself that would square with ordinary social roleplaying or with any accepted notion of rights, duties, virtues, and obligations of the citizen. He claimed that no real knowledge of the world was possible within traditional modes of thinking; it was only accessible to the "solitary man," and "thaumaturge" who, as writer, artist, or philosopher, would remain outside the academy and believe only what he saw with his own eyes. Hilbert is the caricature of what Sartre would have considered a lonely but legitimate negative force, blown up into an extreme, pathological, and thus instructive, case-history.

Simone de Beauvoir writes that in the early thirties she and Sartre were fascinated by newspaper accounts of extreme cases of abnormal behavior, which, like psychoses and neuroses, presented in exaggerated form attitudes and passions common to so-called normal men and women. They were convinced that these anti-social explosions always entailed the revelation of some important truth. They gave special importance to those which seemed to indicate a personal liberation for someone and to those which laid bare the *tares* and hypocrisies that were concealed behind the facades of bourgeois households and conduct. They paid special attention to those crimes and trials which had psychological or social significance and were quick to smell out the mystification involved when the social order was in question and defending itself. Like Hilbert, they were intrigued by the case of the Papin sisters, wanting to see in the murder by the maids of their tyrannical mistresses, as did Janet Flanner, not a murder so much as a mini-revolution, a drama of social and political retribution, the revenge by members of an exploited working class against a society responsible for the orphanage where they grew up and their servant status, an absurd and unjust social system created by and for the *bien pensants* and which systematically spawned all manner of psychotics, murderers, and freaks. The horror inspired by the system could be properly denounced only by an exemplary counter-horror: the two sisters had made themselves the instruments and the martyrs of a "somber justice." When in the course of the trial it became evident that the elder sister was an out-and-out psychotic and that the younger one had participated in her illness in a bizarre, incestuous, Lesbian *folie à deux*, Sartre and Beauvoir were disappointed, concluding that the crime was not, as they had hoped, the "savage unleashing of a freedom" against a repressice establishment, but merely the blind, terrified striking out of a psychotic, and with no social meaning. They were wrong, of course; that the raving Christine lacked the class consciousness necessary for a political murder would take little away from whatever social significance there might be. She did strike, after all, as opposed to, say, cutting out paper dolls, and it was the mistresses who were slain, and not some random dog or cat. Hilbert, in any case, seems to represent what Sartre might have wished the Papin sisters to be. He, at least, had "more serious reasons" for killing, more serious, that is, than the fancied ones, that "they" hated him and were forever jostling him in the street.

Hilbert's more serious reasons (his theoretical anti-Humanism) would have been shared by Sartre, who possessed a generous dose of good feeling for his fellow men but an exasperated antipathy towards the liberal intellectual Establishment whose timeless, abstract values, silly optimism (200 years after Doctor Pangloss) and systematic reverence for Culture called nothing into question, fled any genuine attempt to understand the human condition, and rationalized handily any real problem, such as the brooding presence of an exploited working class on the edge of town. Hilbert tells us in his letter that the Humanists have monopolized the meaning of life. Not sharing their state of grace, he has been forced to abandon everything he has undertaken; otherwise "they" would turn it sooner or later to their profit. All of the available tools including language, come down to us from "them," so that a man can't even formulate a thought by himself: " . . . j'aurais voulu des mots *à moi.* Mais ceux dont je dispose ont traîné dans je ne sais combien de consciences; ils s'arrangent tout seuls dans ma tête en vertu d'habitudes qu'ils ont prises chez les autres at ça n'est pas sans repugnance que je les utilize en vous écrivant." (" . . . I would have like to have my *own* words. But those at my disposal have kicked around in I don't know how many other consciousnesses: they arrange themselves in my head on their own, thanks to habits they've picked up in other people's brains and it's not without repugnance that I utilize them in this letter.") One is reminded of Sartre's own situation (which, in *Qu'est-ce que la littérature,* he extends to his class): condemned by his bourgeois situation (and a doting grandfather) to a *lycée* education, the University system, and a career in letters, all within an ordered culture and a policed society — in which books "grow naturally" like trees in a garden, make their appearance fully-grown in their perfected, classical form, received as a matter of course the seal of collective approval, are accepted automatically as national monuments (Didn't De Gaulle say that Sartre, *also,* is France?), and provide material for the *explications de texte* of the future—Sartre felt obliged to spend a lifetime contesting this enforced patrimony and to this day does his best thinking "again himself." Hilbert find himself alienated and uncomfortable in a material and social world contaminated with *a priori* meaning and value and unable to share with others their complaisant acceptance of it and the smug sense of their own preordained legitimacy in the scheme of things. Incapable of doing anything *with* them, he can at least, with his revolver, do something *against* them; he can really and symbolically blow a few of them out of the human tub (taking, of course, the baby with the bathwater) in a futile, symbolic attempt, as Sartre said of the Surrealists, to leap outside the human condition, or, like Abraham's paranoid, destroy the world.

Hilbert's inhibited thought processes are typical of the paranoid, who often feels that others can read his mind, steal his thoughts, and put ideas in his head, or that his brain, like his body in a crowd, is entrapped and suffocated by any concrete environment—originally within the family where, as a child all his thinking and responses were felt to be restricted and imposed upon, and later within the family's neurotically-sustained extensions, such as marriage, as if thought itself were impossible without first breaking away from the stifling presence of the Other. But we don't want to reduce Hilbert to psychology, because for Sartre the delusion of influence is a fundamental aspect of human reality, implicit in the very fact of verbal communication. In a world populated, scandalously, by other people any verbal expression at all needs, for better or for worse, the collaboration of the Other in order to come to have objective meaning. The presence of the Other is always in some sense "alienating" because our utterance, once in the public domain, is at the mercy of interpretations and its intention is always more or less distorted. Likewise, one must read Hilbert's conviction that his projects were doomed to failure, or absurd and frowned upon, or diverted to the profit of "them," as both the rationalization of failure by a clinical paranoid and the ground for a serious theory of alienated effort which poses the very necessity of alienation from available socializations. In Sartre's system, the presence of the Other makes any expression of "self," verbal or otherwise, alienated by definition: " . . . je m'éprouve dans mon aliénation au profit de l'Autre." (" . . . I experience myself in my alienation to the profit of the Other.") And being in the world with others, from the point of view of *L'Etre et le néant* and common sense, is an inescapable aspect of the human condition.

Sartre himself, in the blurb he prepared for his publisher, emphasizes Hilbert's attempt, and failure, to deny his "human" condition, which involves, besides an ontological relationship to the universe at large, a social or intersubjective element which even supplies a necessary, if bothersome, dimension of ourselves, the Being-for-Others. The fainting scene at the beginning provides a preview for Hilbert's ultimate failure to put himself "above the human" that he admits is in him. Seeing a man dead and bleeding in the street, Hilbert claims emotional invulnerability, telling himself that there is nothing "human" about the tragic scene, that the blood is no more moving than fresh paint. It doesn't work; he feels weak and chooses to faint, what Sartre would probably call a "magical" attempt to alter a world with such creatures in it. He is brought to his senses by some anonymous passers-by and is of course furious at their intervention, the fraternity of their act, and his dependence on them.

His attempt at assassination is no less a failure, from the points of view both of psychology and "Existential" humanism. Psychologically, Hilbert's sensibilities are so blunted that by the time of the shooting his "hatred" has no substance and his project founders in useless agitation. For Sartre, Hilbert's "hatred," which fails in real life, is no different from the abstract "love" of the Humanist, which fails on the political level: it is just as impossible to hate Man as an entity as to love him. Hilbert wants no more to inflict pain on others than on himself. Cornered in the toilet, he finds excuses not to shoot himself and wonders, hopefully, if his victim might not live. In the end he puts off his project as long as possible and assures his capture by "forgetting" to leave his door unlocked, then conveniently running the wrong way in the rue d'Odessa, towards the populated Boulevard du Montparnasse instead of back up the street to the relatively quiet Boulevard Edgar-Quinet, as planned. Like the depressed suicidal, Hilbert wants nothing more than to reestablish human contact, but he can't bring himself to understand it or do it; thus the ironic: "J'aurais donné n'importe quoi pour quitter ma chamber, mais je ne pouvais pas descendre à cause des gens qui marchaient dans les rues." ("I would have given anything to leave my room, but I couldn't go out because of the people walking around there in the streets.") Freud's view that the paranoid's hatred is disguised love seems applicable to Hilbert's case. His solitude like that of Sartre's Baudelaire, is, ironically, a kind of social tie, a superior isolation being his only means of participation; and ultimately, the crime constitutes a kind of twisted link with humanity, a way of forcing attention, recognition, and perhaps love. In his study of Baudelaire Sartre quotes (twice) a remarkable statement from *Fusées* which could serve accurately as Hilbert's epitaph: "Quand j'aurai inspiré le dégoût et l'horreur universels j'aurai conquis la solitude." ("When I will have inspired universal disgust and horror, then will I have conquered solitude.") Taken in its broadest significance, *Erostrate* can represent the foundation in fiction of what will later become an "Existentialist" humanism having its ground, not in some abstract myth of static Human Nature and so-called Human Dignity, but in the lucid comprehensions of the reality of the human situation intrinsic to which is a fluid, immediate relationship with others, alternately free and alienated, sadistic and masochistic, and from which derives a dimension of ourselves that must be dealt with constantly—the Being-for-Others. Sartre will spend much of the rest of his life grappling with this social problem, first in terms of close intersubjective relationships, in *L'Etre et le néant*, and finally within a much broader, Marxist context, in the *Critique de la raison dialectique*.

DOMINICK LaCAPRA

Early Theoretical Studies: Art Is an Unreality

Sartre's early series of theoretical studies are rarely read today: *The Transcendence of the Ego* (1936–1937), *The Imagination* (1936), *Sketch for a Theory of the Emotions* (1939), and *L'Imaginaire* (1940). In a preparation for the examination of Sartre's more famous and influential works, a brief and highly selective analysis of the early ones, explicitly addressed to the issue of continuity and discontinuity in Sartre's thought, is pertinent.

The analysis of imagination and emotion as structures or activities of consciousness is especially interesting in these early works. It fills gaps in the dominant line of argument of *Being and Nothingness* (1943), although more submerged but still forceful tendencies in the later work go beyond its limits. The early theoretical notions—especially in the case of *L'Imaginaire*—are situated and indirectly contested in *Nausea* (1938). And they are more directly challenged in Sartre's views on language, literature, and art in *What Is Literature?* (1947) and "A Plea for Intellectuals" (1965). But, in certain respects, Sartre returns repeatedly—as, for example, in the existential biographies—to notions or modes of conceptualization developed in the early studies, notably in the very important *L'Imaginaire*.

Sartre's early theoretical studies are organized around the phenomenological conception of consciousness. Consciousness is intentional, that is, it is always consciousness of something. The thing is the object of

From *A Preface to Sartre: A Critical Introduction to Sartre's Literary and Philosophical Writings.* © 1978 by Cornell University Press.

consciousness, but not its content. To see consciousness as itself a thing or as having contents is to fall into the naturalistic "illusion of immanence." Consciousness is a structure or an activity, which for Sartre is appropriately understood through the metaphor of an empty spontaneity. Indeed, in an important sense, which Sartre never takes as problematic, a series of metaphors structures the proper usage of "consciousness" as a concept. (Consciousness is masculine, pure, limpid, clean, hard, active, mineral-like, erect yet devoid of content; its adventure is a flight from "feminine" passivity, maternal immanence, viscosity, "a stinking brine of the spirit," "moist gastric" intimacy, self-love, formlessness, mud, and indecision.) Consciousness as an activity that transcends the thing or object is, moreover, closely connected with human freedom. Sartre never makes theoretically explicit the precise nature of the relationship between freedom and consciousness: he often uses the two terms interchangeably. And these two terms are linked to a third: nihilation, or the ontological basis for processes of negation—a linkage explicated at length in *Being and Nothingness*, yet already crucial in *L'Imaginaire*.

Two relatively clear aspects of Sartre's early studies impugn common interpretations of his early thought. First, Sartre's early thought does, in one of its movements, directly relate freedom or consciousness to action and projects in the "real" world. The "mind" is not seen simply as activeless. Second, consciousness is not originally specified in terms of the individual. It is initially treated as impersonal, or at least as nonpersonal. It is individuated but in a sense initially contrasted, not with the social, but with the universal or generic. And it is always "mine" but in a sense specified in *The Transcendence of the Ego* as nonpossessive and purely designative. One explicit criticism of Husserl in this work is of his view of ego as the center and subject of consciousness, thereby giving consciousness a content. The ego for Sartre is not the subject or center of consciousness: it is the intentional object of consciousness in the world. Indeed, the early works of Sartre explode the notion of identity and individuality in the ordinary sense. As Sartre later put it in *Being and Nothingness*, the for-itself is what it is not and is not what it is. Sartre, in one important movement of his thought, does conceive consciousness as initially isolated in the world, but this isolation is not at first identified with that of the lonely or uncommitted individual.

One central equivocation in the early Sartre, however, continues throughout his works and allows, if it does not invite, systematic misreadings. There is a dominant tendency in his thought that presents freedom (or consciousness) as initially pure and total within itself and radically transcendent in relation to the world. In this sense, freedom—split off from the world—is initially isolated. A submerged tendency in Sartre's thought indicates that freedom is always already implicated in the world in a sense that undercuts and may give rise to the opposition between transcendence and immanence.

In his early theoretical works, Sartre's dominant tendency is especially powerful. In terms of it, freedom is conceived as having two basic "options." On the one hand, it can choose to direct itself toward perception, reality, action, desire, truth, and morality. On the other hand, it can attempt to escape this series of involvements in the "real" world and, in its negative purity, transcend them toward imagination, emotion, unreality, contemplation, artifice, error, evil, and art. The first series might be termed that of proper reactions to the world or proper uses of freedom and intentional consciousness. The second series is an object of suspicion and anxiety but also, paradoxically, a possible source of salvation (through art). At the most basic level, Sartre explicitly resists any ambiguous overlap or undecidable interplay between the two series of free choices or activities of consciousness even at the margin of borderline cases. But his texts do at times indicate the submerged and unspeakable intercourse or interplay of the two series in a manner that is not "raised to consciousness" as an object of theoretical reflection. In his early theoretical works, moreover, Sartre not only explicitly resists supplementary relationships; he also fails to discuss the possibility of complementary relationships through dialectical mediation and possible synthesis. Instead, he "relates" the two series through the nonrelation of segregation or a taboo on contact and relies on an extreme form of analysis to mark the divide. An analytic logic of identity and difference presents the only relationship between the two series as mutual avoidance or, upon contact and the impairment of purity, mutual annihilation. Sartre himself attempts to play the good shepherd of theoretical concepts that clearly separate the two series and prevent the encroachment of the one upon the other.

Sartre explicitly relates his enterprise in his early thought to Husserl and Descartes and in a sense repeats Husserl's own recapitulation of the Cartesian heritage—but in a form more uncompromising and *outré* than the endeavors of his predecessors, for Sartre makes no explicit allowance for exceptions or areas of permeability in his clear and distinct ideas. Subversive and misguided inclinations in Husserl and Descartes are duly observed and excoriated. Sartre will not wink where his predecessors nodded. His short but powerful essay "A Fundamental Idea of the Phenomenology of Husserl" begins with words calculated to produce a shock effect in the reader:

> "He ate her with his eyes." This sentence and many other signs
> mark the illusion common to realism and idealism, according to

which to know is to eat. French philosophy, after a hundred years of academicism, is still at this point. We have all read Brunschvicg, Lalande, and Meyerson; we have all believed that the Spirit-Spider [*l'Esprit-Araignée*] attracted things into its web, covered them with white spittle, and slowly swallowed them, reducing them to its own substance.

The rejection of what Sartre terms an alimentary philosophy, which presents consciousness as digesting contents, prefaces his own association of phenomenology with what might be called, by an extension of the metaphor, an emetic philosophy, which evacuates consciousness and throws it explosively into the world. For alimentary philosophy, consciousness is itself immanent in reality: it is sucked down by an alien "other," which makes it flesh of its flesh. For Sartre, consciousness is radically transcendent but in a sense that immediately presents it to the world. It has no contents or attachments to serve as barrier between its pure, empty spontaneity and the world. It is altogether *disponible*. The concluding words of this brief essay are as insistent as its opening lines:

> If we love a woman, it is because she is lovable. Thus we are delivered from Proust. Delivered at the same time from "interior life": in vain do we seek like Amiel, like a child that kisses its own shoulder, the caresses and pamperings of our intimacy, since at last everything is outside, even ourselves: outside, in the world, among others. It is not in I know not what retreat that we discover ourselves: it is on the road, in the city, in the midst of the crowd, thing among things, man among men.

Sartre takes his distance from Husserl in criticizing the tendencies that betray the phenomenological project of liberation by either filling in consciousness or diverting it from an orientation toward reality. In *The Transcendence of the Ego*, the transcendental ego as subject was rejected by Sartre precisely because it blocked the empty spontaneity of a wind-swept consciousness. And Sartre accepts the *epochè* or phenomenological reduction only in so far as it does not simply bracket reality or put it out of play but rather seeks to transform everyday life. In *Being and Nothingness*, Sartre accuses Husserl of taking a turn toward subjective idealism in seeking an intuition of ideal essences. In *The Transcendence of the Ego*, Sartre concludes by insisting that for centuries philosophy has not experienced so realistic a current as phenomenology and so intense a concern with plunging man back into the world. A political, historical concern with "real problems" is directly indicated: "It has always seemed to me that a working hypothesis as fruitful as historical materialism never needed for a foundation the absurdity that is metaphysical materialism." (This is, of course, the theme that was later developed in the 1946 essay "Materialism and Revolution.")

Yet the critique of Husserl is not without attendant difficulties in Sartre's early thought. Sartre's rejection of the transcendental ego and his purge of the "I" from consciousness still enable him to assert that consciousness is "quite simply a first condition and an absolute source of existence." And the desire to affirm a primary orientation toward reality fosters Sartre's extreme analytic tendencies, for he sometimes takes ideal types (or eidetic essences) and projects them onto "reality" as inclusive and exhaustive definitions of things in terms of categorial opposites or antinomies. This tendency marks his early analyses of emotion, imagination, and perception (as well as his later analysis of prose and poetry).

Before turning to these analyses, one may note Sartre's attested affinity with Descartes. As Sartre expressed himself in an interview of 1944: "In our country [chez nous], only one person has profoundly affected my mind: Descartes. I place myself in his lineage and proclaim my relationship to this old Cartesian tradition that has been conserved in France." But the criticisms of Husserl in *The Transcendence of the Ego* were implicit criticisms of Descartes, and Sartre—in expelling the ego from consciousness—was engaged in displacing the final "o" from the *cogito*. Sartre attempts to explicate his relation to Descartes in an essay of 1945, "La Liberté cartésienne." Cartesian freedom and Husserlian intentionality are intimately linked in Sartre's mind, for the freedom of Descartes applies to consciousness in the world.

As Sartre sees it, freedom in Descartes is total but not absolute, for in Descartes, as in the Stoics, a crucial distinction is made between freedom and power. The purity and totality of freedom depend upon its clear distinction from power in the world. "To be free is not at all to be able to do what one wants [*pouvoir faire ce qu'on veut*] but it is to be able to will what one can do [*vouloir ce qu'on peut*]." Action, however restricted its field, is free to the extent that it is informed by the project of intentional consciousness. Freedom is total, but power is limited by the situation. One may note that this conception, which Sartre holds on a possibly dominant level of his thought, depends upon an identity between freedom and intentional consciousness and a dichotomy between freedom and the situation. The conception is placed in question to the extent that these associations are challenged. On this conception, moreover, freedom is related to power through an activist leap made in the interest of man's mastery of the situation. Sartre finds in Descartes "a magnificent humanist affirmation of creative liberty," which constrains us to take up "this fearful task, *our* task *par*

excellence: to make truth exist in the world, to make the world be true. . . ."
Sartre, of course, objects to the Cartesian role of divinity as fail-safe. But—in
a turn of thought that seems to confuse Heidegger with Feuerbach—he
insists that the reliance upon traditional religious ideas does not detract from
Descartes's ringing affirmation of man and freedom:

> Little does it matter to us that he was constrained by his epoch,
> as by his point of departure, to reduce human free will to only a
> negative power to refuse itself to the point of finally giving in and
> abandoning himself to divine solicitude; little does it matter to us
> that he hypostatized in God this original and *constituting* freedom
> whose infinite existence he seized by the *cogito* itself: it remains
> that a formidable power of divine and human affirmation runs
> through and supports his universe. Two centuries of crisis will be
> necessary—crisis of Faith, crisis of Science—for man to
> recuperate this creative freedom that Descartes placed in God
> and for one to suspect finally this truth, the essential basis of
> humanism: man is the being whose appearance makes a world
> exist. But we do not reproach Descartes for having given to God
> what is our proper due [*ce qui nous revient en propre*]; instead we
> admire him for having, in an authoritarian epoch, laid the bases
> of democracy, having followed the requirements of the idea of
> autonomy to the end, and having understood, well before
> Heidegger in *Vom Wesen des Grundes*, that the unique foundation
> of being is freedom.

Thus, the task of human freedom is to repossess what was formerly
"hypostatized" in divinity. In his early theoretical writings, Sartre explores
the adventures of freedom through an analytic framework that is probably
more demanding than Cartesianism in its insistence upon clear and distinct
ideas. Analysis in the early Sartre functions as an extreme ritual of
purification. Where Descartes, for example, allows for a possible confusion
between the real and the imaginary, Sartre insists upon their radical
discontinuity. Perception for Sartre is informed by a logic of identity and
difference, and it is geared to reality through a linkage with instrumental
action that tests the real. Perception has no points of contact with
imagination. Perception, imagination, and emotion are total, or totalitarian,
structures of consciousness that can be experienced only alternately, not
simultaneously. Their relation is purely diachronic, not synchronic. But all
three are structures and activities of consciousness, which cannot be seen on
the analogy of the thing or through the naturalistic "illusion of immanence"

which would fill them with contents and implicate them in causal series. Sartre presents perception as central and guiding in its logical, adult relation to freedom and action in reality. By contrast, emotion and imagination are "perceived" in structurally analogous ways as escapes from reality and freedom—emotion as an evasion "from below" and imagination as one "from above." Both emotion and imagination are compared to magic, "prelogical" thinking, or childlike behavior. Both are what orthodox Freudians would call forms of substitute gratification and what Sartre later discusses in terms of the game of "loser wins." For both are prompted by some failure in reality and constitute inappropriate responses to real problems.

In one of the few significant studies of an important area of Sartre's thought, Joseph Fell makes observations that apply beyond the problem of emotion in the thought of Sartre:

> The question [is] whether instrumental [related to perception] and magical [related to emotion] attitudes are only *limiting cases* on a continuous scale whose intermediate points mark attitudes which are combinations or syntheses of the instrumental and magical attitudes. And are the corresponding perceptual fields which are intended by these attitudes likewise partially instrumental and partially magical, with wholly instrumental and wholly magical worlds representing only limiting cases? We said that in order for Sartre's theory to cover cases of delicate and weak emotion it would seem necessary for him to qualify considerably his apparently stark dialectical opposition of instrumental and magical ways of being-in-the-world. In presenting Sartre's theory of imagination I raised the question whether the following dialectical formulation was to be taken literally: "The image and the perception . . . represent the two irreducible attitudes of consciousness. It follows that they exclude each other." We concluded that weak and delicate emotions could not be regarded as emotions at all unless such statements were taken as descriptions of limiting cases, not formulas descriptive of *all* emotions or *all* cases of imagination. Yet such a conclusion seems contradicted by remarks such as this: "It is easy to see that every emotional apprehension of an object which frightens, irritates, saddens, etc., can be made only on the basis of a total alteration of the world."

Fell himself strains to make his critical observations apply only to exceptions (such as "delicate" and "weak" emotions) requiring seemingly minor modifications that Sartre's theory might accommodate (by recognizing, for example, the status of his analyses as "descriptions" of limiting cases, not of all cases). But certain of Fell's comments fail to be contained in this framework of criticism. He astutely notices, for example, that Sartre's analysis of the emotions is radically contested by Sartre's own understanding of an emotion that is central in his thought—*angoisse*, or anguish: "[*Angoisse*] is reflective; it is neither transformative nor deceptive because it is recognition of the freedom of consciousness hidden by all other emotions; it may, certainly, be accompanied by bodily changes, it does not even seem to be a purposive act. It thus seems a thorough misfit, failing utterly to fall within the categories of Sartre's theory."

One might add that the purifying reflection related to the recognition of anguished freedom can effect a radical conversion in being-in-the-world only if that freedom is lived on the prereflective level and "is" an emotion. The very core of Sartre's early thought escapes the analytic categories of his dominant framework. Not only is it a question of "describing" limiting cases, it is also a question of "recognizing" the status of these limiting cases or analytically defined polar opposites as fictions more or less approximated in reality—a status that itself places in question any rigid categorial opposition between fiction and reality. The analytic type (which Fell curiously but revealingly refers to as the "stark dialectical opposition") is itself a pure form that attempts to center and master the "ambiguous" supplementary interplay that it simultaneously indicates and represses. It is not simply a question of "weak" and "delicate" emotions, but also one of possibly strong emotion (or imagination) as the *proper* response to the situation—the status Sartre implicitly accords to *angoisse* itself. Sartre's equivocation on these matters "is" very much his equivocation about freedom (pure/impure, initially unengaged/always already engaged) and bad faith (escape from pure freedom and unproblematic reality/escape from ambivalence itself). One might reformulate Fell's criticism by arguing that Sartre "describes" emotion and the imagination only in so far as they are responses in bad faith. But, given his own equivocation about the nature and status of his "descriptions," his own analysis is in "bad faith."

Perhaps the most important of Sartre's early theoretical studies is *L'Imaginaire* (badly translated both in title and content as *The Psychology of the Imagination*). This work is a crucial supplement to *Being and Nothingness*, which largely assumes the theory of the imagination directly related in the earlier work to the problems of freedom and nothingness:

> The imaginary represents at each instant the implicit meaning of
> the real. . . . And if negation is the unconditional principle of all

imagination, reciprocally it can never realize itself except in and through an act of imagination. One must imagine what one negates. [*Il faut qu'on imagine ce que l'on nie.*] In fact the object of a negation cannot be *real* since that would mean affirming what one denies—but no more can it be a total *nothing* because precisely one denies [or negates—*nie*] *something*. Thus the object of a negation must be posited as imaginary. And this is true for the logical forms of negation (doubt, restriction, etc.) as for its active and affective forms (defense, consciousness of impotence, of lack, etc.). . . . Thus the imagination, far from appearing as a factual characteristic of consciousness, is revealed [*devoilée*] as an essential and transcendental condition of consciousness. It is as absurd to conceive of a consciousness that could not imagine as to conceive of a consciousness that could not effect the *cogito*. [*L'Imaginaire*]

The dominant line of argument in *L'Imaginaire* may be seen as an attempt to disentangle in terms of clear and distinct analytic dichotomies the *noeud de vipères* embodied in this quotation. The ambiguous overlap of the imaginary and the real, of imagination and perception—indeed of affirmation and negation—are at times implicit in the language Sartre uses ("negation . . . can never realise itself"), but it is not recognized, and is in fact explicitly denied on the level of theory. In the interest of purity, a logic of identity and difference analyzes, controls, and guides a conception of the imagination and art. Sartre employs analysis to distribute "ambiguity" or the supplementary interplay of the same and the other (the imaginary is the same as the real but as differed) into discrete categories, or distinct boxes, of experience. Negation implies not the transformative reconstruction of its object but its "nihilation," the escape into the imaginary, and the postulation of a sharp divide. Life is one thing. Art is another. Reality is one thing. Imagination is another. Perception is entirely different from imagination. Perception is presented as excessively rich: we can always learn more about the perceived "real" object as we walk around it and acquire new perspectives on it. Imagination is poor. It gives its object all in one go, and it corresponds to a lack in reality created by freedom itself. Excess and lack are thus squarely placed on opposite sides of an unbreachable barrier. This "conception" of the imagination is indeed necessitated by Sartre's definition of imagination as an intentional structure of consciousness that "nihilates" reality and "presents" its object as not present, absent, or not existing. And imagination is related to the two faces of freedom that never come face to face. Imagination "is" freedom as a nihilating, empty spontaneity. It marks the paradox of freedom, for it liberates man from reality only to entrap him in a fatalistic world of escapist images that is poverty-stricken. Again, the silenced problems are those of overlap and mediation, supplementarity and dialectical relationship between "opposites"; Sartre himself seems unable to provide "viable" relationships among elements that threaten to constitute the world of hollowly repetitive fatal splits both explored and replicated in his early works. And again there are at least marginal, unexplored elements in the text that place his dominant view in question—for example, the fascinating case of the woman impersonating Maurice Chevalier in such a way that an interplay between perception and imagination is generated, which threatens to undermine or contaminate the decisive analytic opposition between the two. But the most interesting part of *L'Imaginaire* is the concluding section, in which Sartre offers a sustained analysis of the relation of imagination to art—a problem that will continue to preoccupy if not haunt him in his later works. Toward the end of *L'Imaginaire*, Sartre presents seriously, but not explicitly as a means of salvation, the conception of art that he later presents toward the end of *Nausea* as a possible means of salvaging existence, although it then takes on an ironic quality. It is a conception of art derived from a rather literal reading of the theory of symbolist poetics: the aesthetic object is the rose missing from every bouquet. And it is a conception of art that Sartre later attributes to Flaubert and envisions himself as having outgrown.

What, then, is art in *L'Imaginaire*? As a product of the imagination, "the work of art is an unreality." It negates reality and transcends it, not toward some heaven of real forms or essences, but toward an absence. The only point of contact between the real object and the aesthetic object of beauty is the material that serves as "analogon" for that imaginary derealization of the real. And this point, as Sartre interprets it, is a zero point that almost effaces itself. The relationship between the real and the aesthetic is purely analogical. Sartre's argument places a great deal of interpretive weight on the analogon as a feeble point zero of contact. It is a kind of sense datum in the real that somehow indicates the unreal. Sartre attempts to eliminate all ambiguity in the analogon's role as real reference point of the ideal but nihilating aesthetic object. There is a total divide between the sensible paint on the canvas and the painting as art, between the words on the paper and the poem as an aesthetic object, between the notes on the score sheet or even the performance of a piece and the other-worldly sounds of music:

> What is real, one must not tire of repeating, are the results of the strokes of the paint brush, the coating [*l'empâtement*] of the canvas, its grain, the varnish one has placed over the colors. But precisely all of that is not in the least the object of aesthetic

appreciation. On the contrary, what is "beautiful" is a being that cannot be given to perception and which, in its very nature is out of the world [*isolé de l'univers*]. . . . The painter has not in the least *realized* his mental image: he has simply constituted a material analogon such that each of us may seize this image if only he considers the analogon. But the image thus provided with an exterior analogon remains an image. There is no realization of the imaginary; at the very most one can speak of its *objectification* [*tout au plus pourrait-on parler de son* objectivation]. [*L'Imaginaire*]

It is interesting that, in a significant slip, the English version translates the last phrase as "nor can one speak of its objectification," thereby transforming a weak affirmation into a strong negation. Given Sartre's conception of the analogon (which is far from clear and distinct), it is difficult to see how one can speak of the objectification or objectivation of the imaginary in the art object. In the distinction he makes between the analogon and the aesthetic object, Sartre repeats and displaces problems associated with the relationship between the world and divinity in theology or with the relationship between the *signans* and the *signatum* (signifier and signified) in the philosophy and theory of language. In Sartre's "iconoclastic" theory of the imagination, art functions as a secular, humanistic "surrogate" for a God that is not simply hidden but absent: it allows for a transcendental signified (a terminal concept, often identified with a referent, ultimately holding everything together in a meaningful way) that is purely imaginary. And the analogon generates theoretical problems "analogous" to those raised by any immanent sign in relation to a transcendent signified. The analogon is a purely external sign, or index, that must somehow remain purely external in relation to what it signifies but nonetheless function as a signifier pointing to the absent object. And the problems surrounding it create the anxiety of contamination. The objections raised to Sartre's early theory from more "immanent" conceptions of art (but does not modern art explore precisely the strokes of the brush, the texture and grain of the canvas, the varnish, as media of composition and as aesthetic objects?) often seem like pale shadows of religious debates.

The problems circulating around Sartre's theory of art are those found in his conception of freedom, for freedom is imagination as a nihilating consciousness. In his later works, Sartre returns to these problems, often in paradoxical or internally divided ways. One may note that in *L'Imaginaire* the drastic separation between the real and the imaginary, life and art, is applied to all forms of art and literature. It drives a wedge between morality and the aesthetic as well as between desire and the imagination. Commitment in art is out of the question: "It is stupid to confound morality and aesthetics" because "the values of the Good suppose being-in-the-world, aim at conduct in reality, and are subjected first and foremost to the essential absurdity of existence" (*L'Imaginaire*). The moral problem is apparently to come to terms with the "rich" but nauseatingly ugly and absurd world given to us in perception. In relation to the "real" world, freedom in art is deadly. The aesthetic negates and transcends the nauseating absurdity of contingent existence, and it seems, at least implicitly, to indicate a possible path of "salvation" from the real world. But it does so at the price of furnishing an escapist illusion that carries with it a touch of evil. Indeed, Sartre interprets the feeling of letdown after an artistic performance in terms of the abrupt transition from a consciousness captivated by the imaginary to a renewed contact with reality that "provokes the nauseating disgust that characterizes the realizing consciousness." There is no mutually contestatory and possibly re-creative interplay between art and reality, only a passage from one to the other through the narrow gate of the analogon. Nor is art rooted in erotic experience or related to bodily desire even in terms of "sublimation." Sartre, rather, carries the divorce between desire and beauty to the point of swallowing the paradox that one cannot desire a beautiful woman—a perverse paradox that in effect presents all desire on the analogy of the impotent look of the *voyeur* gazing at frigid, glacial beauty.

In *What Is Literature?* Sartre tries to reverse fields by subtracting prose from complicity in pure art and by developing a theory of committed literature that demystifies the escapist illusion and plunges at least certain forms of literature into the "real world" of morality, desire, and politics. But he thus risks making a mystery of that which is literary in his conception of prose. And he will continue to ground his argument upon uncompromising analytic dichotomies that explicitly resist both supplementary interplay and dialectical mediation. His later turn to dialectics may in part be seen as an attempt to heal the wounds aggravated by his own extreme analytic tendencies.

One might argue that the deadly dichotomies of Sartre's early theoretical works replicated and reinforced the traits of the dominant culture against which he was revolting in other ways. The ugliness of reality is accepted and sanctioned as an ontological given, as is its divorce from aesthetic considerations. Art and life cannot possibly take on a relationship of mutual testing and affirmation. Sartre's conception of freedom seems to function as an ideology superimposed on extreme splits and contradictions presented in terms of a logic of mastery and repression. But the very uncompromising nature of Sartre's early thought has the ability to drive tensions to the breaking point of bewildering paradox if not of patent absurdity. Negative dialectics was already implicit in his early form of ultra-analysis. The idea of art as a pleasing escape from the cares of ugly reality seems acceptable up to a point. But when it is taken to extremes, its implications become too disconcerting for comfort. In so far as Sartre follows the analytic distinctions that structure common sense and have a familiar resonance in the metaphysical tradition, he seems to underwrite conventional attitudes and the "wisdom" of ordinary language. But he never does this alone. He carries those distinctions to a point of opposition that evacuates them and, however blindly, brings out their fragility and proximity to shocking paradox. The familiar is defamiliarized, and the reassuringly recognizable opens onto the mad but extremely "logical" world of the paranoid schizophrenic. The important if obvious difficulty that Sartre is theoretically unequipped to confront in his early works is whether his approach to problems threatens to reflect both dominant tendencies and extreme reactions to them in a manner that provides little insight into critical and constructive alternatives.

HAZEL E. BARNES

Sartre's Concept of the Self

The word "self" appears to mean all things to all people; it is often used in the vaguest possible way by psychotherapists who should know better. For some it is the hard kernel of unchangeability in the person, and for others it is an ideal to be realized. If Sartre's concept of the self has often been misunderstood, this is largely because he uses the same term to refer to different things in distinct contexts, which he himself keeps clear but his readers do not. Also, his emphasis on one rather than the other of these has changed as his interest and thought have developed. I should like here to do three things. First, I want to differentiate among various ideas of self as Sartre has defined them in his early theoretical work and see how they stand in relation to his overall view of what the individual is. Second, I will consider what became of these theoretical formulations when Sartre, much later, set out to study the case of Flaubert. Third, by way of conclusion, I want to point up a paradox. At either end of Sartre's career readers have complained that somehow Sartre lost the living person. In *Being and Nothingness* (1943) the radically free and isolated individual seemed to be too little in touch with the everyday world to be real. All that remained was an abstract, impersonal consciousness. In *L'Idiot de la famille* (1971–72), by contrast, some readers were disturbed ny Sartre's claim that every person is "a singular universal" (*un universel singulier*). Gustave Flaubert appeared to be only the *product* of

From *Review of Existential Psychology and Psychiatry* 17, no. 1 (1980–81): 41–65. © 1981 by Humanities Press, Inc.

his familial and societal conditioning. History demanded and in effect wrote
the novels signed by his name. Suppose that we ask: Who *was* Flaubert?
What would we mean if we were to answer, "He was himself"?

I

There are three sharply defined usages of "self" by Sartre: first, the self
of prereflective consciousness; second, the self as ego or as personality; third,
the self as value. To these I am adding a fourth category of the self as
embodied consciousness. Sartre himself is not inclined to use the word "self"
to represent the total person as embodied consciousness, but clearly that is
his goal when he wanted to discover "what we can know of a man today . . .
Flaubert, for example." The "person" includes all of the first three notions of
self, none of which can be wholly dissociated from the body. In *Being and
Nothingness* he was concerned primarily with defining the ontological status of
consciousness, ego, the body, their differentiation and their interdependency;
the stress was always on consciousness. In *L'Idiot de la famille* ego and the body
received far more attention.

The Self of Prereflective Consciousness

Every consciousness is a self-consciousness, Sartre declares, for
consciousness is always aware if itself as consciousness. The self of
prereflective consciousness derives from the fact that in being aware of an
object, consciousness is aware of not being the object. To be conscious of a
thing is to be aware that the awareness and the thing are not the same. For
example, if there is suddenly a bright light, the immediate reaction is not that
I am seeing a bright light; consciousness of the light implies that the light is
somehow *there*, in front of consciousness, but not consciousness itself. I am
referring, of course, to the famous "nihilation," of which Sartre makes so
much. The human individual, whom he calls being-for-itself, is that part of
being which effects a psychic withdrawal from the rest of being (being-in-
itself). To nihilate is to be conscious *of* something as an object not identical
with consciousness.

Thus there are two inextricable ingredients in any act of consciousness:
of the object and a self-consciousness which Sartre indicates by putting the
"of" in parentheses: *conscience* (de) *soi*. The latter is consciousness' awareness
of itself as being aware. Sartre says that prereflective consciousness is
personal in that there is a return to self, a slight displacement such as is

indicated by some of the French reflexive verbs—for example, *il s'intéresse à* . . . (he interests himself in . . .). The adjective "personal," while it may be correct grammatically, is misleading here. The awareness of being aware is totally void of individualizing psychic qualities. It is the condition of all consciousness rather than the differentiating "selfness" of a particular consciousness. If by "personal" we refer to the traits of a personality, I should say that this self-consciousness is individual but nonpersonal. It need not be empty of emotion. It may be a pain or a pleasure consciousness, for instance, but it is not accompanied by any sense of "I" or "me." It is pure intentionality, directed toward an object. One might be tempted to call it instaneous, but that is not quite correct. All consciousness involves temporality for Sartre, for it is always directed toward a future and posited against the background of a past.

His insistence that the prereflective consciousness is egoless is heavily consequential for Sartre. By separating it from what is normally thought of as the personality, he postulates a radical freedom from psychological determination as traditionally conceived. It is the prereflective consciousness which makes the original "choice of being," or fundamental project, by which we relate ourselves to the world. In *Being and Nothingness* Sartre argued that it is this nonpersonal self-consciousness that gives me my uneasy, usually unacknowledged realization that there is nothing absolutely fixed or necessary in this choice, that it might have been entirely different, and that it could—at least in theory—be replaced by another choice and consequently a different personality structure.

The Self as Ego

Another way to express this idea is to say that the familiar personal self is not part of the structure of a consciousness but its product. As a consciousness reflects back upon earlier acts of consciousness, it begins to impose a unity upon those experiences. The result is a network of interlocking responses in which the activity of an agent must always be assumed. The true agent, of course, has been the original prereflective consciousness, but as it is objectified by the reflective consciousness, it seems to take on qualities inseparable from the accumulation of particular interactions with the world. Here we have the emergence of the ego. We must not confuse this with the Freudian ego, which comprises only a part of the psychic structure. The Sartrean ego is coexistive with all of one's psyche; but note that psyche, for Sartre, refers to all of the mental and emotional *objects* of the reflective consciousness, not to the original prereflective consciousness. The ego, including both the "I" and the "me," is what most people mean by self in popular usage. In what we may call the natural attitude, it is made up of a bundle of character traits and a structured personality. It is what I *am*, manifested in a thousand external acts and reactions. The *I* both creates the *me* and springs forth from it so that, at least theoretically, I can study it in its now quiet past and therefore know the form it will take and how it will appear in the future. The ego is my permanent, enduring self, which distinguishes me forever from all other selves. Nevertheless, Sartre insists that the existence of the ego is purely ideal. It is the purely formal unity that a present consciousness perpetually imposes on its past and future intentional acts.

There is a difference according to whether it is the past or the future that we are considering. The essence of what I have been in the past is a part of my being—that being-in-itself which I (as being-for-itself) drag along behind my present existence—like a mermaid with a tail. Thus it is correct, if rather pointless, to say that I have a self in the past, but the statement is true only from the point of view of the present. It is this self—the essential core of one's personal biography—which is the object of what Sartre calls "impure reflection." This last is ordinary introspection such as we frequently indulge in when we are recalling past happenings, trying to evaluate and to understand ourselves, to pin down our half-formed hopes and vague unhappiness. It is closely associated with the psychological analyses by novelists who seek to reveal to readers the complexity of emotional states. (Sartre alludes especially to Proust.) Impure reflection is a process of isolating and categorizing emotions, for example, as though they were things in themselves, and the whole procedure is carried out well within the framework of our fundamental project. Our psychic life, the object of our introspection, can indeed be grasped by a consciousness, however inadequately, either my own or that of therapist or biographer. Yet despite our familiarity with our autobiography, we recognize the sense of frustration that accompanies our attempt to pin down the real me or true self. The explanation lies in the fact that I apprehend an object where I thought to lay hands on a subjectivity. What is original about Sartre's rediscovery that the subject who thinks is not the subject thought of is precisely the fact that the original self-consciousness is not the personalized self. To ask what kind of self I am is to formulate the question improperly. Instead, I should ask what kind of self "my" consciousness has created. This is indeed to raise more than a psychological question. Sartre has noted that it is on the level of *pure reflection* that morality is posited. For a consciousness to look at its own product and to pass judgment on it is the original ethical act. But what is pure reflection? Is it an attainable goal or an illusion?

Sartre acknowledged that he had never adequately clarified his intention with regard to pure reflection. I think I know why. There is a troublesome ambiguity in the term itself. It hints at an ethics, and it suggests a form of self-knowledge. But Sartre states explicitly that consciousness cannot know itself knowing. If taken as a self-knowing, the ideal of reflection is impossible to achieve. For Sartre knowledge is consciousness' direct presence to an object in-itself. The self prereflective consciousness cannot become the object of knowing at the same time that this consciousness is the reflecting agent. Perhaps it is easier to represent this in French than in English. We have seen that in every conscious act there are two things:

1. *conscience de l'object*
2. *conscience (de) soi*

In reflective consciousness (assuming it to be a form of knowing) we would have the same situation.

1. *conscience de soi (= l'objet)*
2. *conscience (de) soi*

There is no way to suppress the second line. We attempt simply to combine these in a single line

Conscience de conscience (de) soi

But this would be to suppress the self-awareness of the reflecting consciousness. It is equally impossible to perform the act which might be expressed as

Conscience (de) soi de conscience (de) soi.

That is, we cannot do it if we intend that the second *conscience (de) soi* is the same as the first one. The intermediate *de*, which is the verbal equivalent of the act of nihilation that accompanies every intentional consciousness, separates them as surely as they are separated in their position on the page. We may say either that there is not enough separation between the two: the reflecting, since it *is* the reflected-on, cannot get outside it. Or we may say that there is too much separation: the object of consciousness is no longer the present consciousness but a past consciousness. The reflecting is no longer the same as the reflected. Sartre expresses the dilemma in a homely image. A donkey tries to reach a carrot attached to a stick fastened to the shaft of the cart he is pulling. Every movement to touch the carrot pushes it out of reach. We cannot make of our consciousness an object without falling to the level of impure reflection.

Pure reflection, Sartre says, is not a full knowledge but rather a *recognition*; it is not a new consciousness but an internal modification of the prereflective consciousness. Sartre compares it to the situation of a person writing while aware that someone else is watching him. Indeed, pure reflection is the first faint hint of my having, factually, an outside, of my being-for-others. Ever if alone, a consciousness can be, as it were, its own witness, but it can be so only if an external object is retained. In the midst of an activity I may suddenly reflect on myself as performing it without ceasing to keep the job to be done as the object of my consciousness. As I reflect, I am aware also that I am *not* the activity any more than I would be a tree that I observed. Joseph Catalano gives a particularly clear example taken from sport.

> If I an now reflecting on my playing tennis, I am aware of myself as playing tennis; I am certain that the self-that-is-playing tennis is the self reflecting on my tennis playing. . . . When I reflect on my tennis, I am aware that I can never perfectly *be* the self that is playing tennis. But this very nihilation (which is reflection), namely, that I can not-be a self that is identified with my tennis playing has its origin within the act of tennis playing, within the *being* of the original pre-reflective awareness that the being of consciousness is not identified with the being of tennis playing.

Sartre himself chooses for illustration of the difference between prereflection and reflection Descartes' enterprise of doubting and points out that in "Cogito, ergo sum," the cogito is already in the reflective level.

Whether we consider the reflecting tennis player or the French philosopher seeking to prove his existence by trying to doubt it, we are immediately aware that reflection involves temporality. To be aware of myself doing something is to be aware of myself relating what has just been to what is to come. Pure reflection reveals to consciousness that as a nihilating intention, it is a pursuit of self, not a self that *is*.

It is easy to grasp that this over-the-shoulder glimpse of consciousness is possible, but why does Sartre assign to it so much importance? How can it possibly serve, as Sartre at the end of *Being and Nothingness* suggests that it might, as a basis for a new ethics?

Where Sartre has not spoken, we cannot make assertions for him with any confidence, but I believe that he has given us a slight hint. Sartre recognized that it is possible to reflect on the memory of a nonreflective experience. I think we can see here the germ of one form of pure reflection —the attempt to hold up to consideration the elements and intrinsic qualities of the spontaneous conscious act, stripped of the overlay of associations after-the-event; the intent would be to examine a choice or an act as it was in itself at the time of its making. Precisely this is the aim of Hugo in *Dirty Hands;* but Hugo fails. Forced to rely on memory, he is unable to establish with certainty the reasons why he shot Hoederer in the past; he can only determine now the meaning he would like the act to have for the future. Granted that years had elapsed and Hugo had changed. But his failure perhaps explains why Sartre never developed the concept of pure reflection. Is it ever possible to be sure that one has isolated a former act of consciousness from its later overlay? Perhaps Sartre believed that we might train ourselves to look at our only-just-past reactions and to isolate what was genuinely spontaneous from what was influenced by individual and social presumptions. But this is to state a truism, or else Sartre envisioned some technique which he lacked the capacity, ability, or will to spell out. Sometimes I wonder if pure reflection is anything different from Sartre's habit of thinking against himself, of being willing to throw everything into question—both the existing structures of society and the furniture of one's psychic habitation. Sartre seemed to say as much in a late interview: "You know, I have never described [pure reflection]. I said that it could exist, but I showed only the facts of accessory reflection. Subsequently I discovered that the non-accessory reflection was not a way of looking that was different from the immediate, accessory way of looking but was the critical work you can perform on yourself during a whole lifetime, through praxis."

Sartre certainly suggests elsewhere, and perhaps implies even here, that the self which is the goal of pure reflection is indeed the original *conscience (de) soi,* but the purpose of reflection would not be to discover that self as object but to liberate it from the incrustations of ego. This view would fit in with a remark by Sartre in *The Transcendence of the Ego.* There he says that in pure reflection the ego may be present but only "on the horizon" and as something which consciousness overflows and maintains by a continuous creation. He adds, "Perhaps the essential role of the ego is to hide from consciousness its own spontaneity." The reason, of course, would be fear of what the full realization of our freedom would entail. Paradoxically, the revelation of the selfness of prereflective consciousness brings the realization that there is no self as substance, that a free consciousness has never been identical with the self it has made in the past or with the self that it projects toward the future.

The Self as Value

So far we have not discussed the future dimension. Sartre, we recall, claims that the ego is the ideal unity imposed by consciousness on all its psychic activity. Unlike the past, the future does not belong to being-in-itself. As the not yet, it depends on the nihilating action of the for-itself, which transcends what exists here and now. The future, so far as particular futures are concerned, has a purely virtual existence. There is no way to predict the dispositions and reactions of that "I" who will keep the rendezvous with the future that I presently project—not even if the world and other persons should perform their parts perfectly. The ego here is called on to unify acts still wholly imaginary. To speak of a future self is to postulate that a consciousness will continue to create a self that can be grasped only retrospectively. But Sartre now introduces an entirely different concept of self, one which does not belong to the ego and which is by definition never realized. Under the heading "The Self and the Circuit of Selfness," he discusses a self that is purely ideal, a value that we try to realize. It is metaphysical (or ontological) rather than psychological. We might think of our pursuit of this self as a corollary to the curtailed project of pure reflection.

Sartre argues that the for-itself is a lack of being which seeks to achieve being. Several other ways in which he expresses this idea might be formulated as follows: Consciousness is process, not substantial entity. It exists only as directed toward something other than itself. Consciousness is consciousness of something (Husserl). It is born, supported by a being which it is not (Sartre). Human reality is not what it is in the way that natural or manufactured things are. Human reality is what it is not and is not what it is. As a lack of being, the for-itself reaches out toward being. Consciousness is not a self and does not have a self; but as a self-making process, it pursues a self. Or, as Sartre says, it seeks to come to itself.

This future self Sartre links with desire and equates with value. He calls it a value because it is always the still unattained object of my desire. If I am thirsty, he says, what I desire is not just a glass of water but a thirst satisfied. I want to be simultaneously a desire as lack and a desire fulfilled, to be conscious of myself as a lack that is filled. Thus the ultimate desire or value, of which all other desires are tributary expressions, is that I should *be* the self I have to make. This ideal is, of course, the desire to be in-itself-for-itself, which Sartre describes as the self-contradictory passion to be the Self-cause, or God.

Clearly one cannot have both unrestricted freedom to grow and a built-in program. If each consciousness is a continuous self-projection, we cannot say that the future self exists or will be grasped in the way that for the traveler the city of his destination exists and will eventually be reached by him. Yet we may raise the question as to whether pure reflection, in the extended sense in which we interpreted it with respect to the past, is relevant as regards our future consciousness. Obviously there can be no reflexive reaction on the future, but I think there is one way in which pure reflection can function so as to keep the future open to a free consciousness. The pure reflection which reveals to me that my spontaneous prereflective consciousness is not imprisoned within an ego can act to prevent me from preparing to make the future a repetition of the past, out of anxiety or insecurity. Frequently one rehearses so thoroughly the part one will play in a future event that one blinds oneself to unexpected possibilities and blocks off in advance any chance of spontaneous choice. A pure reflection not only would open up the past to new meaning but would regard the future as provisional.

At this stage we can see the wide variations in Sartre's use of the term "self," and we can recognize how distinctively and how precisely "self" must be employed in a Sartrean oriented psychotherapy. Obviously any notion of self as a two- or three-tiered structured psyche, such as Freud or Jung conceived, is out of the question. So is the humanistic concept of self-actualization if it is attached to a coherent pattern of inborn potentialities—what I like to call the "acorn theory" as presented, for example, in the work of Fromm and Maslow. The primary task for the person who would live in good faith (in Sartrean terms) is to keep the various categories of self clear in one's attitude towards one's life. This means, as Sartre puts it, that I should live with the realization that my nature is a demand but not a recourse. The ego is neither the cause of my actions nor a pattern to guide them; it is not a fixed self though it may be thought of as the self to which my consciousness has become accustomed. My spontaneous self-consciousness (the prereflective consciousness) is responsible for each new choice just as it has been the author of what I have made myself in the past.

The Self as Embodied Consciousness

Up until now I have been considering consciousness and psyche almost as if they were unembodied, but such was never Sartre's intention. In everyday experience my sense of my own self and of the Other's self is inextricably linked with the body even if, on some occasions, I may feel that there is a certain incongruity between external appearance and the inward life. It is natural for us to want to use the word "self" to refer to the total person even though Sartre tends to avoid this usage. In any case we cannot adequately grasp the sense in which Sartre's three kinds of "self" come into play unless we include the body. For a philosopher who has sometimes been mistaken for an idealist, the early Sartre assigned considerable importance to the body. In *The Emotions*, while he rejected the James-Lange theory which claimed that bodily reactions *caused* the emotions, Sartre nevertheless kept body on the active side; it is not a mere passive receptor or register of psychic reactions. Speaking of emotional behavior rather than of purely internal states (if indeed we may claim that these exit), Sartre claims that my consciousness assumes the emotional mode as a magical way of altering a lived situation in which I cannot modify the world itself. By effecting bodily changes, I alter my relation to the world. For example, I faint in the path of a menacing monster, thus "annihilating" myself since I cannot annihilate the beast. Or a woman patient is racked with uncontrollable sobbing *in order that* she may be unable to articulate a painful confession to the therapist. In short, emotional behavior is purposeful and seeks to effect its purpose by means of the body. In *The Transcendence of the Ego* the body stands for "the illusory fulfillment of the I-concept" on the nonreflective level. It supports the empty, purely formal "I-concept" which allows me to answer, without intermediate mental process, the question, "What are you doing?" when my action has been nonreflective. If I am breaking up sticks, I say, 'I' am breaking up sticks, and I see and feel the object 'body' engaged in breaking the sticks. The body thus serves as a visible and tangible symbol for the *I*.

Being and Nothingness has a long chapter devoted to the body. Sartre claims that we must recognize that it has three ontological dimensions: First, there is the Other's body—or the body for the Other. Here Sartre stresses the fact that I always consider the Other's body as the expression of a consciousness, not as an inert object in the world. Second, there is my-body-as-known-by-the-Other. At times the body (whether my own or the Other's) is pure object, as when I probe for a sliver or diagnose the extent of an injury. Of more concern to us here is the third dimension—the body-as-for-itself. This is the lived body or—as Sartre phrases it—the body I exist. Sartre denies any dualism. Sensations are not a hybrid something—not quite subjective, not quite objective—which are sent to consciousness by the body. The body *is* conscious. It is in and through the body that consciousness is present to the world, that it is individualized, that it has facticity, that it has a past. But consciousness does not use the body as an instrument for its separate needs. The relation is not that of agent and tool. A non-thetic awareness of body is inseparable from consciousness: "The body is what this consciousness *is*; it is not even anything except body. The rest is nothingness and silence."

The last half of the quotation reminds us that we cannot reduce consciousness to body. It is nothing except body, but we must read this in the sense that consciousness is no thing, that it is a nihilating process. As for-itself, the body is not the object *of* consciousness as it is in the other two dimensions. Consciousness does indeed nihilate the body in the way that Being-for-itself nihilates all Being-in-itself. But its nihilation of its own body is different from its nihilation of perceived objects in the world. The relation is closer to the bond that links present to past acts of consciousness. Mentally, as physically, the point of view of consciousness has the body as center of reference. If my eyes pain me as I read, my reading consciousness is also a pain-consciousness, and I do not separate the two, except in reflection, any more than I separate my view of a landscape from the conditions of light and air that enfold and reveal it.

The purely physiological aspects of body are virtually ignored in *Being and Nothingness*. When Sartre does mention them, he always adds that a free consciousness determines one's reactions. It is my basic choice of being that decides whether my fatigue enhances the pleasure of a hike or serves as an excuse for resting or turning back. Even under the sadist's knife, my consciousness decides when and whether I can no longer endure the torture. In the caress and embrace of sexual desire, the lover seeks to *incarnate* his own and the beloved's consciousness, in the vain hope of grasping the Other's entrapped consciousness as one skims the cream off milk. Moments of ultimate physical closeness (not the completion of orgasm) are supremely satisfying in realizing symbolically the impossible union in oneness of consciousness. What normally passes for a psychosomatic phenomenon was of no interest to Sartre at this date. It becomes of major importance in his study of Flaubert.

Let us turn now to *L'Idiot de la famille* and observe how Sartre uses the different notions of self when he attempts to understand the concrete reality of a once living person.

II

L'Idiot de la famille, a three-volume study of Flaubert which attempts to combine the approach of existential psychoanalysis with that of Marxist sociology, offers a final synthesis of Sartre's thought. As compared with his earlier books, the work shows no glaring theoretical inconsistency in its analysis of areas where Sartre or we would use the term "self," but the difference in emphasis and the added significance that are assigned to ego and body give us a much different picture of the interplay of subjective consciousness and conditioning and of how personality is developed. These nearly three thousand pages do not lend themselves to an easy summary of what Sartre believes to be "the truth of Flaubert." I will limit myself to a few observations which are especially relevant to the various uses of "self" by Sartre as I have outlined them.

The Self of Prereflective Consciousness

In the Flaubert study we find virtually no discussion of the free prereflective consciousness as such, but existence is everywhere implied. We see this partly by what is omitted. There is a total absence of any mention of genetic or endocrinological determinism. Sartre explicitly rejects the existence of innate genius or talent, and the idea of intelligence as something biologically given and measurable. Far from positing that Gustave Flaubert had any natural facility with words, Sartre argues that it was Gustave's difficulty with language which led him eventually to literature. He gives considerable weight to the psychosomatic, but the emphasis is always on the underlying intention. He insists that Flaubert's famous nervous crisis in 1844, which all biographers recognize as a turning point in his life, was due to hysteria, not epilepsy. Where Benjamin Bart, for example, sees Flaubert as a novelist whose will to succeed triumphed over the ravages of a disease which impaired his powers, Sartre views the crisis as the neurotic but successful solution of an otherwise insoluble conflict. To Flaubert himself it seemed like a death and rebirth. It was in fact a self-effected liberation, won at great psychic cost.

Freedom has not been lost in *L'Idiot de la famille*, but it appears chiefly in the paradoxical form in which Sartre presented it in an interview at the time of the first publication of the work. "A man can always make something out of what is made of him. This is the limit I would today accord to freedom: the small movement which makes of a totally conditioned social being someone who does not render back completely what his conditioning has given him."

Sartre periodically directs our attention to the indispensable "small movement" amidst what would otherwise pass for a classic study of psychological determinism and unconscious conditioning. He does this partly by relying on his early concept of bad faith as a lie to oneself, in which the subject is never wholly ignorant of what he refuses to reflect or acknowledge. But now he attaches less of moral condemnation and speaks rather of the opaqueness of the lived experience (*le vécu*). A distinction between knowledge and comprehension, mentioned in *Being and Nothingness* but not fully developed, becomes crucial in the Flaubert study. A person may be wholly aware of an impulse, a wish, may vaguely sense its connection with an underlying structure of personal significances, without holding it up to a purifying reflection that would result in the kind of knowledge demanding deliberation and decision. What happens is something like what occurs more overtly when one looks at a set of papers piled helter skelter on the desk. One feels, "I ought to look over those. Some of those things certainly need attention. But I won't get into it now." Sartre claims that behavior such as "failure conduct" or the will to fail (*conduite d'échec*), is intentional (i.e., purposeful) but not deliberate. He notes that Flaubert himself referred to the "fulgurations" or sudden revelations of the stageset of his life world. One of these was expressed in the adolescent Gustave's unexpected realization that he envied, in a person he despised, the man's capacity for immense and genuine feeling. In later life a moment of retrospective self-understanding effected the confession to George Sand, "I was a coward in my youth."

Pervading the pages of *Being and Nothingness* was the presence of an anxious consciousness seeking in vain for meaningful structure outside itself and forced to recognize that rational order and purpose were only the thin human overlay imposed upon an incomprehensible world of matter. Flaubert himself was not disposed to recognize the terrifying responsibilities of this lovely freedom though he did in fact seek refuge in art from what he conceived to be the futility of existence in a world that failed to meet our high aspirations. We find a truly Sartrean echo of our despair in the face of an alien world, in one of his important digressions; somewhat surprisingly, the context is a discussion of practical jokes.

Sartre observes that it is through the world that I come to know myself. (Recall that all consciousness is consciousness *of* something other than itself.) "The world is what separates me from myself and announces me to myself." Most of the time I exist with the assumption that things are indeed roughly what they seem. Despite my knowledge that my senses have on occasion deceived me, I cannot live without assuming that there is a broad area of daily life in which they can be trusted. Yet I retain a slight awareness of the ultimate unknowability in the things of which I am conscious. While the anguished awareness of this uncertainty is not present in every act, it exists as part of our "global feeling of our insertion in the world." What Sartre is speaking of is not just my realistic fear of accidents but a fundamental sense of estrangement. The practical joke is an attempt to evoke deliberately a rupture in the normal world of the person who is duped. Suppose that I, the victim, am offered what looks like a sugar cube for my tea but is actually a piece of celluloid. When it floats, I have a momentary but total feeling of disorientation. "I appear as a stranger to myself, my customs are disqualified, my past abolished, I am naked in a new present which is lost in an unknown future." Suddenly my secret suspicion is confirmed: "My relation with being, with *my* being, was only an appearance; the *true* relation is discovered. It is horrible; I come to myself, a terrifying monster through a monstrous world."

To be the dupe of one practical joke is unlikely to be fatal; it may even be salutary. A prolonged series of practical jokes perpetrated on the same victim, especially if it is a child, might well induce, Sartre suggests, "an artificial psychosis by forcing him to live his normal adaptation to the real as a permanent disadaptation."

The Self as Ego

This last statement by Sartre takes us away from the abstract, isolated consciousness confronting the world and others as objects and reminds us of the way that the Other as subject may intrude into the most private recesses of my relations with myself; that is, with my self in the sense of ego. In L'Idiot de la famille there are at least three important contexts in which Sartre uses his own distinctive concept of ego as the product of consciousness, not as the subject synonymous with consciousness. The first concerns what Sartre believes to be Gustave's nonverbalized belief with regard to his own ego and its formation. For reasons which we will note shortly, the child Gustave, Sartre claims, failed to develop as an active agent. Instead, he conceived of himself as being made by the Other. By means of other people's acts and words, he hoped to learn what he was. In short, his ego was an alter ego, both in his own mind and, to a degree, in reality. In Sartrean terms we may say that Gustave widened the breach between basic consciousness and the ego, feeling that his ego was the product not of his own consciousness but of others' and that there was no escape from it. Sartre finds evidence in Flaubert's adolescent writing that he felt other people (his father especially) had made him what he was. At the same time he retained obscurely a resentful consciousness of being a free impulse which did not want to be limited to this nature that had been bestowed upon him

Sartre appears to share this view. In his discussion of the gradual development of Flaubert's adult personality, he brings to bear all of the familiar elements of family conditioning—my second point. Gustave's "prehistory" includes the background and character of his parents, his relation to siblings (not only the older brother and younger sister who lived, but also the two brothers who died before he was born and the expected sister whose place he usurped). "Protohistory" is Sartre's term for the early years of childhood. We may subdivide it into what he calls "constitution" and "personalization." Constitution refers to the fundamental patterns of affectivity which Sartre believes are set by the infant's relations with its mother. Personalization, beginning in protohistory but extending beyond it, refers to the way that the child internalizes and unifies its lived situation in the family. Although the mother's role is still important in personalization, Sartre gives primary emphasis, in the case of Gustave, to the influence of the father and less directly of the brother. We will look more specifically at the parental influences when we consider Sartre's treatment of psychosomatic factors in the fully embodied consciousness we know as Gustave Flaubert. For the moment I will simply point out that the discussion of Gustave's psychic formation, although it is superficially closer to a traditional psychoanalytical approach than one might have expected, remains distinctively Sartrean. Parental influences are fully as significant in Sartre's analysis as in Freud's, but they are handled differently. Though Sartre may refer to the Oedipus complex, for example, his discussion of the child's psychological development bears no relation to the patterned stages of sexual and personal evolvement as outlined for males and females respectively in psychoanalytical texts.

A third illustration of Sartre's use of his concept of the ego occurs when he is discussing reading. As one would expect in a work by Sartre on Flaubert, considerable weight is given to the effect on Gustave of the books he read. Sartre is interested in the nature of the literature itself, both as an expression of the social factors which produced it and as a molding influence on a new generation of writers. What is more relevant to us here is his discussion of just how we as readers empathize with an imaginary character and why fiction is so effective in helping to form a personality and even on occasion to alter our points of view. Sartre's explanation works only if we accept his basic position on consciousness and the psyche. Since the basic consciousness which I am is not structured, there is always implicit in me the awareness that my ego stands apart, at the horizon, as it were, of my consciousness, as the result of my structuring of experience. Therefore, since the ego is a quasi-object in the field of the reading consciousness, I as reader am free to project my ego into the ego of the character. As I identify my self with his, suddenly the reactions of the hero become part of my own past. As Sartre reminds us, our memory often confuses real events with imaginary ones. (We recall the way in which one's dream of a person may color one's attitude toward him or her in waking life.) I cannot move into the fictional world of another being without modifying the color of the world in which I live when I am not reading.

Something else happens, too, Sartre says, while read empathetically. Although the "I" of my ego and the "I" of the hero are merged, I retain the feeling that each is inextricably linked with a transparent consciousness. Since the hero has been objectified by the author, I seem to grasp the hero's free consciousness—and my own—as objects even while I remain subject.

Suppose that I am reading the tale of a Castilian nobleman. Sartre writes, "The Castilian is [the reader] himself appearing to himself at last as the object which he is in the world, and at the same time the Castillian is his [the reader's] own subjectivity as it appears in *itself* to an impartial all-knowing observer. In short, it is the in-itself-for-itself finally achieved.

The illusion depends in part also on the particular relation that exists between me and the author. It seems that out of the black marks on the page I freely create the fictional character and his world. But my creation is a re-creation in so far as it is guided by the inscribed intention of the author. One is inevitably reminded of Augustine's declaration—that our freedom consists in voluntarily doing God's will.

The Self as Value

Unexpectedly, we have moved from ego to the self as in-itself-for-itself, or value. It should not surprise us that this impossible goal is achieved only in an act of imagination. With respect to Flaubert and the ideal of self-coincidence, Sartre makes two important points. First, even as a child Flaubert thought of himself as living out a preordained destiny. As an adult he liked to think that he was incapable of change and inwardly impervious to anything which might touch him externally. He was what he was, once and for all. He refused, insofar as it was possible, to live with a future dimension. His life was a cyclic repetition. When political events transformed his society, he felt that he had outlived himself. And in fact critics have remarked that despite innovations in plot and setting, his last books have the same themes and attitudes as the early ones. Flaubert tried to defy time, not by remaining youthful in spirit but by considering himself already an old man when he was in his early twenties. Second, he chose art over life. Rather than to live as a man in time, he wanted to *be* the artist who creates imaginary eternities. He tried to make himself a work of art, partly by role playing, partly by casting himself in a form that excluded the transient and the spontaneous.

The Self as Embodied Consciousness

The somatic plays a major role in Sartre's analysis of Flaubert, both in the initial conditioning of his "constitution" or basic affectivity and in the climactic nervous crisis which established one and for all his "fundamental project"; that is, his way of being in the world. We observed earlier that Sartre attributes to the mother the primary responsibility for the baby's constitution. While denying that he himself has been influenced by Lacan, Sartre is like Lacan in stressing the symbiotic relation of the baby to its mother in infancy. Psychic and somatic are inextricably intertwined. Sartre claims that Madame Flaubert was overprotective but unloving in her treatment of the son who came when she wanted a daughter and whom in any case she did not expect to live very long. Maternal love, Sartre declares, is not an emotion but a relation. The underloved child's first experience of himself as body is that of being a thing, dependent on another, but with no sense of reciprocity. The result in Gustave's case was a basic passivity fundamental to all of his reactions in later life.

On the sexual level, passivity and not a latent homosexuality or unresolved Oedipus complex was at the root of a certain femininity in Flaubert's character which his contemporaries noted. This hypothesis explains his intense, somewhat dependent relations with Louis Bouilhet and Maxime du Camp and his uneasy liaison with Louise Colet. Letters show that Flaubert was not impotent, but he appears to have feared Louise's strong sexuality as much as he longed for it. He saw her as seldom as he could manage, even at the height of his professed ardor. Like Léon in *Madame Bovary*, he seemed in some ways to be her mistress more than she was his. He expressed the wish that Louise could be man to the waist and woman below, that the two together might form, as it were, an hermaphroditic couple. What he really wanted, Sartre claims, was to be roused to virility by the caresses of the hands of the strong woman—in other words, the phallic mother.

Psychological consequents outside the sexual context were even more important. Nonvalorization was one of them, and Sartre claims that Flaubert never did develop the self-esteem that is requisite for being at ease with oneself. Sartre argues that the underloved child develops no sense of being an active agent in control of his destiny. To make the child feel that he is a sovereign around whom the world revolves, that it is he who decides what will happen, that the world awaits his striding down the path he will choose— all this is not to be regarded as the temptation of an overfond mother but rather the duty of an intelligent one. When we recall Sartre's view of the human being as a "useless passion," inhabiting a universe without support for human values, where nobody is privileged, we must conclude that Sartre is advising now the deliberate inculcation of a falsehood. But its intent is to instill in the child the true notion that he is an active agent who will make his own destiny.

Sartre claims that the unloving overprotectiveness of Gustave's mother imprinted on the child's "constitution" (perhaps we could more naturally speak of "psychic disposition") a dependent passivity. There are still other consequences which Sartre obviously would expect to find in any child in a similar situation. First is a certain aboulia, a lack of capacity for true desire, which manifested itself even in Gustave's childhood as ennui or distaste for life. Sartre believes that if a baby is fed and cared for strictly by an adult's schedule with no concern for his specific hungers, thirsts, and discomforts, he fails to make the natural association between desiring and satisfaction and may never learn the pleasure of being satisfied. Then, too, helplessness creates a feeling of unreality. Sartre cites an episode from his own life and one from Gide's *Journal* to illustrate the way that one's sense of being totally out of control and at the mercy of external forces can leave one with the feeling that what goes on is not really happening, is like something in a dream (in dreams as we remember them, of course, not as we are immersed in them). Finally, Sartre adds, Flaubert's inability to feel clearly the distinction between real and unreal resulted in his confusing truth and belief—or better, in not recognizing the existence of truth as an absolute criterion. So strong was this feeling in Gustave that Sartre associates it with Flaubert's later decision to become a "worker in the imaginary," a creator of fiction. The mother's influence came first and laid the foundation for Gustave's passive constitution. Sartre speaks of this as "the first castration."

The father not only reinforced the damage the mother had done, but exerted the decisive influence on Gustave's "personalization." Sartre dwells at length on the difficulties of a second son in the kind of patriarchal family in which the first boy plays the role of heir apparent. We have evidence for Gustave's jealousy of his older brother Achille. But Sartre goes far beyond the simple postulation of sibling rivalry. To be the younger son was to be marked as inferior, a pale copy or replica, at best a standby. Sartre thinks that there was a fatal interplay between Gustave's gradual realization of what it meant to be a second son and the natural difficulties inherent in moving from childhood to boyhood. Sartre speaks of the crisis of the "second weaning," which takes place when the child reaches the age of six or seven. This is the time when the engaging helplessness of the toddler is seen as clumsiness; the prattling cherub is suddenly a chattering nuisance. It marked the abrupt end of the "golden age" when Dr. Flaubert took Gustave along with him on his house calls. Gustave now is left at home, and his mother tells him that he must learn to read. Family documents record that Gustave had great difficulty in grasping the skill of reading, whereas Achille had mastered it easily. Sartre makes a great deal of this incident. He gives three reasons for Gustave's troubles. (We may observe once again the absence of physical explanations such as dyslexia or other natural disability.) First, he was suddenly called upon to act, but his constitutional passivity had not prepared him for the role of active agent. Second, he had regarded words as things which came from the Other. He had not learned reciprocity. It was not natural for him to reconstruct their meaning for himself. Finally, his presentiment of what would be demanded of him made him reluctant to leave the golden age of childhood. Gustave did indeed finally learn to read, but the crisis was catastrophic. Dr. Flaubert concluded that his son was retarded. Gustave accepted the pronouncement of his inferiority. It is from this episode that Sartre gets his title: *The Family Idiot*.

In the literary pieces which Flaubert wrote in his early and mid-adolescence, Sartre finds documents to support his picture of Gustave's life-world. The boy lived in an environment both theological and feudal. God the Father had justly condemned his evil son, but the prodigal longed and secretly hoped for forgiveness. The Father was a feudal suzerain who had no use for the homage of the vassal who loved him. The son exiled from Paradise simultaneously accepted the malediction and resented it. He loved his father and wished for his death. He resolved to live out his unhappy fate to its extreme in the hope that at last the cruel father would pity the son he had destroyed.

When Gustave went to school, his pride in being a Flaubert and his shame at being the rejected, inferior cadet resulted in two modes of behavior: compensating daydreams and aggressiveness. These were two sides of a coin. The fantasies were sado-masochistic. Sometimes Gustave imagined himself to be a Giant looking with scorn on the stupidity and baseness of the human ants below; often he identified himself with a cruel, destructive, powerful figure like Nero. In the schoolyard he was bitingly sarcastic in his taunts and not above joining with others in verbally tormenting the weak. He seems also to have been the leader in creating an imaginary character, the Garçon. Taking turns at the role, the boys used this fictional being as a mouthpiece by which to mock both bourgeois values and the dreams of the Romantics. Sartre claims that this spontaneous social psychodrama was therapeutic for the group and for Gustave but in quite different ways. For most of the boys it was effective in ridding them of the temporary aberrations induced by empathy with Romantic heroes—metaphysical despair and temptations to suicide. They became, like the Garçon, reconciled to enjoying the benefits of being bourgeois, even as they scoffed at its refined pretensions. Gustave enjoyed the double reward of being loved as one of the group and yet believing that he had demoralized his companions. To demoralize, Sartre insisted, remained Flaubert's chosen mission as a writer. *Madame Bovary*, for example, shows us that, except in art, there is no alternative to the foolish, self defeating dreams of Emma and the gross materialism of the successful Homais.

In describing how Gustave finally came to grips with his family situation and by the same stroke launched himself on his career as an artist, Sartre ties together the constitutional passivity, paternal conditioning, and the psychosomatic. At the lycée Gustave's record was respectable but not brilliant. When he excelled, it was in those fields least propitious for a prospective medical student—in history and literature. Rather than explaining this record as the result of natural interests or talents, Sartre sees it resulting from Gustave's resolve not to imitate Achille but to demonstrate the inferiority to which his father had condemned him. This was the first manifestation of what Sartre calls "failure conduct" or, to use the more familiar term, the will to fail. It is an obvious strategy to be employed by a "passive agent." The latter is Sartre's term for one whose constitution is marked by passivity. When he acts, as all of us must do, willy-nilly, he tries to convince himself that he is coasting with the current, giving in to circumstances beyond his control, refusing to acknowledge his own part in shaping the circumstances.

A bourgeois son was expected to work at some sort of profession. Since Gustave showed no talent for medicine, the obvious alternative was law. He hated the very thought of it, but he was duly enrolled and even made a show of studying. Sartre describes him caught between two impossible demands: His passivity makes him incapable of defying his father, but he is equally unable to obey his father. To do so would be to sentence himself to a life in which he must not only acknowledge his mediocrity but seem to be contented with it. The sole solution is to show that he *cannot* obey. This means that he must accept total disgrace. He does in fact fail his first set of exams. But this is not enough. He will be expected to repeat them. Somehow he must demonstrate his inability to hold any kind of job. Now the negative strategy becomes a positive calculation. If he can stay at home, like an unmarried daughter, supported by his father until eventually he inherits his share of the estate, then he will have everything he requires. The dependent, feminine aspect of his personality will be fostered. He, and not the brilliant Achille, will live in the bosom of the family, who will be forced to pity him, to care for him, hence to love him. And he will be free to write. Radical failure will be a form of salvation. Loser will win.

It would have been easy for Sartre to defend such a hypothesis if he had been willing to resort to the concept of an unconscious. Sartre tries to work without it. The will to fail, he says, can be sustained only as a project in bad faith. But a divided intention, auto-suggestion, and somatic reactions are essential accompanying elements. The conflict was genuine and manifested itself on at least three levels. First, Gustave's fear of public failure and parental displeasure was acute, as painful in immediate anticipation as was the more remote hatred career. Either outcome was intolerable. Second, Gustave at times tried to assume the role of active agent. He declared to a friend his resolve to work disdainfully until he had won his law degree and then refuse to practice. But the habit of passive obedience was so strong in him that he must have known that this was sheer bravado. If defiance were to be his solution, now was the time to announce it. Finally, two attitudes, deriving respectively from the family's attitude and from his reading in Romantic literature, were mutually contradictory: the Flaubert pride demanded that the greatest must show himself able to do the least. But opposed to this was the ideal of the Romantic hero whose greater vision prevented him from seeing how to perform the lowly task at his feet—the eagle that loses the footrace, or Plato's philosopher newly descended into the cave. Each set of attitudes poisoned the other. Gustave would in all sincerity force himself to study and try to succeed—as indeed he did on his retake of the first examinations. But most of the time his efforts were self-defeating. He would postpone study until the last moment; then in a sudden panic he would try to do too much in too short of a time. Having decided in advance that the legal code was meaningless jargon, he attempted to master it by sheer memorization, refusing to take the intellectual steps which, by viewing law as the evolutionary accretion of historical development or as logical construction, might have made it interesting and easier to retain. He neglected his physical well-being so that ill health by itself might render him incapable. Finally, as it became that only a desperate solution would save him, he called on his body for more decisive intervention.

Sartre cites several pieces of evidence to show that Flaubert, however confusedly and inaccurately, was aware of the interaction of psychic and bodily reactions. Gustave applied to himself the theory that in some persons agitations of the senses, instead of stimulating intellectual or artistic creativity, passed into the nervous system, causing physiological disturbances. This is what happens, he said, in the case of those musically talented children who will never be Mozarts. A second indication that Sartre finds is Flaubert's reference to a prolonged period of sexual abstinence at just this date. Combined with his confession to a sudden impulse toward self-castration which came over him one day, Sartre argues that probably Gustave found himself impotent in this time of pressure, not an unlikely thing to have happened. But Sartre goes on to hypothesize that Gustave associated the wish and the reality. Had a momentary, rejected impulse been accepted and acted on by the body? A third point refers to earlier days at home. Gustave had amused himself and the family by doing imitations of an epileptic, a former journalist who had been reduced to beggary by his affliction. Gustave recorded that he threw himself into this performance to the point of almost being in the other man's skin and added that his father, fearing it might have some harmful affects on his son, forbade any repetition of the act. Sartre claims that Flaubert was afraid lest his imitations of madness and his habit of imagining abnormal mental states might, through the power of suggestion, induce his body to succumb to insanity.

If we follow Sartre, Gustave during the months preceding January 1844 awaited something decisive that would come to him from outside—the quintessence of "active passivity." Certainly the timing of his nervous crisis suggests "intentional" hysteria and not a purely accidental epilepsy. After failing the second set of examinations, he had gone home for the winter holidays. If nothing happened to save him, he would have to return to the law books and try again. One night as he was driving with his brother a cart suddenly appeared out of the darkness, not colliding with the Flaubert vehicle, but coming close. As though it was a sign, Gustave fell rigid to the floor. He did not lose consciousness but suffered sever pains, hallucinatory perceptions of strange lights, etc. During the subsequent weeks attacks returned, accompanied now by convulsions, but Flaubert appeared strangely relaxed and without anxiety. It was as though the worst had happened and there was nothing more to fear. Was this simply because he had consented to the ignominy of failure and disgrace and now, having paid the price, could look forward to reaping the reward? Or was it also as Sartre suggests, relief that he had risked death and insanity but had avoided them? Dr. Flaubert died a little more than two years later, in 1846. Soon afterward, and despite the fact that his beloved sister had died in childbirth shortly before the father's demise, Gustave declared that at last he could get to work at writing again. The attacks diminished in frequency and finally, after ten years, ceased entirely.

Sartre is speaking of hysteria, of course, not playacting and knowing deception. Obviously the nervous crisis was not the effect of a rational act of will any more than Gustave's failure to pass the examinations was due to feigned ignorance. Yet Sartre insists that Flaubert had a certain comprehension of the intentional structure behind the crisis. This is implied in his many references to his having sacrificed everything for art, to his having renounced all real passions in order to be able to depict then in art. His language constantly suggests that some sort of bargain had been made. When the last years of his life were disturbed by financial worries, he regarded it not merely as unfortunate but unjust. His laments sound like complaints over a broken contract. Finally, at Flaubert's great moment of disillusion, there was another psychosomatic occurrence. The fall of the Second Empire and the Prussian invasion of France were cataclysmic for Flaubert, who looked on the defeat of France as the end of Latin culture. In retrospect he felt that the Court of Napoleon III, in whose circles he had been lionized, had all been a sham, like a staged court in an opera. Science had triumphed over art. Imagination, instead of creating a higher reality, had helped to insure the real humiliation of the German occupation of Flaubert's own home at Croisset. Sartre states that at this date Flaubert found his whole life called into question and felt that after all loser had been self-deluded in thinking he had won. Statements in Flaubert's letters testify to his acute sense of having outlived himself. In his anger at his fellow citizens he wrote, "I would like to drown humanity in my vomit." Significantly, it was at this time that he was afflicted with spells of nausea so severe that he was convinced that he had developed a stomach ulcer. He consulted a physician, who could find no organic cause. Gradually the symptoms disappeared. Sartre explains the imagined ulcer as the expression of Flaubert's wish that he could vomit up himself because of his guilt at having enjoyed and been an accomplice of the regime responsible for today's dust and ashes. He rejected both the fossil he saw himself becoming and the deluded man who had not foreseen the outcome. Sartre expresses it, Flaubert could only wait for death since he had lived beyond the period for which he had programmed himself.

III

Who was Flaubert? Some critics of Sartre's biography of him have claimed that the study of conditioning has been carried to such an extreme that "Gustave" has been lost, that we are left with the feeling that any younger son in that family—or even a changeling—would have become the author of *Madame Bovary*. I hope I have shown, even by my few examples, that this is to misread Sartre, that Gustave as a passive agent still directed the course of his life. Sartre has remarked that Flaubert was at least free to choose to become the novelist we know, or a poor physician, or nothing but a typical bourgeois. I would add that there are a number of places in the book at which one feels that his preference for the imaginary might also have induced him to choose psychosis.

John Weightman charged Sartre with a deficiency in his theory. In Weightman's view, Sartre's early rejection of "human nature" as a psychological given led him to miss "the physiological uniqueness, the given genetic identity of the individual Gustave." Weightman asks, "If there is no density of the given individual nature, if there is no weighting to be derived from the various possibilities within the temperament, how can anyone get the inner leverage necessary for the exercise of freedom? Freedom cannot be rootless; it must be the margin of uncertainty in the possibilities of the given."

The last sentence we may dismiss with the observation that Sartre himself might have written it; but for him the margin of uncertainty would be located at the moment of internalization of the given, and the given would refer to the subject's situation, not to genetic coding. The rest of

Weightman's accusation reveals an inability to grasp—or else an unwillingness to accept—the distinction between consciousness and ego. Like most people in our Western tradition, he is unable to conceive of life as a true self-making and wants to see it as an unfolding. The differences between a rolling snowball and a Roman candle! The free consciousness that made Flaubert continued to manifest itself through layers of personal ego which it itself laid down and within the structures of the life world it had formed out of its environment.

If to the question, "Who was Flaubert?" we were to reply, "He was himself," the statement is correct or incorrect, in Sartre terms, according to which use of self we have in mind. I like to think that there are two forms of self-realization consistent with Sartre's psychology. The first is spontaneous self-realization and is based on my recognition that the core of my existence is inextricably bound up with nonbeing, the "nothingness" of which Sartre speaks, the separation between consciousness and all its objects (physical and mental)—my freedom itself. I need not (indeed *cannot*), in any absolute sense, *be anything*, but I am free to project being whatever I choose. I am separated from my past, from my future, even from my self (as fully personalized ego). Spontaneous self-realization is the realization of the power and the independence of the preflective consciousness. In contrast, temporal self-realization depends on my acknowledging my responsibility for my own past and future; it necessitates that I relate them to the present in some coherent pattern. By my actions, Sartre tells us, I carve out my being—in the world; the image of what I have made myself is formed by the marks I have left on the total environment in which I have moved. What I am is what I have done —at this moment. "You are your life," Inez tells Garcin in *No Exit*. Obviously both kinds of self-realization are essential for full development of our freedom and responsibility. Spontaneous self-realization by itself results in the weathervane personality, the irresponsible and finally valueless life. But to live wholly within the framework of one's chosen value system, even if once it was freely created, is to become "uptight," resistant to growth, incapable of enjoying the psychic refreshment of the "moral holidays" which William James one said, are essential to our psychological well-being.

Sartre claims that Flaubert, insofar as he was able, refused spontaneous self-realization and chose to identify himself first with the ego "given" to him and then with his own carefully shaped self-image as artist. In reality both of these and the person history knows as Gustave Flaubert were the product of the original, nonpersonalized, prereflective self-consciousness, which neither Flaubert nor we could ever grasp and objectify.

S. BEYNON JOHN

Politics and the Private Self in Sartre's Les Chemins de la liberté

To move from the world of *La Nausée* and the short stories to that of Sartre's unfinished tetralogy, *Les Chemins de la liberté* (1945–49), is to pass from an almost morbidly private to a public realm where the characteristic and recurring Sartrian myth-makers are no longer insulated from the larger interests of society. The novel sequence ceases to exploit politics as mere violent background, which is what happens in "Le Mur," or as a kind of laboratory model of the psychology of fascism, which seems to me what occurs in "L'Enfance d'un chef." On the contrary, the novels reflect the view once expressed by Thomas Mann: "In our time, the destiny of man presents its meaning in political terms." In *Les Chemins* we are dealing with a work which bears on the nerve of contemporary politics and in which an acutely personal experience of the life of our times has been disciplined and subdued to a larger ironic awareness of the movement of history, though there are moments when the force of private feeling disturbs the ironic balance.

All creeds emerged from *La Nausée* as equally irrelevant to the scandal of contingency, but in *Les Chemins* allegiance to Communism emerges as a serious and dominant theme. Indeed, what chiefly makes the novel sequence distinct from Sartre's previous fiction and unifies its separate volumes is its way of connecting men with the world of politics and of conjuring up that world as the natural, and perhaps inevitable, arena of human choice. This

From *Australian Journal of French Studies* 19, no. 2 (May–August 1982): 185–203. © 1982 by Monash University.

aspect of the novels is the one I should like to concentrate on, though it must also be seen as inseparable from the general movement of the novels, which is to do with freedom and the illusion of freedom working themselves out in a variety of contexts among characters who are self-deluding and in flight from the full implications of personal responsibility. In effect, one of Sartre's most distinctive achievements is to relate the private microcosm, with its play of evasion and moral ambiguity, to the political macrocosm with its strains and conflicts. The author's alertness to the change and detail of the external world is never divorced from his acute feeling for the motions of the individual consciousness. The political character of the novel sequence becomes progressively more explicit as the narrative proceeds and this general movement also represents a change in scale. We leave the small, self-absorbed world of Parisian friends and lovers in *L'Age de raison* for the broader canvas of European politics and the threat of war in *Le Sursis* and the brutal impact of military defeat in *La Mort dans l'âme*. Sartre's invented world is juxtaposed to actual historical events and personages so that we are driven to judge of some part of the truth of the fictional experience by an appeal to life outside the novels. To put it another way, our sense of the quality of the moral insight and formal order we encounter in the novels cannot quite be divorced from our feelings about the adequacy of the fiction as a picture of European political life between 1938 and 1940. Judged in this way, I would have thought that *Le Sursis* and *La Mort dans l'âme* fail to render the full complexity of the political events which inspired them, though they are uncannily sensitive to the mood of bafflement, anxiety and confusion which prevailed in Europe at the time of Munich.

The actual dates on which the separate volumes in the sequence were composed suggest the outside pressures which helped to shape the general sense of the tetralogy. In the summer of 1938, as Simone de Beauvoir records, Sartre first intimated that he had an idea for a new novel sequence. So we are dealing with a work conceived in the wake of the Austrian *Anschluss* of March 1938 and in the climate of violent propaganda designed by the Nazis to prepare the way for the break-up of Czechoslovakia in September of the same year. The dominant theme of the new novel sequence was to be freedom and its general title *Lucifer*. The first volume was to be called *La Révolte*, the second *Le Serment*, and an epigraph was to suggest the nature of the central problem: ["The misfortune is that we are free"]. On 2 November 1939, while Europe was still adjusting to the tensions of the phoney war, Sartre dispatched a hundred pages of the manuscript of volume one to Simone de Beauvoir. The first draft of the completed first volume was finished by May 1940 and rehandled between 1941, when he was released from a prisoner of war camp, and 1945 when its definitive version appeared under the title of *L'Age de raison*. A fragment of the text (Brunet's invitation to Mathieu to join the Communist Party) was published in August 1943 in *Domaine français*, a special number of the periodical *Messages* appearing in Geneva, and another (Daniel's attempt to drown his cats) in the same month at Lyons in the review *L'Arbalète*. So a novel originally conceived in the pre-war months of appeasement and bitter disillusion was modified and reshaped under the impact of military defeat, foreign occupation and clandestine resistance. The second volume, as Simone de Beauvoir recalls in *La Force de l'âge*, was written by July 1943 and its opening pages, under the title "23 septembre 1938" (the date of Hitler's Godesberg memorandum on Czechoslovakia), appeared in an issue of the periodical *Les Lettres françaises* in November 1944, prior to publication of the novel in its entirety in 1945 when it too was given a new title, *Le Sursis*. Both new titles seem to me to suggest more ironic detachment than the rather melodramatic originals and perhaps point to the author's growing concern with distancing his material. The general title of the novel-cycle reflects the central importance which the idea of freedom is given in the fiction, though the form and texture of the novels cannot be said to *configure* the idea of freedom in quite the astonishingly apt way in which the form and texture of *La Nausée* embody the notion of contingency.

To judge from a reference in *La Force de l'âge* the third volume of the cycle, as envisaged by Sartre in late August 1939, was to turn on a dramatic reversal of roles in which the Communist Brunet, alienated by the Nazi-Soviet non-aggression pact of 23 August 1939, was to quit the Party and seek Mathieu Delarue's help. It is significant that this reversal, which looks dangerously like an attempt to show a chastened and fictionalized Paul Nizan appealing to a lucid and fictionalized Sartre, does not actually figure in *La Mort dans l'âme* (1949), the third volume of the cycle, which was written between 1947 and 1948 and serialized in the pages of *Les Temps Modernes* between December 1948 and June 1949. The roots of this volume clearly lie in Sartre's own experience, as is partly confirmed by the two fragments of his wartime diary that have been published. These offer a vivid and direct account of Sartre's own involvement in the French military defeat, an account that is particularly good at rendering the ghostly emptiness of the small provincial town, all dust, silence and sunlight, where the French troops are holed up. It is true that with the brutal death of Schneider/Vicarios in "Drôle d'amitié," the one fragment of the abandoned fourth volume that has found its way into print, Brunet reaches a crisis of disillusionment with the Communist Party over the issue of Nazi-Soviet relations in 1940. But the irony in this situation is not dramatically reinforced for us by showing him appealing to Mathieu (who does not, in fact, appear in this fragment).

A reversal of Mathieu and Brunet's situations does take place in the scheme Sartre originally planned for the abortive fourth volume but, according to Simone de Beauvoir's notes and recollections, this reversal in no sense suggests Brunet's abandonment of the Party in favour of Mathieu's own brand of politics. Brunet's predicament is painful enough in this context but his crisis of faith is not contrasted for effect with Mathieu's lucidity. Sartre's original plot for this volume appears to have provided for the recapture of Brunet who then determines to establish contact with the Party outside the prisoner of war camp. To this end he enlists the help of the camp escapes-organizer who turns out, by a coincidence which strains credulity, to be Mathieu. He has missed death on the church-tower in that scene, heavy with intimations of a final catastrophe, which concludes the first part of *La Mort dans l'âme*.

In Simone de Beauvoir's version of this projected outline for the fourth volume, Mathieu epitomizes the break with his old and uncommitted way of life by participating in the execution of a camp spy. Brunet escapes and reaches Paris only to find that, with the entry of the USSR into the war, the French Communist Party's previous policy toward Nazi Germany now lies in ruins. He helps to rehabilitate Schneider/Vicarios' reputation and resumes his activities as a party functionary in the Resistance, but his experiences have undermined his faith in the Party. Ironically he discovers his own freedom and subjectivity at the very moment Mathieu chooses to move away from subjectivity to commitment. The latter joins the ranks of the Resistance, embraces the collective discipline of clandestine struggle and commits himself fully to a cause. He eventually dies under torture—"heroic because he has made himself a hero"—to quote Simone de Beauvoir's account. This looks pretty extraordinary stuff, but that some form of positive and voluntaristic ending was part of Sartre's original intentions for the tetralogy may be judged from a remark he made in an interview with Claudine Chonez as early as 1938: ["*La Nausée* has been accused of being overly pessimistic. But let's wait until the end. In my next novel, which will be a sequel, the hero will right the machine. One will see existence rehabilitated, and my hero acting and enjoying the taste of action"].

Philippe, Daniel's last homosexual conquest, also joins the Resistance as a gesture of resentment against the masterful Daniel and as a way of proving he is not a coward. He is killed in an affray at some café and Daniel, distraught with grief and anger, uses one of Philippe's hand-grenades to blow up a meeting of important German officials to which he has access as a prominent collaborator. Sarah, a refugee in Marseilles, throws herself and her small son Pablo out of the window in order to avoid arrest by the Germans; Boris is parachuted into the anonymity of the *maquis*.

If I have laboured the matter of the dates at which the novels of the cycle were composed and the plots projected and discarded, it is not simply to emphasize the strong and persistent intertraffic which occurs between Sartre's real-life experience of politics and specific elements of plotting and characterisation which are a feature of the novels themselves, but also to indicate how Sartre's own struggle, in the world of post-war politics, to divest himself of subjective and simplistic explanations leads him to abandon aspects of the novel he had planned. The rather eccentric segment of Parisian society which Sartre introduces to us in *L'Age de raison*, and with which he himself was familiar, is surely quite deliberately stylized so as to inflate the tedium, triviality and aimlessness of private life on the eve of the Second World War. It is a picture of that society seen *after* the deluge, its shallowness rendered grossly culpable by the knowledge we, as readers, share with the author of the historical catastrophe which is to overwhelm what the characters themselves assume to be a normal and permanent way of life.

Similarly, parts of the political argument of *La Mort dans l'âme* and "Drôle d'amitié," especially in their relation to Brunet, seem to me to reflect the frustrations and divisions typical of French domestic politics immediately after the Liberation and, more narrowly, Sartre's own estrangement from the French Communist Party between 1947 and 1948. The real world infects the imaginary life of the novel. One result is that Sartre's outraged personal feelings about the campaign of slander mounted by the French Communist Party against himself and the memory of his old friend, Paul Nizan, who had defected from the Party on the issue of the Nazi-Soviet Pact, fill certain pages of "Drôle d'amitié" with a very special urgency and rancour. For instance, Vicarios' defence of himself against the lies and fabrications of the Party has an intensity that does not relate quite naturally to the gentle and rather mysterious figure the author has created. I suspect that here Sartre's own voice comes dangerously close to drowning the autonomous voice of the character. In the same way, the viciousness with which Chalais, the Party's hatchet man, is portrayed and the glee with which the author displays the hollowness of Brunet's relationships with his Communist comrades, both tend to overreach the ironic detachment required in this part of the narrative if the human inadequacy of political bureaucrats of the Left is to be exposed without also exposing the author's intrusive judgement.

So far as the abandoned fourth volume, *La Dernière chance*, is concerned, its character (to judge from Simone de Beauvoir's summary) is almost wholly sensational. Its structure reflects a schematic irony which serves in a crude way to diminish both Daniel, the symbolic representative of the incipient fascism of French capitalism; Philippe, the confused and egotistical rebel against the bourgeois family; and even Brunet, the militant Communist, who is left in a state of political schizophrenia. Only a reformed Mathieu, symbolizing the fusion of the liberal mind and the collectivist ethos, rises to the level of events. The world of the Resistance is viewed in somewhat Wagnerian terms as the end of an epoch and, in its edifying distribution of rewards and punishments, seems to me to fulfil a private fantasy rather than to embody the imaginative realization of the great and meaningful themes of freedom and commitment which had animated the volumes preceding *La Dernière chance*. The "resurrection" of Mathieu is perhaps the most profoundly significant feature of this outline. It points without ambiguity to Sartre's need (at least, at this stage of his life) to show the socialist intellectual if not actually triumphing over the Communist Party, at least as offering a valid alternative to it. In this sense, the dialogue between Communism and the uncommitted intellectual of the Left has to be artificially revived in the person of Mathieu, even though this runs counter to the effects actually produced by the skill and energy of the writing in that scene of *La Mort dans l'âme* in which Mathieu appears to share the death of his comrades on the church-tower.

In the light of this plan for *La Dernière chance*, the abandonment of the tetralogy, which is confirmed by the failure to publish any sequel to the episode in "Drôle d'amitie," reflects Sartre's awareness that the relatively simple conflicts of loyalty and principle he associated with the Resistance, however skilfully and imaginatively conveyed in retrospect, were likely to offer too facile and schematic a picture of authentic political involvement to the French reading public of 1949, disenchanted as it was with the peace, conscious of its own divisions and of the complex, shifting and ambiguous character of politics in postwar Europe. In the last resort, of course, we must judge *Les Chemins* in its incomplete state and this very incompleteness reinforces its ambiguities. The final impact of *Les Chemins*, in the form in which we now read it, remains negative and ironic in all that concerns personal relations and political choices (or so I shall argue in what follows). The ironies are rooted in an acute awareness of the ways in which men deceive themselves and mask or deny the reality of their freedom, and in an equally strong sense of how the meaning of their actions can be distorted or even nullified by historical events and processes from which they cannot escape. Hence Sartre's own description of *L'Age de raison* and *Le Sursis* as constituting "an inventory of false, mutilated and incomplete freedoms."

At one level, this ironic sense is present in the nature of Mathieu's predicament in *L'Age de raison*. It is that of a humane, decent, self-doubting intellectual whose moral and philosophic scruples are lavished on a comically conceived private crisis at a time when great public issues are at stake: the fate of republicanism in Spain, the clash of Communist and Fascist ideologies. I say "comically conceived" because Mathieu's fumbling and ineffectual attempts to solve it, like the ease with which he can be deflected from dealing with it, are sources of comedy and even farce. At another level, the irony is embodied in the dramatic reversal of fortunes undergone by Mathieu and Brunet by the time the tetralogy breaks off. With what are apparently his last shots from the church tower the hesitant and isolated intellectual involves himself in violence and, however dubious and subjective his motives, vividly affirms his solidarity with others. On the other hand, the loyal party functionary, heartbroken by the ruthless liquidation of Vicarios, is left alone and despairing in the night of the prisoner of war camp. The contrast between the vertical tower in the full light of morning and the barbed-wire cage of the darkened camp emphasizes graphically Mathieu's involvement and affirmation of self (however mistaken these may be from an objective point of view) and Brunet's humiliation and effacement.

As elaborated in the unfinished version of the tetralogy the respective fates of Mathieu and Brunet illuminate symbolically the political direction of the work. The relation between Mathieu's private life as a slightly raffish school-master and the world of political conflict around him is initially established early in the narrative, in that encounter between him and the drunken beggar which opens *L'Age de raison*. Mathieu is making his way dutifully to the flat where Marcelle, his mistress of seven years standing, expects his regular visit when he is accosted by a beggar smelling of drink. Mathieu gives him money and then protects him from harassment by an officious young policeman. In return, the man insists on giving him a postcard with a Madrid stamp on it. He fingers it reverently before handing it over and expresses maudlin remorse for not having gone to Madrid himself. As he moves off, Mathieu registers irritation:

[Mathieu walked away with a vague sense of regret. There had been a time in his life when he used to wander through the streets, hang around in bars, when he would have accepted anyone's invitation. That was all over now. That kind of thing never produced anything. It was amusing. Yes! He had wanted to go and fight in Spain. Mathieu hastened his step, he thought with irritation: "In any case we had nothing to say to each other." . . . He remembered the guy's face and the expression he had assumed in order to examine the stamp: a funny passionate look. Mathieu examined the stamp in his turn without stopping his walk, then he put the postcard in his pocket. A train whistled and Mathieu thought: "I am old."]

This passage is revealing. The author/narrator is discreetly effaced here but his presence is sensed in the devices he uses to signal to us the significance of this encounter. The "vague regret" which he attributes to Mathieu is carefully planted to suggest Mathieu's residual nostalgia for his old, carefree, unattached days and, more particularly, to hint at the resentment he now feels for the life of habit and obligation he shares with Marcelle, a resentment that will loom larger and more explicit as the plot develops. Similarly, Mathieu's "irritation;" as reported by the narrator, is deliberately linked with his private reflection that he has "nothing to say" to the beggar precisely so as to throw doubt on the truthfulness of that remark and to imply that Mathieu and the beggar share a sense of guilt and remorse about the Spanish Civil War. Indeed, each of Mathieu's reactions in this episode emphasizes how ambiguous is the quality of his moral response, how uncertain his sense of personal involvement. He cannot side with respectable society (in the shape of the policeman) against the beggar, but his casual charity, like the ease with which he deflects the policeman, merely serve to show how much a part of that society he is and how "superior" to the object of his attentions. His subsequent refusal to join the beggar in a drink confirms his social embarrassment. In juxtaposing Mathieu's reference to his ageing to the whistle of a passing train, with its evocation of a world in which others are on the move to new destinations, the narrator skilfully marks the break from a war-torn Madrid, briefly conjured up by the postcard, to a Paris which frames Mathieu's own settled routine. Here, in his unexpected meeting with the beggar, Mathieu's listlessly regular life is abruptly exposed to another, more intense and painful world coloured by failure, guilt and suffering. The theme of the Spanish Civil War, introduced so suddenly and obliquely, recurs like a leit-motiv throughout the novel, a perpetual (though discreet and hidden) threat to the private relationships with which it is chiefly concerned and a perpetual (though indirect) reproach to the narrowness and complacency of those relationships. The Civil War in Spain distracts Mathieu from his worries about whether his salary, the symbol of his bourgeois security, will last out until the end of the month; recurs in conversation with his solid and assured Communist friend, Brunet: wells up in self-recrimination in the Sumatra night-club, and spoils the taste of the sherry he drinks with the homosexual Daniel.

By providing a specifically political dimension the novel-sequence as a whole expresses an enlargement of the scope of human action, at least in comparison with *La Nausée*. In spite of this, *L'Age de raison* itself never becomes a fully political novel but remains essentially the description of a world of individuals insulated from the life of politics. It offers a criticism of the pseudo-freedoms pursued by these individuals and, particularly in the case of Mathieu, a revelation of the disturbances which accompany the recognition of freedom, though the tone surrounding some of these disturbances is distinctly ironic. Significantly, most of these characters live in the margins of respectable society and their relationship with the workaday world of tasks and professional responsibilities is tenuous. Mathieu is a teacher on vacation, Marcelle a model of enforced idleness, Boris and Ivich students untouched by any strong sense of intellectual interests, Sarah a housewife never shown at her chores, Daniel apparently a stockbroker, though never seen at work at the Bourse. Certainly Lola works as a night-club singer but the exotic nature of the setting tends to place her apart from the life of office, shop or factory. In fact, the world of jobs and routine is purposely held at bay so that interest can focus on personal relationships, on inner, rather than social, experience. And these relations of dependence between individuals, the wary and often disaffected attitudes towards society, the habit of strenuous self-scrutiny, the preoccupation with time, all express a deep and painful uncertainty about the nature of the self and its relation to the world outside.

It is, of course, true that Mathieu's career of drift is contrasted with the energy of Gomez, the absent but unforgotten painter who is an officer in the International Brigade, and with the assurance of Brunet, the party activist, though descriptions of the latter ("a Prussian cast of face," "a great tower") are not unambiguously admiring. But though these two symbolize modes of political commitment, they are marginal to the action of the novel which is principally concerned with private individuals making and regretting decisions, displaying integrity, bad faith or confusion in their friendships and love-affairs among the distraction of bars, night-clubs and art galleries. At this stage one can say of Brunet and Gomez (whose abandoned canvas significantly provokes feelings of guilt in Mathieu) that they presage the violence that is to come and are the shadows of public causes falling across purely private dilemmas. In this sense, they make *L'Age de raison* a novel haunted by the absence of politics.

This feeling of politics as existing in a ghostly way at the edges of the narrative in *L'Age de raison* helps to create the sense of strain we experience when we turn to *Le Sursis*, every part of which imaginatively recreates the atmosphere of the Munich crisis of 1938 and is permeated with politics and the threat of war. This sense of strain springs from our awareness that the political content of *L'Age de raison* is too tenuous and latent to be thought of as the necessary prelude to the conflicts of *Le Sursis*. We cannot resist the impression that the second novel of the sequence does not derive naturally from the experience of the first but has had to be imposed on it. Besides, Sartre's preference for rendering reality through the almost solipsistic consciousnesses of isolated individuals is difficult to reconcile with a narrative centred on major political events. There are strains involved in relating the contents of an individual consciousness to a political reality outside it. Actions and events tend to be seen in terms of their value to the private self in its struggle to define itself, and not in terms of the wisdom or utility of particular political choices. Even so, when compared with *L'Age de raison*, *Le Sursis* must be accounted a novel in which the balance between private and public activity has been radically altered and in which a quite new importance is granted to the impact of politics on individual lives. The imagined, and often caricatured, conduct of real-life ministers and diplomats in a variety of European cities combines with vividly rendered episodes of street violence in Czechoslovakia and scenes of mobilization and evacuation of hospitals to create an atmosphere of feverish activity arising from political decisions. The claims of personal life collide with an anonymous external experience which brings individuals sharply up against the nature and limits of their own freedom. Characters keep their different styles of life but are drawn irresistibly into experiences which transcend their private needs and inclinations. As Sartre expresses it in the advertisement for the 1945 edition of the first two volumes of the cycle, the individual is ["a monad which leaks, which will never stop leaking, without ever sinking"]. The shifting chaos of individual lives is everywhere contained within a historical framework, sometimes allusively sketched in with a maximum of fictional invention, sometimes made explicit with almost documentary fidelity. Such is the transcription of Hitler's strident broadcast ultimatum to Dr. Benes which occupies several pages of the chapter entitled "Lundi, 26 septembre" and which reinforces the novel's public dimension while also reminding us of Sartre's debt to the fictional techniques of John Dos Passos, particularly the device of "Newsreels"—a combination of newspaper headlines, stock-market reports, official cornmuniqués, etc.—which the American writer incorporates in novels like *1919*. But, as with Dos Passos, Sartre's use of documentary elements remains an essentially fictive procedure intended to communicate something of the movement and texture of society. *Le Sursis* is still a metaphor about existential choice exercised in a concrete historical situation, not some kind of sociological explanation of why the French were to be defeated in June 1940.

So the idea of politics, of a realm in which man is seen in relation to public obligations and responsibilities, emerges very strongly from the pages of *Le Sursis*. It is embodied in the intertraffic between authority, speaking through the medium of official communiqués and mobilization orders, and the surprised individual shaken out of the torpor and routine of his normal life. But it is only in *La Mort dans l'âme* and "Drôle d'amitié" that politics is presented to us as the collective drama of a nation. This is already reflected in the defeated French soldiers, inhabitants of a "paradise of despair," who roam innocently through the luminous summer landscape in the first part of *La Mort dans l'âme*. Caught in the unreal hiatus between defeat and capture, they carry bunches of flowers and appear to Mathieu to be "angels sauntering at their ease." For a moment they affirm what is precious about private life before private life itself comes to an end, an end brilliantly conveyed in the second part of the novel by the trail of confetti from torn-up personal letters scattered behind them by the French troops as they move across the countryside into captivity: ["The whole road is a long, soiled love-letter"]. The same sense of collective experience is suggested by the animal patience of the captured masses of soldiers. The plight of individuals is effaced before that of the community and the social dimensions of the catastrophe are fully established. That is why we cease to encounter individuals of much variety and interest in the barracks. Brunet is surrounded by social stereotypes who, with the exception of Schneider and the young printer who subsequently throws himself off the train, fail to engage us imaginatively. The poverty of their mental and emotional lives tends to epitomize the degree to which the "inner" life has become irrelevant. Here, as elsewhere in *La Mort dans l'âme*, private relationships—Ivich's botched marriage, the collapse of Odette's love for Jacques, Boris' break with the stricken Lola—dwindle to nothing and are lost in the turmoil of public events: refugees streaming south, the dazed defeat of the French army, the entry of the Germans into Paris.

So in its second and third volumes, as in the fragment we possess of the abandoned fourth, *Les Chemins de la liberté* affirms itself conspicuously as a political novel. This is something different from a social novel which I take to be one in which the novelist affords us fresh insight into the way in which the experience of individuals is shaped by their social medium. Sartre's skill lies rather in communicating the distance between the vivid life of consciousness, always so brilliantly in focus, and the confused movement of social and political events, always shifting and blurred. In *Les Chemins* we gain small sense of individuals as exhibiting styles of life that spring from concrete economic and social conditions, but a strong sense of discrete minds of varying degree of lucidity and sophistication worrying away at the problems of personal freedom and political involvement. The specifically political strain is, perhaps, too narrowly and technically conceived in the intense and elaborate discussions about the policies of the French Communist Party which characterize parts of the second section of *La Mort dans l'âme* and parts of "Drôle d'amitié." On the other hand, the almost theological acrimony of the debate between Schneider and Brunet or between Brunet and the inflexible Chalais is imaginatively consistent with the desperation felt by these men as events confront them with a cruel test of their political faith and loyalty.

Nowhere in the abandoned tetralogy do we learn unambiguously what sort of commitment in politics is proper for a person living in good faith, though we learn a lot from the fates of Mathieu, Gomez and Brunet about what does *not* constitute authentic commitment. Certainly freedom is not to be equated with Mathieu's irresponsibility or Daniel's slavery as he veers between self-indulgence and expiation. It is yet to be discovered beyond the bankruptcy of these modes of behaviour. The motives and acts of these four characters, in particular, reinforce for us a sense of the fundamental difficulty and complexity of the moral life and, more especially, of the problems involved in connecting private and public choices. As the sequence proceeds, there is a greater sense of honesty and lucidity, a sharper awareness of the risks of living in a changing world, but if we concentrate on Mathieu, Gomez and Brunet in their public or political roles, we are struck by the ultimately unpersuasive character of all their modes of commitment. None of them embodies a fully satisfying style of life. The failure of *L'Etre et le néant* to transcend a kind of social stalemate is here transposed, in a fictive way, into the field of politics.

If we look closely at Mathieu's one outstanding act of involvement in a public cause (his last stand on the church-tower), we need to say at the outset that it is rendered by a vivid and effective narrative of action. Indeed, in making Mathieu the sole survivor of a particularly bloody encounter, the Sartre who envisaged him as resurrected in the projected fourth volume positively invites us to deny the imaginative power of the scene itself and to suspend disbelief about Mathieu's death simply so that he can take up again a particular argument about valid commitment. Mathieu's actions on the tower are primarily seen in personal terms as a revenge on a botched life, on his own inadequacy and indecisiveness, and as an act of destruction that will make up for all the hesitations and frustrations of his past: [" . . . One bullet for Lola who I didn't dare to rob, one for Marcelle who I should have jilted, one for Odette who I didn't want to screw . . . "]. Though this is recognizably the voice of Mathieu, the recalcitrant schoolmaster and haunter of bars, it is not the idiom of a man responding to philosophic imperatives. Something of these is, however, present in the language with which the author/narrator surrounds Mathieu's act of wild destruction in which military necessities are temporarily eclipsed: ["He was firing on mankind, on Virtue, on the World: Liberty is Terror. . . . He fired. He was pure, he was omnipotent, he was free"]. Here the narrator identifies the act with the concept of "Terror" borrowed from Hegel and though this probably makes Mathieu the only French soldier in the campaign to go down fighting in a blaze of metaphysical notions taken from a German philosopher, it is certainly consistent with the rather cerebral philosophy teacher we have got to know in the course of the novel-cycle.

In avoiding the use of direct speech at this point, the author/narrator emphasizes the distance between himself and his creature, mockingly granting to Mathieu a language that both parodies his normal philosophic self-consciousness and establishes its incongruity in the brutal context in which he finds himself. Such self-dramatizing rhetoric at such a moment effectively punctures any sense we might have that Mathieu's act represents a serious commitment worthy of his sophistication and good will. The whole notion of freedom is here equated with destruction, self-destruction and delusions of omnipotence. The inflated language attributed to Mathieu, like his tendency to see himself as the centre of a falling world are consistent with his earlier thoughts as he takes up his position on the church-tower and prepares for the German attack:

> [I decide that death was the secret meaning of my life, that I have lived in order to die. I die in order to witness that it is impossible to live; my eyes will extinguish the world and will close it for ever.
>
> The earth shrugged its inverted face towards this dying man, the capsized sky flowed across him with all its stars: but Mathieu watched these useless gifts without deigning to gather them in.]

The first paragraph reads like the last spasm of a solipsistic mind; in the second, the lyrical expansion of the language, with its poetic image of almost regal disdain, seems to me to produce a portentous effect and to render Mathieu for us as a self-absorbed actor in some cosmic spectacle. We are coaxed by the emphases of the language, by the stylistic tone of these crucial passages into viewing this heroism as suspect because excessively self-regarding. It is surely significant that of all the snipers left behind to fight this rear-guard action on the tower, Mathieu alone is shown as choosing a rifle carelessly and at random while Pinette makes a deliberate choice, like a workman who knows that the job requires good tools. Equally significant is the fact that we are given access to only one mind, Mathieu's, a mind which expresses itself with a kind of apocalyptic relish that is very much at variance with the plain speech of his comrades. We are being invited to judge this supreme act of violence on Mathieu's part as not very different from the sort of futile romantic gesture which he has performed in the past. One thinks of the incident in the night-club (in *L'Age de raison*) when he drove the knife into the palm of his hand, an incident he significantly recalls during his last vigil on the tower. In fact, we are encouraged to interpret this act on the tower as emblematic of those "false, mutilated and incomplete freedoms" to which Sartre has referred elsewhere. Both these scenes seem contrived in order to establish Mathieu's violence not as an exemplary act reflecting an authentic choice, but as the rather theatrical expression of the tensions and frustrations of a self-deceiving bourgeois intellectual who has yet to find a valid form of commitment in the larger world.

Yet when all this is said, the pages devoted to Mathieu's last stand have their ambiguities. Certain moments in the rapid narrative seem curiously at variance with the ironic spirit which I have argued is central to this episode. It is true that Pinette chooses his rifle more carefully than Mathieu, but, in the end, it is Pinette who is demoralized and paralyzed with fear while Mathieu, finding himself alone among the blood and rubble, stands up recklessly and fires a defiant last burst in a spirit that is oddly close to regimental pride: [". . . it will not be said that we didn't hold out for 15 minutes"]. If it is true that Mathieu's own irate, self-accusing outburst about the women in his life tends to undermine the seriousness of the act in which he is engaged, and even if one admits the discreet authorial mockery at the expense of his endless philosophizing, the ironic possibilities of these moments are at least contained and subdued by the respect and fellow-feeling we have for Mathieu, injured by a beam from the roof that falls in on him and still spattered with the blood from Chasseriau's decapitated body. I am not sure it is possible to accommodate both impulses (the ironic and the affirmative) within this episode without damaging one of them. However, this may simply be the novelist's device for warning us against writing off even those characters whom he persistently surrounds with irony. No matter how trivial or inadequate his motives, Mathieu does, at least, break with a dead past and stand alongside other men in a common, if doomed, enterprise. He may not be an "authentic" man but his essential decency shines through.

If we turn to Gomez, the first thing that has to be said is that he is discredited for us in purely human terms because of the harsh indifference he displays towards the loyal, patient and long-suffering Sarah. And it is precisely this lack of human sympathy which lies at the root of our misgivings about the quality of his *political* commitment. Through Mathieu's eyes we are given a view of Gomez which sharply reduces the admiration we have been willing to grant him as a brave man devoted to the Spanish republican cause. Here the crucial scene is that of the dinner which Mathieu shares with Gomez in *Le Sursis*. It is framed between two episodes involving that self-deceiving mythomaniac, Philippe. The final moment of the scene with Gomez in the restaurant shows him, confident of his military glamour, picking up an attractive actress who is sitting at a nearby table and leading her on to the dance floor. This moment merges with a scene in which the play-acting Philippe is shown dancing with the coloured prostitute, Flossie. In this way, we seem to pass imperceptibly from one kind of actor to another. The meal is lavish. Gomez, newly promoted to general, takes it and the actress quite naturally as his due. Mathieu has his reservations about the Spaniard ["Mathieu didn't think that much of Gomez"] but is prone to feel inadequate in his presence. He is given to hectic bouts of self-reproach but, because of the comic exaggeration of the language he uses, we rather tend to discount these, sensing their false and theatrical character: ["If I eat, a hundred dead Spaniards leap at my throat. I have not paid"]. In fact, Mathieu's zealous self-reproach simply serves to emphasize his own good nature and decency when contrasted with Gomez's hardness, egoism and vanity. We share in Mathieu's shock at the callousness with which Gomez refers to his dead comrades in Spain; and, like Mathieu, we are alienated by the streak of sheer adventurer which Gomez reveals in his appetite for the spoils of war, whether these take the form of gold braid or fifteen year old girls. "Mars and Venus," says Gomez lightly as he shows Mathieu the snapshot of his little Spanish conquest, but the tone suggests he is only half-joking, and that half-joke condemns him. He is brave but the antithesis of Brunet's party activist; an adventurer who embraces causes because they nurture his ego and resolve his personal conflicts. There is nothing in him of disinterested commitment; he is a performer who his found a congenial stage for his activities and who pursues action for its own sake: ["'Mathieu,' he said in a deep slow voice, 'war is beautiful.' His face was glowing. Mathieu tried to disengage himself but Gomez gripped his arm forcefully and went on: 'I love war . . .'"].

Significantly, the last appearance Gomez makes in the novel-sequence, (the opening pages of *La Mort dans l'âme*) shows him in exile in New York, suffering from the humid heat and remote from the events that rack his native continent. He is no longer the dashing lady-killer dining out with Mathieu in *Le Sursis*. We meet him in a mood of despair in which he has lost his faith in politics as a valid and meaningful activity, and his confidence in his own possibilities as a painter or even an art-critic. He is advised to keep quiet about having been a general in Spain and, bitterly contrasting all that past glory with his worn trousers and sweat-stained shirt, reveals his wounded vanity at being seen by the pretty girl at the bus-stop as a "dago" down on his luck. The abrupt shift in the narrative, from this exiled and shabby figure, touting for work and humiliated in it foreign land, to Sarah, bearing the brunt of war as she seeks with fierce maternal desperation to protect her child in the great flood of refugees, emphasizes in the sharpest way the change in Gomez's stature and his virtual displacement in the novel-cycle.

It is tempting to suppose that when we pass from Mathieu to Brunet, we are moving from a world of petty introspection and moral inertia into a world of constructive work and meaningful commitment; from the solitude of the self-doubting intellectual to the fraternal warmth of the party activist. In fact, we gradually become aware that there is no real fraternal warmth or consolation in Brunet's life. Though, in *L'Age de raison*, he is sketched in sympathetically and described in terms of the open air, the calm of the sea and the solid reality of manual work, Brunet is revealed to be just as much the product of a bourgeois upbringing as Mathieu. Indeed, at one level, the writing in both *Le Sursis* and *La Mort dans l'âme* seems intended to break down the idealized image of Brunet which we initially get from Mathieu. It is not simply that Brunet cannot manage to stifle his distaste for the vulgarity of the working-class Zézette, with her red hands, cheap scent and over-powdered face, but that, like Mathieu, he is constantly reproaching himself with harbouring these "class" reactions. When, in *Le Sursis*, he murmurs: ["Intellectual. Bourgeois. Separated forever"], his fit of self-pity undermines him in our eyes, obliges us to see him in a very different light from Mathieu's rather fatuous hero-worship, and confirms the distance between him and the workers who form the backbone of the party. This is reinforced when Zézette's Maurice, a staunch proletarian member of the party, privately expresses irritation with Brunet for parroting the editorial platitudes of *L'Humanité* instead of talking to them in a direct and human way. Brunet's evangelical manner of looking at the workers (["To love them. To love them all, men and women, each and everyone, without distinction"]) simply emphasizes the gulf between his ideological position and his human feeling. His self-reproach is couched in the language of desperation, not the language of fraternity. Brunet's membership of the Communist Party is shown to be as incapable of securing for him the blessings of fraternity as Mathieu's endless cogitation about the true nature of freedom.

Mathieu may fumble for fraternity but Brunet too readily assumes it to be an automatic function of party membership, though his actual behaviour shows at every turn how lacking in human content is this form of political brotherhood. Brunet certainly embodies the stoic virtues but he also displays unfeeling bureaucratic zeal. He thinks of men as material for the party to work on. In his eyes, the soldier Moûlu, trudging into captivity in *La Mort dans l'âme*, is simply poor raw material: ["That one's a petty bourgeois too, just like the other, but more stupid. It won't be easy to work on that"]. This tendency to use men as nothing but disciplined instruments has ugly undercurrents, as when Brunet looks down the straggling line of French prisoners: [" . . . pity this bunch isn't surrounded by five hundred soldiers, bayonet at the ready, pricking the thighs of the stragglers and smashing a rifle butt into the talkers . . ."]. It is not Schneider alone who reproves Brunet's unfeeling laughter when a French prisoner of war is publicly slapped by a German guard, but the human sympathy in each of us who reads the novel. We experience the same reaction when Brunet's authoritarian contempt for human frailty takes the form of forcibly preventing the corporal from scrambling for a slice of bread. We share Schneider's opinion that it is hard to help people when you have no feeling for them. Certainly Brunet is concerned for his comrades but chiefly in the sense of saving them from doctrinal error. He cares for them only insofar as they are already of the Party or can be used for its ends. The rest he sees as "children shouting in the timeless afternoon," and he is shocked to discover that, after they have eaten, his fellow-prisoners are transformed from a cowed mob into something like a carnival crowd. In his eyes, the camp takes on the air of a beach, a fairground, a place of pleasure—and he cannot forgive the French troops for it. For Brunet defeat is the necessary ordeal through which France must pass on the road to a new Communist society. An ultimate optimism about the advent of that society permits him to bear with the ignominy of defeat and the hard life of the transit camp, but he can be sustained in this attitude only so long as the Party is shown to be right and he himself can feel guided, supplanted by its superior wisdom and by the prospect of the inevitable success of its policies. Once Schneider/Vicarios can insinuate into Brunet's mind the notion of a purely opportunistic Soviet Union, willing to sacrifice France and the French Communist Party to its own interests, Brunet is dismayed and disarmed.

It is left to the second section of *La Mort dans l'âme* and to "Drôle d'amitié" to supply the fictional images which will convince us that Brunet's commitment to the Communist Party is no more a form of personal salvation, no more a way of living "authenticity" in the world, than Mathieu's quest of absolute freedom or Gomez's cult of action. It is the crowning irony of Brunet's political career that, as he slaves away in the barracks, and later, in the prisoner of war camp, to rescue the Party from the wreckage of defeat and to animate its few survivors with a new purpose, he has already been overtaken by events. While he believes he is following the party line in fostering resistance, he is, in fact, acting contrary to the French Communist Party's new policy of sympathetic neutrality to the German occupier.

Communism, in the sense of total political commitment of a naive and unquestioning kind, is subjected to critical scrutiny in the person of Brunet both because it holds out an illusory notion of infallible and unchanging truth (significantly, Brunet likens Marxism to the natural laws of the physical universe) and because it fails to respond adequately to the human claims that are made on it by men in deprivation and despair. The Communist Party is

principally condemned not for being mistaken or inconsistent in its analysis
of political change, but for driving men of good will to despair. The
emergence of Brunet as a pivotal figure in the second part of *La Mort dans
l'âme*, and again in the pages of "Drôle d'amitié," is necessary if the argument
about the merits of political commitment is to be fully articulated in
imaginative terms. The worker, Maurice, is too peripheral a figure to have
much significance in this moral scheme, and what we know of him is scarcely
encouraging. One has only to recall his brutal reactions to silly Philippe's
pathetic pleas in the hotel room or his simple-minded mouthing of party
slogans.

By contrast, Schneider/Vicarios is Brunet's necessary complement, the
voice of inwardness, of that "subjectivity" Brunet has learned to suspect and
despise in the service of the Party. Vicarios is both enigmatic and appealing;
appealing, in part, *because* he is an enigma and because we are granted only
scattered glimpses of his past history and quality. We are never allowed to
know him well enough to be able to give him, with complete confidence, the
stature of an authentic Sartrian hero, though he gains immeasurably in our
eyes from the manner of his death, from the way in which he is sacrificed to
a cause that uses men cynically and pretends to infallibility. As the Latin root
of his name implies, he carries vicariously the burden of the Party's errors
and is killed so that no voice can dispute the Party's claim to embody the
truth. It is Brunet's final distinction to recognize this and, at the point at
which we leave him, crouched over the body of Vicarios in "Drôle d'amitié,"
he stands on the brink of what is arguably an "authentic" moral life, though
this remains unrealized in the fiction Sartre has actually published. The
precise nature of this authentic life is at least suggested by Brunet's refusal
either to surrender to the claims of the wholly private self or to continue to
accept the total validity of the Communist view of the world: ["No victory of
men will be able to efface this absolute of suffering: — it's the Party who has
killed him. Even if the U.S.S.R. wins, men are alone"]. Here, in the
nightmarish moment when Vicarios is shot dead in the glare of the camp
searchlights, Brunet also stumbles on another truth, that the love men bear
each other transcends ideology. Paradoxically, it is at the culmination of his
personal crisis of belief, the moment when he renounces the Party and
declares his solidarity with fallible and suffering men, that Brunet really
comes alive for us. And that very aliveness is a criticism of the sterility of the
political creed by which he has previously lived. If passages of *La Mort dans
l'âme* already suggest the unreality of Brunet's personal relations with other
men, "Drôle d'amitié" spells out the disintegration of fraternity as embodied
in the Communist Party. In *La Mort dans l'âme* Brunet learns from the fate
of the young printer who leaps to his death from the train that there are party

members who do not find the Party enough to live by. In "Drôle d'amitié" he learns what Schneider/Vicarios already knows, namely that the solitude of the militant cut off from the party is terrible and complete. Like Vicarios, Brunet discovers in bitterness and anguish that if the Party gives life, it also takes it away.

Vicarios is *murdered* for political reasons, and this sets his death apart from the other kinds of, largely private, violence diffused throughout the novel-cycle. These range from the latent violence contained in Daniel's abortive attempts to drown his cats or castrate himself to the overt violence suffered by Gros-Louis when he is beaten up by petty crooks or Philippe when he is man-handled by the mob of conscripts at the railway station. It is this personal and almost random violence which is communicated to us with the greatest immediacy and vividness. There can be no question about how strongly we feel implicated in the sense of humiliation and outrage experienced by the paralysed Charles as he is clumsily bundled into the cattle-truck, in *Le Sursis*, or the raging desire to dominate by force which is expressed in the ugly wrestling-match between Daniel and his homosexual pickup, in *L'Age de raison*. But political violence, the violence inseparable from radical changes in society—a central preoccupation of Sartre's theatre— is almost never raised, in the novel-sequence, to the same level of expressiveness as private acts of violence. For example, in *La Mort dans l'âme*, what chiefly distinguishes Sartre's treatment of even so portentous a public event as the collapse of the French army in June 1940 is not the concrete realization of violence as the very stuff of political breakdown, but the marvelous skill in conveying how the significance of this violence is blurred and diminished to the level of private dreams as the defeated French soldiers make their individual adjustments to it. It is true that the delaying action fought out on the church tower has the power to recall us to the fury of war, but it is so uniquely centred on Mathieu's introspection that it impresses us chiefly as the lurid enactment of a personal caprice. Only in the brutal death of Vicarios in "Drôle d'amitić" does one see spelt out, in a fully expressive way, the connection between public and private selves, force and ideology, violence and history. At that point in the novel-cycle political violence emerges as a significant theme, though in view of Sartre's subsequent abandonment of the tetralogy, it emerges too late to justify one in speaking of it as a potent and animating idea in *Les Chemins de la liberté*.

CATHARINE SAVAGE BROSMAN

Sartre's Kean *and Self-Portrait*

In 1953, the same year that he began *Les Mots*, and just one year after publishing his massive study on Jean Genet, Jean-Paul Sartre composed *Kean*, one of his two dramatic adaptations (excluding film scripts). The premiere took place on 14 November 1953 at the Théâtre Sarah-Bernhardt; the play was a great stage success. It is a reading in five acts of *Kean ou Désordre et génie* (1836), written by Alexandre Dumas père and included in his complete works, but based on a text composed by Frédéric de Courcy and Théaulon de Saint Lambert for Frédérick Lemaître, the renowned actor, who had met the actor Edmund Kean and, after the latter's death, wanted to play him on the stage. Thus it is at several removes from the biographical reality it would purport to portray; Sartre's Kean is, as he termed him, a myth, the "patron des acteurs," reflecting the author's interest in self-mythification. It was Pierre Brasseur who proposed that Sartre adapt for him the Dumas text. The latter, who had been interested in Kean for some time, was inspired to accept the suggestion, he said, because he had heard laughter at *Hernani*, which he liked, along with the Romantic theatre in general. The play, which abounds in melodramatic situations, does indeed bear some resemblance to the Victor Hugo masterpiece. Sartre considered the subject to be timeless because it dealt with self-identity and allowed a great actor of each generation to take his bearings and test himself, as it were. My purpose

From *French Review* 55, no. 7 (special issue, Summer 1982): 109–22. © 1982 by the American Association of Teachers of French.

is not, however, to study the play as a virtuoso piece for a great performer but rather as an oblique self-portrait, closely associated with the author's autobiographical undertaking. In particular, it illustrates three themes which mark *Les Mots* (1964) and other major works of the period, all three fundamental in Sartre's psyche and catalogue of personal myths, and related to the questions of appearance versus reality, identity, authenticity, and social alienation, which he treats elsewhere. These themes—the major theme of imposture or playacting, the minor ones of treachery and bastardy—and their expression in Kean and *Les Mots* can profitably be examined in terms of both the ontology of the 30s and 40s and the Marxist analyses of the 50s and 60s.

Although Sartre stated that all he wanted to do was to give the play the "petit coup de pouce" that would modernize it enough to make it suitable for the contemporary stage, the changes are considerable and bear a characteristic Sartrean stamp. They include tightening of the plot by reducing the cast and sub-plots, increased banter, great concentration on the two heroines, an entirely different characterization of Anna Damby, and a new interpretation given to Kean and his dilemmas. The emphasis on society reveals Sartre the social commentator as well as Sartre the psychologist, and points to the Marxist social analyses, already adumbrated in *Saint Genet, comédien et martyr*, which would be elaborated only a few years later. Sparkling with humor and psychological insight, the play shows again how its author, sometimes heavyhanded, could rival Giraudoux and Anouilh in Gallic wit, as in the maxim, ["There's no one more punctual than a woman one doesn't love"].

The play is built around four overlapping amorous triangles, which reflect on each other: Kean, the great actor, admired but socially scorned for his illegitimate birth, the Danish ambassador, and Eléna, his wife; Kean, Eléna, and the Prince of Wales, who, as his companion in pleasure, has also been his rival and chooses clothes and women because Kean likes them (a peculiar sexual form of the other as mediator to the self, or the dependence of the for-itself for its reality on the for-others); Kean, Eléna, and Anna Damby, a merchant's daughter, who takes a fancy to the actor and wants to become both an actress and his wife; and Kean, Anna, and Lord Mewill, her fiancé, who is furious that Anna should have jilted him. The dynamics of their multiple relationships are not all pertinent to the present analysis, nor are the probings into masculine and feminine ways of loving and the nuances of class relationships, as Sartre saw them, in early nineteenth-century England. It is useful, however, to quote at the outset Kean's suggestive remark, of both social and ontological import, that he, the prince, and Anna are alike, all victims, all reflections: he was born too low, the prince too high, and Anna a woman. ["You enjoy your beauty through the eyes of others and

. . . I discover my genius in their applause; as for him, he's a flower; in order for him to feel himself a prince, we have to breathe him in"]. All are alienated from the dominant society; none can easily achieve authenticity.

Within this social context, Sartre explores the ambiguous relationships between actor and role and man and actor, in this privileged case of ["an actor whose role is to incarnate his own stage-character"]. These aspects of the more general relationship between self and self and the distance between subjective and objective images introduce the major Sartrean theme of imposture, which he had already considered at length as the phenomenological problem of appearance versus reality. The theme can be expressed as a question of the identity of the self, one of the most characteristic of modern themes. Who is Kean? That depends on who is answering the question. To most of London, he is Hamlet, Romeo, or Othello; that is why Anna is first attracted to him, why Eléna thinks she is in love with him. The latter asks, ["Is there a Kean? The man I saw yesterday was Hamlet in person"]. He is also, socially speaking, an outcast, because he is not well born: his is an extreme case, since he is a bastard, as well as an actor. As Franck Laraque writes, he is ["living inside-out"] through his ambiguous profession, whereas society ["declares it lives right-side out"]. In the first act he distinguishes between the actor—to whom flattering invitations are sent—and the man, noting that his profession is to live by ["false situations"]. Both views are condescending, in the Romantic tradition that makes the audience at once applaud the buffoon and scorn him, misunderstanding his genius; they are also anguishing and objectifying, as is any judgment of the other. ["You're ripping me to pieces with your admiration and your contempt!"]. To the prince, Kean is a charming companion, to whom many boudoirs open; the prince is not unaware that Kean takes pleasure in spiting the aristocrats by seducing their wives as well as by dominating them with his talent, thus excluding *them*, whereas elsewhere he is excluded. To Kean himself, he is a subject, a project, felt and lived from the inside, ["the true Kean that I alone knew"], carrying with him the past of his humble beginnings, which he validates in a sense by his success but which he feels in some way he has betrayed by catering to those who despise him and to whom, in the true Romantic vein, he feels superior. He is also, for himself, an actor and a pariah, since others see him thus; their judgment has been internalized. He thus reveals simultaneously lack of self-image and megalomania. As elsewhere in Sartre's works, the for-itself and the for-others are conflicting, the latter tainting and objectifying the former since it is its mediator. Even the luxury he has lived with for ten years, being purchased on credit, is ["others' luxury"]. He thinks with nostalgia of the old group of actors who would take him back, if he wished—and the time when, his poverty was a *genuine* one, whereas now he is surrounded by furniture he does not own and flowers which, because he has not really paid for them, are an optical illusion. Yet ["it pleases me to reign over mirages"]—he lives now on such illusion, which can be multiplied indefinitely.

In addition, Kean is the roles he has played; that is, he no longer distinguishes between private and stage selves, chiefly because the public will not allow it, for social reasons. ["I'm a false prince, a false minister, a false general. Apart from that nothing. Ah! Yes: a national glory. But on the condition that I don't decide to exist for real"]. Using the contrast of weight and lightness which often serves in Sartre's imagery to indicate the reality of human beings, he says he would prefer to ["weigh with my own weight upon the world"] and perform acts rather than gestures. He even reaches the point of acting himself—that is, conforming to an image he has previously created, which he and others expect to see in him. ["Fear nought, it's only Kean, the actor, playing the role of Kean"]. He epitomizes one type of player which Sartre has described. In contrast to the ordinary actor who, when he has finished work, goes back to being just another man again, he is the sort who ["plays himself at every second. It's a marvellous gift and a curse, at the same time: and he's the real victim of it, never knowing who he truly is, whether he's playing or not playing. . . . [He] even plays his own life, no longer recognizes himself, no longer knows who he is. And who, in the end, is no one"]. Acting is not self-expression but self-creation, in an almost dialectical movement of reconciled contraries, but which has no permanence. ["One doesn't act to earn one's living. One acts in order to lie, to lie to oneself, to be what one cannot be and because one has had enough of being what one is. One acts in order not to know oneself and because one knows oneself too well. . . . One acts because one loves the truth and because one hates it. One acts because one would go mad if one didn't act. Act! Do I know when I'm acting? Is there ever a moment when I stop acting?"]. He recognizes that even his love for Eléna is illusionism. When he tries to cast off his actor's personality, and be simply Kean (whatever that may mean), it is socially impossible: Eléna, who like so many previous mistresses is in love with the actor, or rather with his roles, accepts his suit only if it is expressed dramatically, the prince finds him amusing only because he is an actor, and Lord Mewill can applaud him but never fight him in a duel.

In short, Kean the impostor cannot locate his true self. ["I am nothing, my chick, I play at being what I am"]. Having expressed all passions, he chooses every day which one he wants to assume, and thus chooses what he shall be. C. R. Bukala has observed that Kean's "forgetting of himself as a man suggests the nothingness which Sartre speaks of as situated at the very center of his being." Indeed, it is because man is nothingness, consciousness being always occupied by its object, and thus is not what he is and is what he is not, that role-playing is possible; it springs from the aspiration to *be* as the in-itself is, absolutely and with total identity, which aspiration is a negative result of human freedom. As Sartre had argued in one of his earliest and most interesting philosophic texts, there is no transcendent ego, no contents of the self. Moreover, man is always temporally as well as ontologically distant from himself, projected ahead to what Valéry termed the ["ever future hollow"]. All emotion, as Sartre showed, is behavior, a free choice (and a "magical" one which aims at simplifying the world); we are not identical to our emotion but rather adopt it as a reaction, that is, play it. ["We actors, when a misfortune happens to us, we have to mime the emotion in order to feel it"]. The emotions Kean displays are no more nor less genuine because they are those of a character. In fact, he suggests that life is a poor copy of art. ["I wonder if true feelings aren't just feelings badly acted"], that is, where they dominate rather than being under control. ["Do I hate women or do I play at hating them? Am I playing at making you feel frightened and disgusted, or do I want, very really and very wickedly, to make you pay for the others?"]. As Robert J. Nelson writes, "Kean's esthetic (if he may be said to have one at all) contains no idea of experiencing all the passions which are to be shown on the stage, for the actor, having no real self to expose to experience, has no real passions to present." Furthermore, man is always non-positionally conscious of his choice of behavior: there is no such thing as an unconscious consciousness, or consciousness being an obstacle to itself. Thus, to find any authenticity at all is a difficult, perhaps contradictory enterprise which the actor illustrates most clearly, but which is shared by all, and to which, Sartre later asserted, only a totally changed society can offer a solution.

In short, everyone on the world's stage is indeed a player, the professional actor merely carrying his role to a higher degree. Readers will recall countless memorable instances of role-playing in Sartrean works. In *Kean*, the prince plays at being a prince, Kean at being an actor, Eléna at being in love (and she is the best, he says). Like *Nekrassov*, it is a ballet of imposture and illusions. Sartre commented that his personages are struggling with shadows which are their own characters. Only Anna Damby, he added, achieves some authenticity. Leaving her social circle and the expectations others have about her, she chooses Kean; she announces her purposes honestly, is aware of the role she is playing when she first comes to him, and uses it for a purpose which transcends it. Even when employing familiar feminine stratagems to make herself loved, she at least acknowledges them, so that her public and private selves are much closer to being identical. It is appropriate that she should win out by getting what she wants, as she puts it, taking the banished Kean to New York, away from the audiences who

loved only Kean-playing-Othello. Perhaps there both Kean, who had
forsworn the theatre after his outburst of act IV, and Anna can act again. This
ending does not solve all the problems associated with the multiple, illusory,
and alienated selves, but it is suggestive, for instance, of the influence that a
more democratic society could have in fostering authenticity. Kean has
accused his idle aristocratic audiences of not respecting the work of others,
whereas American society (however much Sartre may criticize it elsewhere)
is founded first of all on work. When Anna lies to the prince to make him
think Kean still loves Eléna, so that he may continue to find her interesting,
illusion again assumes its proper place in a society based on illusion
(hereditary privilege), opposed to the genuine love of Kean and Anna, which
needs no such lie.

In the fourth act, which is built around the play within a play, Sartre
replaced, at Brasseur's request, the scene from *Romeo and Juliet* in the Dumas
text with the final scenes of *Othello*. They have the advantage of making Kean
attempt to reproduce on stage the emotions he is truly feeling, or extend to
the "real world" the dramatic illusion. The closer connection between the
stage scene and Kean's own drama is developed effectively, as the real
jealousy he feels when he realizes the prince of Wales is courting Eléna also
and will be in her box prohibits him from playing Othello successfully. As he
had said, ["I have all the gifts. The nuisance is that they are imaginary. Let a
false prince steal a false mistress from me this evening and you will see if I
know how to shout. But when the real Prince of Wales comes and says to my
face, 'You have confided in a woman, and yesterday that woman and I have
flouted you,' then rage leaves me helpless and makes me stutter"]. Sartre's
interpretation recalls Diderot's well-known thesis in *Le Paradoxe sur le
comédien* that a player is more effective if he is emotionally removed from his
role. Provoked by Eléna's flirtations with the prince and the latter's loud
comments, he ruins his career by interrupting the scene and addressing first
the prince, then other spectators, even stuttering. Declaring his
emancipation from his role, and baring his schizophrenic multiplicity, he
taunts the nobles, especially their most illustrious member, the prince, and
suggests their fundamental misunderstanding in taking the stage for illusion
(on which they feed) and themselves for real, whereas they are greater
impostors yet, the true hypocrites who lie to themselves. They feed on the
imaginary grandeur of being descended from Plantagenets and fear true
reality. Instead of chicken blood, he would like to make human blood flow.
["You came here each evening and you threw bouquets on the stage crying
'Bravo.' I ended up believing that you loved me. But tell me: *who* were you
applauding? Huh? Othello? Impossible: he's a bloodthirsty madman. So it
must be Kean"]. He rubs off his makeup: ["All the same it's curious, you only

like what is false"]. The spectators are in bad faith; they have the *esprit de sérieux* like the bourgeois in *La Nausée* and the alienating society of *Saint Genet*. They have created the actor so that he can amuse them and his obvious imposture will hide their own; he is a sacrificial monster. ["What am I but what you have made of me? . . . You and all the others. Lord! So serious men need illusion. . . . They take a child and change him into an optical illusion. An optical illusion, a phantasmagoria, that's what they've done with Kean"]. In his final outburst he accuses them—not Othello—of murder: ["Kean died in his infancy. Shut up, you murderers, it was you who killed him. It was you who took a child and turned him into a monster!"].

He had earlier felt that only in the presence of real people—those who do not have social prerogatives, whom Sartre elsewhere calls *prolétaires*—did he have a sense of his potential real self. For his former actor friends, ["I am a man, d'you understand, and they believe it so strongly that they will end up by persuading me of it"]. This explains how in act V he can seriously renounce his career and propose taking up the identity of "Monsieur Edmond, [jeweller]." Moreover, he has committed an irreparable act, or what he hopes is one, by insulting the prince. Like Sartre in *Les Mots*, and characters such as Hugo in *Les Mains sales* and Goetz in *Le Diable et le Bon Dieu*, other plays where the stage motif is featured, he meditates on the motivation and reality of his own actions. At one moment his outburst seems to him just another gesture: jealous of Eléna, his Desdemona, he took himself for Othello. ["I was peopled with gestures"]. As Goetz asks, ["And so, then, everything was lies and playacting? I've committed no acts, only gestures"]. But by its consequences—a prison sentence—it is an act, which he espouses, even if he was committing only a "suicide pour rire" and it was the *public* who loaded the pistol. ["If they put me in prison it's because they consider me a man. . . . Prison, believe me, that'll be real"].

This major theme of imposture conveys the author's primary self-expression in the play. The parallels are numerous between Kean and Poulou in *Les Mots*, surrounded by ["the faded theatricality of the Schweitzers"] and by ["virtuous playactors"], especially his buffoon grandfather, who, like Victor Hugo, took himself for Victor Hugo, writes Sartre, if not God the Father. As Kean observes, ["When a man is false, everything around him is false"]. The reader will recall the childish histrion inventing scenes and dialogues, assuming the identity of romantic heroes, living out adventures under the table in his grandfather's study: ["I would throw myself recklessly into the imaginary and more than once I thought of letting myself be engulfed entirely by it"]. This was in order to cover, as well as possible, the void he felt in himself, in a world where his behavior was dictated by the others—the adults—who made him conform to their view of a model child.

["I was born to fill the great need that I had of myself"]. That is to say that he sought objectification or being through the approval of an audience, the for-others, and then release in private fantastic reveries, played out for himself. He has noted elsewhere that children in general are actors, attempting to work on their parents by their antics, as does Lucien Fleurier in "L'Enfance d'un chef." Speaking of Genet at the age of ten, Sartre contrasts him with ["We [who] were only busy playing the servile buffoon to please"]. Jean-Paul's earliest experiences were satisfying, since playacting and falsehood were all he knew. But he later came to fear that his lack of justification and the great transparency he felt were also those of adults. He then suspected that, since they too were perhaps actors, there was no *real* reality beyond playacting which could give it its guarantee, no audience, but only other actors. Using the same distinction between acts and gestures which he had already attributed to Goetz and Kean, he writes, ["I was an imposter. How can one playact without knowing that one is acting? . . . I was a false child, I was holding a false salad basket; I could feel my actions changing into gestures. Comedy hid the world and men from me. I only saw roles and costumes"]. Yet behind the imposture of the adults there was nonetheless something he could not reach, the genuine concerns of whispered family conferences of those whose "acting" really counted, when the "petit chéri" was sent out of the room. ["They had persuaded me that we were created to play-act with each other. I accepted the play-acting, but I insisted on being the main character. Now . . . I perceived that I had a 'false leading-role,' with a text, lots of stage-presence, but no scene 'for me'; in a word, I was giving the grown-ups their cues"].

To offset this realization that, while others ultimately had being, his masks merely covered an empty for-itself, and the consequent feeling of contingency and inferiority, he attempted to cultivate a sense of necessity and superiority (like Kean's Romantic pride), a sense bestowed by the ostensible family beliefs (that he was a gift from heaven, his grandfather's greatest joy), but undermined by the falsehood on which these beliefs rested, as well as by the existence of an autonomous and indifferent world. As he put it, he wished that at every gathering at which he was not present there would be someone missing—Jean-Paul—whose absence, far from being accessory, was the most imposing fact of the situation. The boy's predilection for heights, never outgrown, is representative of this sense of superiority, which may be associated with the lack of superego which Sartre ascribes to the absence of acquaintance with his father, his moral bastardy. It is likewise related to his conviction that he would become a great writer, a conviction both sincere and a sham. After his dramatic and even "cinematic" experiences, in which he tried to *realize* by acting a mental image—an eminently romantic project—

he could no longer hide his imposture from himself. Speaking like the self-aware Kean, he states, ["I pretended to be an actor pretending to be a hero"].

He then adopted the stratagem of transferring his images into words, an activity which remained integral to him for something like four decades: ["The imposture was the same but . . . I took words to be the quintessence of things"]. Unlike his playacting, this new imposture, which allowed for a distance between self and self (the writer and his hero), gave him a new autonomy with respect to adults because the writing self bore a type of authenticity, which might be compared to Kean's realization that he is acting (unlike the audience, which does not recognize its imposture), and his conscious and creative adoption of the passions suited to that role. Noticing his nothingness, he nevertheless managed at a second stage to find his being: ["I was almost nothing, at the very most an activity with no content; but no more was necessary. I was escaping from the play-acting; I was not yet working, but already I was no longer playing. The liar found his truth in the elaboration of his lies. I was born from writing: before it there was merely a game of mirrors; from my first novel I knew that a child had entered the Hall of Mirrors. Writing, I existed, I escaped from the grown-ups"]. This "child," who is an authentic being, can be contrasted to the monster which society makes of Genet and Kean, before each learns to divest himself of the alienated self. Unfortunately, in the young Sartre's life the adults contributed to this early authenticity a new element of imposture by their lip-service recognition of his talent, as an ornament and a "destiny," that is, their version of the myth of the writer, by which he could however never presume to live, since, as they emphasized, it had so many disadvantages. Thus labeling it and him, and giving him a mandate to write because he would thus fulfill his supposed destiny, they removed the freedom he had gained and made of him too something of the monster which he identified with Genet and Kean, what has been called the ["writer-messiah of a dechristianized bourgeoisie"]. He wrote that he lived in the unreal, both "prince et cordonnier," that is, future genius writer on the one hand and pitiful boy duping himself on the other. In time, as he adds, this mandate became his character, an ingenious solution to the problem of alienation, which he later had to unlearn.

Sartre documented his playacting as a child in order to demolish it, as well as the teleological view of his (and any) destiny, the myth of literature, and its promise of salvation, that is, his profoundly neurotic false departure which lasted, he repeatedly emphasized, until the early 1950s. He wished also to illustrate the lie of bourgeois family life, since Charles Schweitzer's roles were no more genuine than Poulou's, just overlaid with an additional layer of unconsciousness. He wanted to show (somewhat paradoxically, of course) that without the "impossible Salut," he was just an ordinary project—["A whole man, made of all men and who is worth them all and whom anyone is worth"]—much as Kean, wanting to leave the stage, says ["I will be able to be anyone"]. His approach to the theme of imposture in *Les Mots* is thus critical in the first instance, as he denounces his own role-playing and that of an entire society, indeed, of the whole of bourgeois France and the Occident, the image of which in his mind was derived first of all from his family. ["The radical *imposture* of the actor sends us back, in fact, to the contradictions of our society"], writes Jeanson. Yet the corresponding portrait of the actor in *Kean* is nevertheless sympathetic, as is that of Poulou himself to a considerable degree. In this connection it will be remembered that as a university student Sartre acted in student produced reviews, and that he was an excellent mimic. His interest in the production of his own plays included concern for the techniques of acting, and his attention to the drama as a cultural manifestation, as well as an artistic genre, is amply documented. Moreover, he continued to write for the theatre well after he had abandoned the novel, apparently seeing no contradiction between it and his evolving political views. His critique of role-playing, then, pervasive as it may be, is not without an element of fascination and comprehension, as is to be expected because it is self-criticism. In fact, Sartre's whole approach to existence may be seen as close to that of an actor, who must *put on* being or essence, rather than having it already given; his criticism of the Schweitzer milieu would then refer to the content of the playacting, and its unconsciousness, rather than the acting itself, which is inevitable, at least in a society the basis of which is alienation.

One can in fact be both "comédien" and "martyr," like Genet. Sartre's developing social orientation of the 1950s made him see that this universal role-playing in order to create a being for oneself, as he had analyzed it in *L'Etre et le néant*, was not done in a vacuum but rather was also a response of an original freedom to the pressures of an unjust, but self-righteous, society: the for-itself which adopts a mask is conditioned by the mask around it, and may indeed, through its playacting, develop a very creative response. Similarly, as it has been observed, Sartre's denunciation of literature in *Les Mots* came in the form of a highly literary autobiography, and in the years following the denunciation he produced works of considerable literary value. It must then be seen as qualified; as Sartre later saw, in an alienated society the person must be alienated also, and in this desperate situation the actor, like Kean, reasserts his freedom despite his roles; he defines himself as Camus wrote, by his "comédies" as well as by his sincere impulses.

Similarly, Sartre's interest in the allied figure of the traitor, illustrated variously by such imaginary figures as Philippe and Daniel in *Le Sursis*, Goetz and Heinrich in *Le Diable et le Bon Dieu*, and his portrait of Genet and analysis of the character of collaborators, as well as by Kean, has a positive aspect, closely allied to his own self-understanding. This obsessive theme has been insufficiently recognized, as John M. Hoberman has recently noted. Jeanson, one of the few who have approached it, has analyzed the basic identity of the bastard and the traitor. In Kean's case, he "betrays" the conventions under which society has allowed him to operate, thus society itself, which he dares to show up in the fourth act as an illusion and an imposture. As Hernani is an outlaw, Kean is an actor; he is, notes Laraque, a revolutionary, criticizing hereditary privileges due to birth and the idleness of the aristocracy. ["I raged against the nobles; since their blood didn't flow in my veins, I wanted to make it flow out of theirs"]. As an actor Kean is king on the stage. Though playing for an audience, he is not phenomenologically dependent upon them; rather, they derive their justification from his identity with his role. Moreover, by pointing out his own role, and thus undermining the security of the audience, forcing it to make a response other than the aesthetic one, he turns himself into the other—the judge, the accuser—rather than allowing society to continue to be his. He points out that the prince too is a creature of illusion, a reflection, like himself, in others' eyes, but the prince has no counterbalancing stage existence and would give anything to be Kean. Yet Kean remains the imposter *par excellence*, whence the irony of this judgment.

Sartre similarly considers himself a traitor. ["I became a traitor and I have remained one. In vain do I put myself entirely into whatever I undertake, or give myself wholeheartedly to work, to friendship, in a minute I will deny myself, I know it, I wish it and I betray myself already—in the midst of my passion—by the foreboding of my future treason"]. He betrays himself partly through the momentum of his project, always ahead of himself, projected beyond today to tomorrow, with the past having no claim on him. This is symbolized by Sartre's personal unwillingness to save money—capitalize or collect a patrimony—and even to keep his books and other such possessions, which, as Simone de Beauvoir noted, he usually gave away—much as Kean refuses to save what little cash remains and instead gives it to a street musician in a grand gesture, not wishing to be possessed by money. Most of all Sartre is a traitor to his family and his class—by his political ideas—to his early readership, which his later works denounce, and additionally to a certain deep self, by a movement of self-opposition and denial which is not unknown among other writers, especially of Protestant background. ["I am doubly a traitor—a traitor in the conflict between the generations and a traitor in the class-struggle. The generation of 1945 thinks that I have betrayed it because it was taught to know me through *Huis clos* and *La Nausée*, works written at a time when I hadn't yet realized the Marxist implications of my ideas"]. His interest in André Gorz, whose volume *Le Traître* he prefaced in 1958, is another instance of acknowledgement of the profound fascination which moral treason exercises on him.

Similarly, in one sense Sartre espouses morally the bastardy which, after *Saint Genet*, both *Kean* and *Les Mots* illustrate. Though he was born legitimate, his father's early death and his consequent upbringing by his mother and grandparents gave him the sense of being fatherless, a circumstance which, it is well known, he viewed as an advantage, since the basic paternal role, which is to exercise authority over the freedom of the child, is corrupt. This attitude recalls Gide's contention that the bastard, freed from the obligation to fulfill an image and carry on a family destiny, is able to invent his values, and ultimately himself; he alone is authentic. However, Sartre puts greater stress on the social pressures exercised on the illegitimate child and on a kind of schizophrenia induced within him by the fact that to others he is flawed from birth, whereas, like everyone else, to himself he is an absolute, perfect freedom. His status is thus originally false; society receives him only to exclude him; he is born an impostor. This is the case with Kean. As one can judge from such works as *La Nausée* and *Les Mots*, this feeling of being unjustified is the *original* feeling, not confined to illegitimate children; but in their case, nothing counteracts it. As a result of this social judgment, the other becomes internalized, and the theme of illegitimacy rejoins those of imposture and treachery, since the bastard, not knowing which self is real, the inner project and freedom or the internalized other, plays himself and feels untrue to himself.

Bastardy is also, however, something of an advantage in Sartrean context, as the previous remarks indicate. Kean asserts to Lord Mewill that his own name is rising, whereas the lord merely "descends" from his ancestors, who are psychologically speaking an immense superego. Sartre later agreed that all intellectuals were bastards, in the positive sense. Observing this connection, Jeanson points out that both are forced to see what other men succeed in dissimulating, and that, conversely, lucidity makes one a bastard, stripping away the false justifications and *raisons d'être* which give to the "just" their prerogatives, and making consciousness separate from action. The problem is to explain why some intellectuals become cognizant of this status and others do not; Sartre has been unable to shed light on this, as in the case of Raymond Queneau, for instance, who has remained a bourgeois writer, except by referring to the data that analysis might produce upon examination of his childhood. In Genet's case it is partly thanks to pederasty; in Sartre's own, there is no clear answer.

If Kean is an impostor, fabricated by a flawed society against which he turns in self-defense, and who therefore as artist depends upon an erroneous, vicious circumstance, the question can be raised concerning what the position of theatre would be in an authentic, unalienated society the sort whose coming Sartre imagines in *Critique de la raison dialectique* and other late writings. In *Qu'est-ce que la littérature?* he affirmed that the contemporary artist—at least the novelist and dramatist—could function effectively and authentically by presenting a critical literature intended for his own time, according to techniques which suit changing circumstances. In *Saint Genet*, it is writing, including poetry, which is one of the forms in which Genet's self-creative genius asserts itself against society. In later writings on the theatre he emphasized the critical function of plays such as *Les Séquestrés d'Altona*, yet suggested that he no longer believed literature and theatre could change things, that is, overcome the alienation and falsehood of the entire society to which they are directed. Art, like ethics (as he suggested in *Saint Genet*), would seem to be impossible. Only in a new society, based on radically different modes of production which would eliminate scarcity, would the position of the writer and artist no longer be adversarial and critical. What this would produce has to be left to the imagination. Until such a revolution takes place, the artist and actor remain in a false position and work, even if creativity, through falsity itself.

Sartre's severe self-portrait in *Les Mots*, like his more sympathetic one of Kean, must thus be understood as a self-accusation in the first instance only; his mirrors reflect back on society and the autobiographical enterprise is a social one. Reminding us of Sartre's great predecessor Rousseau, it concludes that corrupt individuals are produced by corrupt institutions. We are all, he would say, playactors, traitors, and bastards, but in *Kean*, the mirror is held up to our slavery, and our freedom.

THOMAS B. SPADEMAN

Rights and the Gift in Sartre's
Notebooks for an Ethics

T he concept of (legal) right has been the source of some particularly knotty problems for legal theorists following Marx. If Marx's assessment, that rights are peculiar to capitalist society, is correct, one might be led to wonder: what form would social mediation take in a post-capitalist society? Current debate in legal theory reflects a high degree of uncertainty with regard to this question. On the one hand, many in the Critical Legal Studies movement (the "crits") advocate the abandonment of rights discourse as essentially oppressive, while on the other hand many critical race theorists defend that discourse on the pragmatic grounds that it still serves a liberatory function, whatever its theoretical deficiencies. The disagreement between these theorists may simply reflect an assessment of timing; rights have been particularly useful for the oppressed in the U.S., especially in the last few decades, while the crits are, for the most part, white academics in positions of privilege, and hence do not, perhaps, experience rights talk as a positive form of discourse. At any rate, without some account of the form(s) of social mediation which might replace rights, I think we should be nervous about rejecting them as tools for social change. In this connection Sartre's discussion and criticism of rights in the posthumously published *Notebooks for an Ethics* deserves attention. Sartre develops a notion of social mediation through generosity and the gift, which, I argue, has some interesting programmatic implications for the search for an

From *Philosophy Today* 39, no. 4 (Winter 1995): 421–430. © 1995 by DePaul University.

alternative to rights. In this essay, then, after a brief look at Marx's comments on rights in "On the Jewish Question" as background, I examine and interpret Sartre's extension of Marx's position and synthesize Sartre's somewhat fragmented (and fragmentary) remarks in the *Notebooks*, with an eye toward developing some of those programmatic implications.

Marx's "On the Jewish Question"

In his well-known essay "On the Jewish Question," Marx criticizes Bruno Bauer's nearsighted view of emancipation. Bauer sought a solution to the "Jewish problem"—really the problem of oppression—in political emancipation, rather than human emancipation. Political emancipation, or the elimination of legal discrimination (here on the basis of religion) represents a "great progress . . . a real, practical emancipation," but is not the "final form" of emancipation; rather it is the final form "within the framework of the prevailing social order." Mere political emancipation leaves intact a contradiction between the political state and civil society, or as we would say today, the "public" and "private spheres." This split is further reflected in a separation of the self into two aspects. First is the person conceived as a "legal subject," the autonomous, abstracted and universal contractual self, which enters into relations with other similarly abstracted, universal contractual selves. These relations are relations of contract, in which disagreements over substantive issues are mediated through rights discourse, at the level of ideology. Second, is what we might call the concrete, "situated" person, the individual taken within the web of real relations with others, with concrete needs and desires which are only partially and imperfectly translatable into rights discourse. Marx aims at the closure of these two selves—the collapse of the legal subject into the real, situated self, since without overcoming the split real "human" emancipation cannot be achieved. Hence human emancipation takes place:

> when the real, individual man has absorbed into himself the abstract citizen; when as an individual man, in his everyday life, in his work, and in his relationships, he has become a species-being; and when he has recognized and organized his own powers (*forces propres*) as social powers so that he no longer separates this power from himself as political power.

Note, then, that according to Marx there are two "moments" or types of emancipation, political and human, each of which can be understood as operating through certain mechanisms. What are these mechanisms? The mechanism of political emancipation in bourgeois society is the (a) right. Now, it seems to me that rights can function in two ways: to say that "I have a right to do X" is either to posit as necessary and binding the outcome of some previous conflict, or to state the conclusion of some (usually implicit) normative argument that I should have that right. Thus the concept of right, from the perspective of political emancipation, can be at once progressive and reactionary. It is progressive to the extent that a social conflict successfully completed results in a shift of the contested social practice from the public sphere (of legitimate regulation) to the private sphere (where regulation is not legitimate). It is reactionary when the assertion of an already existing right forecloses conflict on a point of social practice, and the ethical aura of such an assertion often functions to obscure the origin in violence of the present distribution of powers (rights) between the public and private sphere. However, neither the revolutionary nor the reactionary aspect of rights goes beyond "egoistic man, man as he is, as a member of civil society." That is, rights are the assurance of "egoism," of the status quo of the capitalist, meritocratic social order, and cannot be revolutionary themselves. It is but a short step to conclude that we should look for some form of mediation beyond rights. For this I will I turn to Sartre's *Notebooks for an Ethics*.

Sartre on Rights in the *Notebooks*

Sartre accepts Marx's basic analysis of the alienating function of rights, but Sartre's language differs markedly as a result of his phenomenological/existential method. It is, however, precisely this orientation that allows Sartre meaningfully to expand Marx's treatment. Of particular interest are two distinctions at the core of Sartre's analysis of rights: (1) the distinction between three historical periods in the development of rights; and (2) the distinction between "spiritualist" and "realist" theories of rights; it is in the context of these two distinctions that Sartre discusses the possibility of transcending rights-mediated social relations through generosity and the gift.

A. Rights in Historical Perspective

Marx was wary of transporting concepts appropriate to the understanding of one historical formation, in the way that the concept of right is appropriate to a market based society, into the analysis of another historical formation, such as feudal society, from which the modern concept of rights is (necessarily) absent. But the seeds of the modern conception of right are to be found in mediaeval usage and legal practices, and Sartre is willing to use the concept of right to schematize the structure of social relations in capitalist and pre-capitalist society, at least as far back as is necessary to explain the transition to early capital. Sartre describes three stages in the development and final surpassing of the concept of right, stages the boundaries of which mark out the transitions in social relations from late feudal to early capitalist society, and from capitalist society proper to post-capitalist society. Sartre identifies these as the stages of the "concrete particular," the "abstract universal," and the "concrete universal." The first transition in the historical evolution from feudal to capitalist order is "The passage from the concrete freedom of one person to the abstract freedom of everyone." A right in this first stage of development is merely an affirmation of "the current state of society considered as what ought-to-be." As such it is connected with a specific, particular claim: the claim of a lord to control a certain property, or the claim of a ruler to rule by divine right, for example. Thus the right originally appears "with a concrete content from which it is not originally distinguished." It is in the process by which it is distinguished that a right with concrete content is transformed into the abstract right of positivist bourgeois legality, universally applicable to each person considered as an abstract holder of rights. Sartre characterizes this shift as one from the concrete particular legal subject to the abstract universal legal subject.

Sartre illustrates this process of transition with a longish series of identifications. The first recognition of a right takes place in the period of the "man/object," that is, in which social relations are between actual people as concrete ("this neighbor"). However, when posited as a right, the concrete relation undergoes a process of abstraction, and with it a transformation in the subjects' perception of oppression, until the period of "man/subject" is reached, in which the social relation is no longer between concrete individuals, but between "abstract" people—between fictional "legal subjects." Sartre further characterizes this transition as the "passage from (concrete) magic syncretism to (abstract) scientific analysis," i.e., from a religious world view to one of enlightenment; "from the concept to the judgment, from the immediate to the mediate . . . from observation to experimentation . . . from naturalism to antiphysis." While some of Sartre's terms here are rather obscure, the general point is clear. The underlying concern with the change in specific social relations recalls Maine's often cited (though somewhat inaccurate) assessment of the shift "from status to contract," with the characteristic Sartrean addition of an emphasis on lived experience within a particular social formation.

Of course, Maine's comment is no more than a useful generalization of one dimension of an ideological shift, and hence oversimplifies or omits forces at work in the shift, specifically material forces. Sartre identifies several material forces which underlie the transition. In addition to changes in the mode of production, he identifies three factors: the increase in population, in which "Man is lost because he is too numerous for himself"; the rise of science; and mechanization, which is the basis for "abstract," alienated labor, or labor as commodity. These factors require a form of social relations that is flexible across varying material conditions, and which at the same time unifies and organizes a complex society into a functioning whole. Thus the abstraction of concrete specific freedoms allows for interaction between members of society who are known to each other only as legal subjects, loci of rights with potential powers, the limits of which are knowable without knowledge of the circumstances of a specific social situation. Sartre gives the striking example of a magistrate who "becomes justice," that is, becomes his function. The judge's desires, that a certain legal outcome be achieved in a given set of circumstances, become rights, so that the judge disappears from the process as a person; he is erased as a concrete subjectivity and becomes pure function for the litigants and for himself. For the actors in the system, especially defendants in criminal proceedings, justice cannot be particular without being seen as arbitrary and hence losing legitimacy. "Justice" must refer to something "above" the actual process, and hence takes on the form of a particular instantiation of a rule, i.e., a right. This "must" is material (the free flow of things as commodities requires the dual abstraction of thing into commodity, and concrete-subject into abstract-legal-subject). But the "must" is also formal (within the logic of the bourgeois legal system) and existential (from the perspective of the system experienced as necessity, from "within"). The judge, whose labor becomes a commodity in the process of abstraction, is universalized as a moment in the reproduction of the material conditions that gave rise to his being-as-function. The judge becomes justice.

The third historical period is present in Sartre's analysis for the most part by implication; it is a period in which the process of transition from concrete particular to abstract universal is completed by the transition to concrete universal. Since a right is a purely negative demand and hence purely formal, we may suppose that rights as such disappear and are replaced by some new form of mediation that neither abstracts from concrete social relations, nor signals a return to the oppressive master-slave relations of the feudal concrete particular. Sartre suggests that relations among people in such a society could be understood through the categories of the gift and generosity. I will return to this suggestion in a moment, after a discussion of the second aspect of rights which Sartre raises in the *Notebooks*.

B. Spiritualist and Realist Theories of Rights

In addition to the analysis of the historical development of rights, Sartre remarks that there are two basic theories about rights, the "spiritualist" and the "realist." These parallel the distinction I drew earlier between the progressive and reactionary functions of rights. Although Sartre's brief comments here are a bit aphoristic (a defect with much of the material in the *Notebooks*), we can infer several features that characterize these two theories. These theories arise only within a society in which rights are relatively fully developed. Hence these are not theories about the structure of the concept of a right, but about possible attitudes taken in situations in which a right might be invoked; we might think of them (internally) as argumentative strategies, and (externally) as oppressive claims made in the name of abstract rights.

Sartre has noted that the affirmation in each particular case of a right is an affirmation of "nonvalue in the realm of being." This "negation of the real" Sartre calls "spiritualist," presumably because it refers to the non-being of the specific right being claimed. The right is a demand; it is not in any way at all a request. Thus a right posits an absent goal that presents itself as objectively necessary, and in so positing treats the concrete person as inessential: it is a formal demand made abstractly, and reduces the complex particular situation that is contested to a formula. Paradigmatic are civil rights: the assertion that Jim Crow laws violated the right to vote resulted in (some degree of) political emancipation, but at the expense of abstracting from the individual projects that created and sustained or were subject to the oppression. Here the goal posited was the removal of some procedural obstructions to the exercise of the vote; but this was not addressed to those responsible as freedoms, and hence as personally rather than legally responsible. As we have seen above, the "spiritualist" theory of rights is double-edged as a form of political emancipation: a purely negative freedom is gained at the expense of the possibility of realizing concrete relations within that process.

The "realist" theory of rights focuses on the aspect of a right in its being, as a recognized token in a legal system based on rights. Such rights are already instantiated and hence are not claims about what ought-to-be, but are mere assertions that certain questions have been authoritatively and finally settled. Rather than being a response to some social harm already undergone, they are merely responses to threats. For example, an assertion of a "right to bear arms" is a claim about an established practice, rather than a demand that the world be otherwise. Sartre's use of the term "realist" here is unfortunate in one respect, in that this theory about rights is similar to claims made by legal positivists such as H. L. A. Hart (and not legal realists), who for the most part ignore the genesis of rights, treating them as timeless universal facts. At any rate, Sartre disparages what he calls the "realist" theory, because it fails to take into account the historical origins of rights as negations.

Most simply, the difference between spiritualist and realist theories can be seen in the structure of confrontations over some particular contested social practice: on the side of the enfranchised, the claim of right is realist; on the side of the disenfranchised, the claim is spiritualist. But in either case, the invocation of rights talk is problematic; "one finds oneself as just a pure universal and one has missed the truth which is that a freedom is an infinitely concrete and qualified enterprise that has to be recognized in its enterprise." A right, as purely negative, thus means: don't treat me as a means; but it never means: help me in my concrete project. This is not simply a restatement of the (dubious) distinction between positive and negative freedoms, conceived as the power to do versus being free from hindrances, since in the case of positive freedom, it is still what Sartre calls negative; it operates on the basis of formal abstractions that negate the concrete individual. In that sense, positive freedom is conceivable under a system of mediations based on rights. But rights, since they abstract from our concrete projects, are incapable of providing a basis for unalienated human relations, and, again, this points to the necessity of defining a mode of relations that is universal, but is not abstract—the concrete universal. Again, Sartre suggests that we find this relation in the attitude of generosity and the gift.

Generosity and the Gift

"The Gift," writes Sartre, is an ambivalent structure with a perpetual instability. Originally stemming perhaps from a contractual desire between two freedoms, it becomes an attempt at magical enslavement and then it again disputes itself at this level through nonthetic consciousness and through reflection.

The gift is not an univocal good; it can be "freedom and liberation," but also can easily be distorted into the "subjugating gift." It is gift in the former sense, however, that is interesting for our purposes here. The liberating gift is "gratuitous, not motivated, and disinterested." Interestingly, Sartre argues that if a gift isn't disinterested, it becomes a contract. In this we catch the first glimpse of the conditions under which contractual relations themselves will be surpassed. Contractual relations, or the social order based on the right to contract which is central to the bourgeois "juridical world outlook"—treat the other as inessential, as means, and thus negate his or her freedom. By comparison, in the authentic gift-giving situation, "my freedom springs forth over the collapse of the world. At the same time, I recognize the other's freedom, for I consider the other as essential and the world as inessential." Of course, gift-giving doesn't exist in abstraction, as a mere "ontological structure"—it is always situated historically. We therefore need to examine the gift in various contexts. The giver's behavior may alter the significance of the gift, resulting in a distortion of the situation of pure gift-giving as liberation into the subjugating gift. More fundamentally, the gift may take place either in an alienated society, in which human relations are mediated by rights, or in an unalienated society.

Sartre indicates that the gift cannot be liberatory absent certain conditions. Not only must it be given "with no strings attached," but it must also occur in conditions in which the recipient is free to accept or reject it. Thus a gift originating in pure generosity can be subjugating if the situation of the recipient is such that the acceptance affirms his or her non-freedom: because the gift is necessary to fend off death or hunger, for instance. Such conditions typify alienated society, and obtain globally, between as well as within bourgeois societies, as a result of the rights of property ownership. Further, the pure gift might be distorted if the recipient is operating within a set of alienating circumstances unknown to the giver, for example, the recipient merely feels some obligation to accept. In such a case the gift operates as potlatch, requiring some response on the part of the recipient. These distortions of the gift from liberatory to subjugative are instructive; because of factors such as material scarcity, actions which are intended to be liberatory will quite often fail and fall back on the actors as sources of non-freedom—not only for the recipient, but for the giver as well.

Should we conclude that gift-giving is pointless in an alienated society? No. Even when made in the context of bourgeois society, if gift-giving originates in a recognition of the other's freedom, it is a positive act, a "break, a refusal to believe, a refusal of being caught up in the world, a refusal of narcissism and of fascination for the world, an affirmation of negativity and of my creative power." As a creative act, it is an expression of pure freedom, a refusal to believe in a system of relations in which, as an abstract universal, the concrete individual is lost, treated as inessential. Sartre characterizes a gift made from generosity in the context of alienated society as "a kind of deliverance." This suggests an interesting posture for those committed to social change, which we might formulate as an imperative: "act in a mode of generosity," even though the meaning of that act is certain to be distorted and turned back on the giver in unexpected and often harmful ways.

Unalienated relations depend on the absence of institutional, psychological or material factors that would distort an otherwise liberating gift. Interestingly, Sartre seems to believe that something close to such a situation can obtain in our (alienated) society, at least partially, and at least in one case. "When the gift is between equals without reciprocal alienation, its acceptance is as free, disinterested, and unmotivated as the gift itself . . . this is the case in an evolved civilization for the gift of the work of art to the spectator." The link between gift-giving as pure generosity with art and creation is worth an excursus.

In "Existentialism Is a Humanism," Sartre argues that the act of making a moral decision is akin to that of artistic creation; neither the moral agent nor the painter can have recourse to a set of values which is pre-established, universal and absolute. Both are creators, the one of moral values, the other of aesthetic values. In *What Is Literature?*, Sartre argues that a painting is at once a demand and a gift: it addresses the spectator as freedom and demands recognition of the artist as a freedom. There is the appearance of inconsistency in Sartre's thought here, since the artist's work is taken as both demand and gift, and in the *Notebooks* rights were characterized as pure demand, on the basis of which Sartre concluded that they treat the other as inessential. But note that in the case of the artist, the demand is for recognition of her or his freedom in the context of a world of alienation. If we take the demand as a result of the artist's need to exact recognition of his or her freedom in the context of a society not structured to allow such recognition, it is reasonable to conclude that the need and the demand would both disappear in a situation of pure gift-giving. Such a painting would have the status of a gift because it originated in a freedom expressing itself as a freedom, through creation, and would be directed to a freedom as freedom as another creator, in a context free of distorting forms of mediation such as is found in rights-discourse. It would place everything "up for grabs" and in that way respect the creative action of the other, without demand. Now, where the creative act of the artist results in the work of art as gift, we may ask a parallel question about work more generally: what is the product of the liberatory gift? Sartre answers: the gift of labor. We must live our labor in the way that an artist lives her or his work of art. If this strikes our ears with a clang of impossibility, recall: in the shift from feudal to bourgeois legal relations, there was a concomitant shift in the conception of work, from that of an obligation to that of a right. A life-world in which labor can be viewed as a gift is very difficult to imagine, from the perspective of one rooted in a bourgeois life-world, in which human relations are lived so completely as property relations.

From Status to Contract to Gift

Of course, the complete re-conception of work and labor as gift is possible only under certain conditions: society must be unalienated, and hence have surpassed or replaced contractual social relations mediated by rights; labor must originate in an act of generosity; and it must be freely received. Under the rule of right or contract, because the property relation is an abstract-formal relation, inequalities in material wealth are for the most part outside the scope of regulation. As a result, argues Sartre, "the sphere of actual behavior, goods and works is left to the jurisdiction of religion and ethics. The gift becomes charity." As long as work is mediated through rights, any extra-legal act involving work, presented as gift, becomes subjugating. We are as yet a long way from knowing the exact form a society would take, if constituted under generosity rather than rights. But some general programmatic results do fall out from the analysis at this point.

1) At the level of individuals, faced with the need to affirm the creative freedom of each other, we need to subvert or convert any practice that defines human relations in terms of function— de-robe the judge, so to speak—and force the actors to see the creative role they play from moment to moment within a social order. A part of the change "from contract to gift" must be a change in the way that we see ourselves as legal subjects—or rather, under the "rule of generosity," as post-legal subjects. This reconception can begin to take place within a system constituted under contract, in the "refusal of narcissism and of fascination for the world."

2) At the institutional level, we need to put in place mediating structures that reveal their own "fascination," so that a break with institutional "false necessity" (in Roberto Unger's apt phrase) become easier—the institutions must always "place themselves into question"—that is, be instantiated with processes that require participants within the relations so constituted to take up the institution in a consciously creative act, rather than in a self subordinating act. In this way the process can be structured to fight its own inertia, and encourage actors within it to realize themselves as creative freedoms.

3) These two levels of struggle, the individual and the institutional, are designed to bring about part of the conditions in which pure generosity becomes possible; neither is sufficient absent the proper material conditions, as yet unspecified by any Marxist. Perhaps the most important lacuna in Sartre's account, as I have elaborated upon it and expanded it here, is the failure as yet to arrive at a theory of the material mechanisms of transition to a

society of the gift, that would be analogous to the material mechanisms of the transition from feudal to capitalist society. I am not sure in what these would consist. Minimally, it seems necessary for material conditions to be present, such that the distortions that arise from scarcity and material want can be overcome. I think we have reason to believe that this much is possible at the present time; certainly we have the capability to alleviate much of the world's hunger and poverty. After all this, I might speculate that our failure to do so plausibly stems in large part from the barriers to relations of generosity and freedom intrinsic to systems of property ownership, and the ways in which property relations are lived in rights-discourse. Hence I think it not unreasonable, strategically, to focus for the time being on the institutional and interpersonal levels of human relations in the manner suggested by the foregoing analysis, at least as a means of encouraging changes at a more fundamental level.

BRIAN SEITZ

Power and the Constitution of Sartre's Identity

1. Mask behind a Mask . . .

Nietzsche's power extends itself into all sorts of curious places in philosophy, and this seems to be the case more in France than anywhere else. It is not necessary to recount the conscious and unconscious transvaluations of Nietzsche we see in philosophers as diverse as Foucault, Deleuze, Cixous, and Derrida. But it may be timely to make some remarks about Nietzsche's usefulness in understanding Sartre, and this may in turn strengthen Sartre's familial connections with the philosophers just named, at least with Foucault, despite Foucault's oedipal protests. The motivation may be predominantly archival rather than more strictly philosophical; to help complicate Sartre's position in the history of philosophy as we near the end of the twentieth century, and to complicate it not by overcoming Sartre but by pointing to traces of Sartre's overcoming of his own reactivity, the vehicle for which is Marx, but the contours of which link him to the less conceptually confining Nietzsche. As an individual writer, Sartre's personal project dissolved at his death, but his writing remains in all of its positivity to be rewritten, which is to say that traces of "Sartre" can be turned to his advantage, or to ours. More specifically, I would like to suggest that the later Sartre provides resources for transvaluing the earlier Sartre, by which I mean not that the later Sartre is an

From *Philosophy Today* 40, nos. 3–4 (Fall 1996): 381–87. © 1996 by DePaul University.

improvement over the earlier—on the contrary—but that, through Nietzsche, the *Critique of Dialectical Reason* offers tools for opening up or problematizing the prominent existential confines of *Being and Nothingness*. If there is a justification for this maneuver, it is that in the long run, *Being and Nothingness* had far more determinative effects on the formation of French philosophy after Sartre than did the *Critique*. Put differently—simplistically, strategically—Nietzsche has won out over Hegel and Marx.

So, rather than getting caught up in a debate about the differences between the early existential Sartre and the later Marxist Sartre, I would like to begin grafting aspects of both Sartres in order to suggest a different composite. Working backwards, then, the integrity of the Sartrean text might suffer as a result of this Nietzschean imposition, but that is the cost of Sartre's overcoming.

In fabricating an account of its own disciplinary heritage—in constructing an account of the history of modern philosophy—academic philosophy links Nietzsche with existentialism, and thus with Sartre; along with Kierkegaard and Dostoevsky, Nietzsche's name enhances the existentialist pedigree, and thus Sartre's. The material for this linkage is there for the taking, even if competing dimensions of the mad professor Nietzsche clearly clash with it. Here, the obvious existential emphasis would have to do with freedom, individualism and, perhaps, absurdity, and this linkage is familiar enough that I need say no more about it.

However, and beyond existentialism—an official signifier with which Sartre himself became increasingly less comfortable—there are other aspects of Sartre that may be illuminated through reference to Nietzsche, reference that might be tougher to make or at least seem more obscure, particularly given Sartre's unhesitant faith in dialectics, the logic in which the constitution of identity seems to be embedded both in *Being and Nothingness* and in the *Critique of Dialectical Reason*. The reference to dialectics is not a stray example in the context of positioning Sartre historically, either, particularly since dialectics is a formal philosophical technique for addressing and disciplining power, from a Foucauldian standpoint nothing other than a way of forcing meaning through a domestication of conflict, an historically cast prejudice that is ironically unhistorical. Or, as Nietzsche writes, "Dialectic and faith in reason still rest on moral principles." "Intoxication by dialectic: as the consciousness of exercising mastery over oneself by means of it—as a tool of the will to power."

The trenchant dualism Sartre establishes in such bewildering detail in *Being and Nothingness* might be read as anything but Nietzschean, particularly insofar as it is not going anywhere, neither toward resolution—for Nietzsche, this means overcoming—nor toward the spectre of resolution, deconstruction. That is, read as a truncated dialectic, and as Sartre himself gleefully argues for hundreds of pages, the relationship between for-itself and in-itself is a hopeless one, hopeless not only because of the impossibility of interpenetration or reciprocity—for-itself's desire for what it lacks is utterly vain—but also because the relationship between these ontological identities—full identity, vacant identity, positivity, negativity—can never really be dynamic, despite for-itself's desperately parasitic attempt to believe the contrary, i.e., despite the bad faith enabling its relentless effort to appropriate that which will only resist it. While it is cast in the language of activity, identity for Sartre is a reaction-formation, a negative reaction to positivity. All that for-itself does is negate, subtended by the bad faith that enables its struggle to nihilate its negativity. Even while it is nothing other than transcendence, for-itself is confined to its own planet.

Or at least that is one reading; represented by *Being and Nothingness*, Sartre would be Hegel's perverse foster child, perverse because of his commitment to failure, the centrality of the concept of possibility inexorably compromised by the impossibility of progress, transcendence an ironic opening onto an empty but nevertheless necessary telos. It is not difficult to provide convincing arguments for this gloss of the text; again, the material is there for the taking.

The *Critique of Dialectical Reason* may seem to be a way out of the dilemma, since the emphasis on totalization, the extended analysis of social formations, and the new language of history opens the dialectic onto the future. That is to say, Sartre remains Hegel's child, but his perverse commitment to nothingness has given way to somethingness. In other words, and through Marx, Sartre remains a Hegelian, but of a more recognizable variety.

However, in its harsh highlight of Sartre's modernist roots in the early nineteenth century, this emphasis on dialectics severely limits what it is that Sartre does or what can be done with Sartre, and the question of doing remains important. For one thing, as both existentialist and Marxist, ontologist and political theorist, Sartre puts doing in the foreground for us. But Nietzsche's ranting and raving—his strategic polemics—have already taught us that philosophy has to do something, something more than staring into the blue. And Nietzsche can teach us something more about Sartre, specifically through the former's understanding of the will to power, which pivots around a relational understanding of activity and reactivity. Can we find Nietzsche's power in Sartre?

At first, the text of *Being and Nothingness* might appear to resist a linkage with the Nietzschean power grid. A literal-minded address of the text might conclude that power languishes or even simply doesn't exist here. The dialectical power of the negative is neutralized by for-itself's inability to make progress. In-itself simply is, and for-itself is utterly powerless to be anything at all other than a useless passion, an unfulfillable desire, a bad dream. Sartre describes the "power" in my objectifying gaze, but I lose it the moment the Other turns his gaze on me, and what had seemed to be power turns out to have been a transient voyeuristic pleasure culminating in self-defeat, an ontological neurosis issuing from the futile desire to be God. Pure power, zero power, same thing. Where is power in this contradictory state of affairs?

The truth is that despite Sartre's obsessive commitment to ontological categories, power is everywhere. Various vectors of the text might afford a point of purchase for reading the theme of power in Sartre's phenomenological ontology, such as—precisely—the prominent role of resistance in the constitution of individual identity; for-itself may despair at or even resist its endless encounter with resistance, but it cannot give that resistance up, since it is what makes it "be" in *Being and Nothingness*. That is, as a differential effect of resistance, Sartrean identity is born of conflict and disturbance. Through his risky understanding of consciousness, which takes intentionality to its limits, the will to power asserts itself in the phenomenological text.

So the play of power is there from the beginning, and it extends itself into the *Critique*, which reinforces a firmer linkage with the dynamism Nietzsche presents through his relational understanding of power as active and reactive. By the time of the *Critique*, Sartre has discovered "history," the field of gray so cherished by Nietzsche. What Sartre calls "history" opens up a new field of possibilities for him, including the opportunity to rewrite the frustratingly skewed account of intersubjectivity in *Being and Nothingness*, and it is here, between the analysis of history and the social, that we find another echo of Nietzsche in the Sartre, one that expands the significance of power, struggle, and conflict. Sartre's rendering of the relationship between, generally, activity (project and praxis) and objectification is clearly not reducible to Nietzsche's power philosophy, but keeping Nietzsche's interest in activity and reactivity in mind may clarify Sartre's analysis and give it some force, and force is of course what the game is about. After all, for Sartre as for Nietzsche what I am is nothing more than the local and historical effects of intersecting lines of force. Sartre assets, "And the quality of being a man does not exist a such." But Nietzsche has already written that "the 'subject' is not something given, it is something added and invented and projected behind what there is." What there is is power. Power is the mask behind the mask in the constitution of Sartrean identity. Or: This is one strategy for indicating a kinship between Nietzsche and Sartre different from the one established by the invention of existentialism, and it is thus also a strategy for helping to prevent the philosophical gaze from objectifying Sartre.

2. Praxis Power

For Nietzsche, the dehiscence of human existence is characterized as the playing out of the will to power—the war of overcoming—the effect of which is the appearance of tenuous identity, the emergence of values and faces that conceal nothing, profiles of specific gains and losses in the play of activity and reactivity. If there is anything that provokes the play of power, it is the desire that locates power in the world. And as is the case for Sartre all along, Nietzsche's desire/power is not a thing but a situated "drive" or a transit. Nietzschean desire is not simply there in itself, and this is true in several obvious and familiar respects for Sartre, too.

To begin with, Sartre's emphasis on transcendence, which begins with the phenomenological observation that consciousness is always consciousness of something other than consciousness, insures that for-itself is always outside of itself, in the world. Using phenomenology in order to criticize phenomenology, Sartre initiates this move in *The Transcendence of the Ego*, which leads to *Being and Nothingness* and the claim that, "I am always beyond what I am, about-to-come to myself." Later, in the *Critique*, this emphasis is tied to Sartre's dialectical understanding of materiality, particularly through the linkage of praxis and the practico-inert; there, for instance, he writes that "he discovers his being-outside-in-the-thing as his fundamental truth and his reality."

Further, and in connection with the question of identity, desire and the other are inseparable—ultimately, identity is dynamically determined by alterity—and so identity is the product of the necessity and possibility of contact with other formations of power. For Nietzsche, and paraphrasing Lyotard, contact with other power formations is necessary; how to contact possibility is contingent. Through the relational play of power, identity appears as both necessary and contingent. Sartre aggressively repeats this pairing of necessity and contingency in *Being and Nothingness*, the specific nature of which is expressed by his paradoxical claim that "We are condemned to freedom," and further, "I am never free except in situation." For Sartre no less than for Nietzsche, the classical opposition between freedom and determinism is nothing more than a ruse, an attempt to resolve the paradoxical conflicts at the heart of human existence.

So far, these general connections between Nietzsche and Sartre remain largely within the framework of *Being and Nothingness*. However, the logic of these connections extends to what Sartre offers in the *Critique*, and this is where things become more complicated and interesting, since the linkage with Nietzsche's understanding of power is newly handicapped by an old critical difference, by negativity.

For Nietzsche, power is positive and negativity is the fantasy of a priest or a professor, both of whom want to retreat from the field of battle, to make peace instead of fighting war, to conjure up definition rather than live with indeterminacy. Nietzschean nature abhors a vacuum; things may be distant from each other, but there are no antitheses and thus no void. It is possible for things to be less than what they might otherwise be, but failure is more a material, martial matter than an ontologically determined order. In short, Nietzsche's desire cannot be characterized as a lack. Power is a tendency to expand, but this tendency is fueled neither by an ontological shortcoming nor by an intrinsically reactive desire for self-preservation but by the movement of life itself, cast in Nietzsche's peculiar biologism. Here is a convoluted intersection with the text of Sartre's *Critique*.

In the *Critique*, the analogue to Nietzsche's power is praxis, but the analogy is initially skewed by a dialectical throwback to Hegel and Marx via the power of the negative. The driving force of negativity in *Being and Nothingness*—lack—was ontologically wild. By the time of the *Critique*, Sartre had firmly grounded it through a Marxist pairing of need and scarcity, beginning with a new biologism that quietly suggests an understanding of the body perhaps quite different from the alienated body with which for-itself grapples in *Being and Nothingness*. The ramifications of the concept of praxis will be the key advantage of a Nietzschean reading of the *Critique*, but praxis is not initially ontologically wild the way that lack was. Sartre grounds praxis via Marxist science, writing:

> Thus, in so far as body is function, function need, and need praxis, one can say that human labor, the original praxis by which man produces and reproduces his life, is entirely dialectical: its possibility and its permanent necessity rest upon the relation of interiority which unites the organism with the environment and upon the deep contradiction between the inorganic and organic orders, both of which are present in everyone.

The circuit Sartre sketches out here goes like this; body, function, need, praxis, relation of interority, deep contradiction. Nietzsche would object to the dialectical rendering of this circuit, starting with the Marxist production/reproduction model in which it is couched, but particularly with the utterly metaphysical notion that there is a "deep contradiction between the inorganic and organic orders." Powers clash with powers, but contradictions are created by philosophers. So as the form of the human situation, praxis is Sartre's way of talking about what Nietzsche calls power, but Sartre derives this concept by means that Nietzsche would ridicule.

However, the relation between praxis and power has some richer dimensions, which strengthen the ties between Sartre and Nietzsche. Sartre writes, "It is the individual's praxis, as the realization of his project, which determines his bonds of reciprocity with everyone." If one's project was that which clarified my absolute distance from others in *Being and Nothingness*, praxis is precisely what puts me in a relation of reciprocity with others in the *Critique*, which is to say that praxis is not only the vehicle for the formation of the social, but also that it is through this formation that individual identity emerges. What is most interesting is Sartre's insistence that although praxis is transformed through exploitation into an inert commodity, it remains a reciprocal relation, "a free exchange between two men who recognize each other in their freedom." As the vehicle of the reciprocity or differential relation at the heart of social formations, even "the inertia of praxis, as a new characteristic of it, removes none of its previous characteristics: praxis remains a transcendence of material being towards a future reorganization of the field"

What I am emphasizing, then, is the sense in which praxis, always concrete and as an analogue to power, is the basis of reciprocity and thus of the social being that could not be accommodated by the radical individualism of *Being and Nothingness*. This may seem like a curious way to assert a linkage between Sartre and the individualistic Nietzsche, and it may seem ironic that the linkage should culminate in the theme of reciprocity. But Nietzsche's disdain for the herd cannot occlude his understanding of power as fundamentally relational if not reciprocal. While Sartre writes of praxis as a transcendence toward a future reorganization of reality determined by reciprocity, Nietzsche writes that, "We are more than the individuals: we are the whole chain as well, with the tasks of all the futures of that chain." But what does it mean that we are more than individuals? In general, it of course means that we are always outside of ourselves or, more precisely, that for both Sartre and Nietzsche the metaphysical line between inside and outside is an attempt to flee power, particularly the power of situation, the field of relational being. Our individuality is never an isolated affair; or we are always more than individuals. However there are different senses in which this is true. On the one hand, there is a relational identity determined by self-affirmation, by saying yes, by actively asserting values; this Nietzschean image might help reinforce and enrich Sartre's analysis of the fused group, always a tenuous affair on the verge of dissolution or consolidation. Just as Nietzschean power tends to coagulate in reactivity, the Sartrean group tends to dissolve into seriality, which, like the morality of the slave, is defined by that which is outside of it. Sartre describes the serial collective in terms of "false reciprocity" and "negative unity," but Nietzsche's understanding of reactive power would enable Sartre to break with these dialectical moralisms, and also to extend Sartre's ambivalence toward elective representative democracy, the unity of which depends upon the serial collective, and upon the interchangeability of the political subject, i.e., upon the objectification of subjectivity, the containment of the threat of unpredictability.

Emerging from the constraints of dialectical reason, praxis is closer to Nietzschean power than anything in *Being and Nothingness*, and it is what provides Sartre with the vehicle for conceptualizing the social, reciprocity. Put more strongly, reciprocity is the residue of *Being and Nothingness*, what *Being and Nothingness* lacked, which is to say that it is the power the text needed, where it had to go in order to transgress its passive nihilism. In other words, repressed by the idiosyncratic dialectical formalism of the text, reciprocity is the lack of *Being and Nothingness*, what was not there but what enabled it to be, its trace of difference.

3. Michel Sartre

Earlier, I described the logic of *Being and Nothingness* as a truncated dialectic, identifiably a dialectical machine, but one perverted by the inaccessibility of its telos, by the impossibility of synthesis, by the anti-dynamism of its determinative dynamic. But what if, through a Nietzachean perspective on key concepts from the *Critique*, we were to overcome not only the more conventional dialectic of the *Critique* but also the truncated dialectic of *Being and Nothingness*? What if, that is—through conceptualizing the dynamic of *Being and Nothingness* via a Nietzschean understanding of power facilitated by importing praxis and reciprocity from the *Critique*—what if we overcame the idiosyncratic dialectic of *Being and Nothingness* and ceased to see it as dialectical? What would we learn? We would perhaps no longer be reading the authentic Sartre, but this move might provide an opportunity to depart from the metaphysical negativity of authenticity and bad faith that linger as symptoms of the limitations of existentialism, and to see how Sartre contributes to the power of Nietzsche in philosophy today. Ultimately, then, this exercise may really be about Nietzsche, whose conflicted possibilities continue to haunt us, whose usefulness is clear but whose ramifications remain obscure. Really, it may be about Foucault.

We have toyed with Sartre, but in the interest of tracing some of the ways that he overcomes himself. And who is Sartre after this mutative procedure? Like Nietzsche and Foucault, he is just a tool in the contempory philosophical repertoire, a tool by means of which to explore not only the subject on vacation—the human subject as a site-specific creation—but also the intimate connections between this vacated subject and power; after all, it is power that ensures that the vacated subject is necessarily a positive identity rather than nothing, power that insures that passion is never useless. Finally, then, under the force of this reading, Sartre points to the priority of history, however not what Foucault mockingly calls "philosophers' history," but history as a resource for understanding that the connections between the subject and power are always specifically located and always open to transformation, even if as a Nietzschean the early Sartre understood that transformation is not about progress or meaning. The only meaning associated with the for-itself emerges in the context of its reciprocal relations with its situation, which is to say that "meaning," for Nietzsche, for Sartre, and for Foucault, is located out there in the world, not a private matter, not the property of consciousness, but a social affair, an effect of networks of power relations. If there is a politics we can use in Sartre, it is neither in his existentialism nor in his Marxism, but in some fugitive, hybrid connections we can cultivate through the imposition of Nietzsche, who himself offers resources for political thought only if we think him through writers like Sartre and Foucault. Foucault acknowledged that he specifically viewed Sartre as the philosopher he needed to overcome. Maybe he did overcome him, but if he did it was because of what Sartre had already given him, which is to say that it was through the reciprocal relation between Sartre and Foucault—a relation of power—that various versions of Nietzsche win out over Marx.

WALTER REDFERN

Praxis and Parapraxis: Sartre's "Le Mur"

I will not tell him the whereabouts of my friends nor
of my enemies, either . . .
            Am I a spy in the land of the living, that I
should deliver men to Death?
                        Edna St. Vincent Millay:
                        "Conscientious Objector."

Où sont les avenirs d'antan?
            Sartre: *Cahiers de la drôle de guerre.*

Prosaic though it may be to say so, the fact that "Le Mur" is narrated by its
central figure, Pablo Ibbieta, forewarns us that he will survive its events,
although of course we do not know *how* till near the end. Like Julien Sorel
on his death-row, Pablo swivels between being momentarily glad of the
company and more often wishing he were alone, for the sake of undistracted
self-concentration. His problems are essentially his own, and this is perhaps
his real problem.

The story's title emphasizes the physical context. Pablo, Tom and
Juan have been switched from a cell in the archbishopric, into a hospital
cellar: a kind of *oubliette*. It is a hint that the focus shifts from the soul to
the body and to human consciousness, though aspirations towards

From *Romanic Review* 88, no. 1 (January 1997): 163–72. © 1997 by the Trustees of Columbia
University in the City of New York.

149

immortality are not excluded. Light filters from above through an open trapdoor, but there is no earthly hope of escaping, any more than from a gallows-drop. Pablo's previous cell had encouraged him to summon up elements of his former life,—beaches, a bar, a bullfight,—but he had not been under a death-sentence there. That earlier world was reflected, upside-down, in the sky; the memory was painful but real. The now smaller patch of sky reflects nothing. He sees a solitary star. "La nuit serait pure et glacée," and thus suitable for the hard thinking he intends to do, unballasted by his past. His whole life has effectively been inverted. Offstage sound-effects of executions proceeding, like hearing a guillotine being nailed together, form a basso continuo for his self-examination.

The walls around him and the others clearly represent the limits of possibility, pictured most powerfully in Tom's imagined sensation of facing a firing-squad and pressing back desperately into the wall. The walls also stand for the difficulties of communication between those enclosed within them. Pablo and Tom think often the same thoughts, but respond differently to them. A barrier separates consciousness and the body, as well as the individual and other, even once cherished, bodies such as Concha's. Above all, the wall of mystery,—what is death?—against which Pablo bangs his head.

Sartre, whose head always buzzed with the already said in others' literature, knew he was rewriting the famous image of Pascal, later recycled by Malraux in *La Condition humaine*:

> On a dit que nous étions dans la situation d'un condamné, parmi des condamnés, qui ignore le jour de son exécution, mais qui voit exécuter chaque jour ses compagnons. Ce n'est pas tout à fait exact: il faudrait plutôt nous comparer à un condamné à mort qui se prépare bravement au dernier supplice, qui met tous ses soins à faire belle figure sur l'échafaud et qui, entre temps, est enlevé par une épidémie de grippe espagnole.

Sartre clearly did not want, as Pascal did, to instill the fear of God in readers, nor, like Malraux, to celebrate orotundly human fraternity, but to exploit the black humour of a fundamentally absurd phenomenon, typified by the aristocrat implicitly alluded to above, quipping on his way to the scaffold (e.g. Thomas More). On a more technically philosophical level, Sartre was equally kicking against Heidegger, whose notion of "Sein zum Tode" Sartre sees as the false culmination of a process already initiated by Rilke and Malraux: the "recuperation" and "humanization" of death. In particular, Sartre objects in Heidegger to a kind of fiddling, whereby "my death" slides into general death. "La mort n'est jamais ce qui donne son sens à la vie: c'est au contraire ce qui lui ôte par principe toute signification." In Sartre's view, death, like birth, is *facticité*, contingent, mindless, and as such beneath contempt. The most virulently anti-Pascalian aspect of "Le Mur" is its firm conviction that no one can prepare for dying, live life guided by its end, live willingly towards death.

Well before their time, Pablo and his fellows are in *un mouroir*, a twilight home, which can be phonetically linked to *miroir*. Each faces himself and the others, in his own inimitable way. This is literally a literature of extreme situations. These men have the most acute deadline conceivable. They are truly backs-to-the wall. At the same time, Sartre's prisoners are not intended as exceptional, for all of us must die, and a death-sentence merely accelerates this common fate. Pablo is, however, unusual to the extent that he refuses any *divertissement*, to use the Pascalian term, even if his fixation on death is not rewarded by any conversion or salvation.

While obsessed primarily with the psychological and philosophical problem of dying, Sartre still makes room for all the expectable behaviour in such a last-ditch situation. The urge to urinate, the chattering teeth, the need to gab, even the altered attitude to the body, soon to be a corpse; the raw nerve-ends, and the irritability against other people and surroundings; the sense of pointlessness; the lethargy caused by lack of sleep. Pablo is "las et surexcité." We the readers are made to feet death-in-the-flesh, as well as death-in-the-head, or on the brain. This is all the more remarkable a fictional feat as death here is seen quintessentially as nameless, indescribable. In the shadow of its coming, all labels, all means of mental control, come unstuck.

Despite his cult of *dureté*, the would-be tough guy Pablo fluctuates. He experiences mood-changes, losses of interest and, in spite of intense concentration, falls to understand much of what he feels or does. Frequently he protests, too much, that he is unafraid of dying and of what might come after death. Perhaps, like Roosevelt in his first Inaugural Address in 1933, he believes that he has nothing to fear but fear itself, yet he does, like Tom, rehearse the execution over and over again.

For his part, Tom piles on the horror masochistically and, for Pablo, self-indulgently, with his tales of men crushed under lorries to save bullets. Pablo slots him into the stereotype of the Irish blarneying gasbag. Pablo's traditional racism embraces not only the national but also the biological. He feels repelled by Tom's flabby body when it does physical jerks to keep warm. Tom's running commentary irks Pablo, who clings for his own part to the Castilian stereotype of tight-lippedness, inner thoughts, and consciously dignified bearing. In addition, Tom's body reminds Pablo of the physicality of dying, and so distracts him from the central issue of the meaning of death.

Their similarity of situation breeds not solidarity but alienation. The polarity, however, is not perfect. Like Garcin in *Huis clos* bemoaning the pain of insentience, Tom believes that imagined agony is the worst kind. Like Pablo, Tom also knows that he cannot imagine death truly: "Je vois mon cadavre: ça n'est pas difficile mais c'est *moi* qui le vois, avec *mes* yeux" (Sartre's italics). Tom knows, then, that there is more to the whole question than he can articulate, but this insight wins him no favours from the watching and listening Pablo: "Je comprenais très bien ce qu'il voulait dire mais je ne voulais pas en avoir l'air." This selfish pettiness betokens a refusal of consolations or of partnership. Pablo is not only a political but also an existential anarchist, of the egoist tendency. His pride in his difference in fact impedes him from learning from others. In many ways, Tom is closer to the (Sartrian) truth than is Pablo. "On n'est pas fait pour penser ça," because death "nous prendra par derrière, Pablo, et nous n'aurons pas pu nous y préparer." For all his spirit of enquiry, Pablo refuses to learn. When he shuts up, it is because he knows Tom is right, and he has an immediate urge to belittle his pathfinder. It is untrue to maintain, as Pablo does, that Tom "parlait sûrement pour s'empêcher de penser." Even when he admits that Tom sees straight, it is begrudgingly. "Naturellement j'étais de son avis, tout ce qu'il disait j'aurais pu le dire [. . .] Seulement, ça me déplaisait de penser les mêmes choses que Tom." As a result, he will not openly acknowledge that Tom has scooped him, when he utters his own version: "Je ne voulais pas penser à ce qui arriverait à l'aube, à la mort. Ça ne rimait à rien, je ne rencontrais que des mots on du vide." Like amputees feeling pain in non-existent limbs, we cannot entertain nothingness, except in the intermediary terms of suffering. And yet, for Sartre, there is a nothingness at the core of being: our consciousness, principally a negating force. We can nihilate, but not comprehend nothingness.

A more estimable instinct in Pablo makes him choose himself against animals, rather than against fellow humans: "Je ne voulais pas mourir comme une bête, je voulais comprendre." To this end, and unaware of the expert advice of Proust's narrator, he actively recalls his past, as if willful memory were reliable. The coming death acts as a watershed, a *ne plus ultra*: there will be a before and an after. "Je prenais tout au sérieux," he reflects "comme si j'avais été immortel." *L'esprit de sérieux*, in Sartre's canon is perhaps an even greater sin than bad faith. The elements (related) of play, acting, and gambling are constants in his thinking, and all of them fight against *l'esprit de sérieux*. It is of course typical of Sartre's often black-and-white thinking that, in order to live fully, one should long to feel immortal. Most would settle for the wisdom of the Pindaric ode brandished by Camus as an epigraph to *Le Mythe de Sisyphe*: "O mon âme, n'aspire pas à la vie immortelle, mais épuise le champ du possible." When Pablo expostulates that his previous life was "un sacré mensonge," why should this unexamined claim be any truer than one which maintained that that life was meaningful? While anyone is entitled to protest at the unfinished business of a suddenly curtailed life, why extend this complaint to a sweeping condemnation of the work-in-progress, the "ébauche"? When he concludes that "la mort avait tout désenchanté," his attitude seems inherently childish ("If these are the rules, I don't want to play this game").

Young Juan begs to be "included out" for different reasons. Like Estelle in *Huis clos*, though free of her guilty secrets, he is convinced that he is a special case. Pablo, like Sartre approached by his young friend Bost, desperate to sign up for service in the Spanish Civil War, is largely dismissive of this greenhorn's blatant fears. He is further repelled by Juan's looks, a pretty-pretty boy transmogrified by terror into the semblance of an old queen. Machismo dictates many of Pablo's responses. He likens Juan's agitation to a fever which, as it indicates the resistance of life to the menace of death, he despises. For all his own sweats and shivers, Pablo wills himself to be unfeverish. When, towards the end, like the wounded mutineers in the film *Paths of Glory*, Juan has to be carried out to execution, he has clearly made himself inert, in a "magic" attempt to deny the reality of his situation. He has not lost consciousness in a faint, but puts himself into a trance, a state of suspension which necessitates portage.

No love is lost, then, between the three co-sufferers. Pablo's creaking shoes grate on Tom. Pablo rejects compassion as a weakening of resolve, and clings to his lifelong prejudices, whether involving the mind or the body, as a means to warding off infection by the defeatism of the other two, their refusal to face facts. With Frantz and Johanna, Sartre promotes with some sympathy the pursuit of "la folie à deux" (while denying its possibility in the case of Eve and Pierre in "La Chambre"); but "la folie à trois" is not even considered. Sartre's frequent use of the mirror motif recurs in Pablo's detesting in the other two his own failings. "Nous étions pareils et pires que des miroirs l'un pour l'autre." Like the trio of *Huis clos*, this one too is locked *in camera*. And yet Pablo sorely needs Tom and Juan as foils to measure and define himself against, as with the Belgian doctor.

Why is he Belgian? Is it merely the weary French cliché, notoriously exploited by Baudelaire, of Belgians as clods? Sartre has at least the grace to spare the doctor sadistic intentions: "Il péchait surtout par défaut d'imagination." His clinical distance from death differs radically from the three men's inability to imagine their own deaths. Like the traditional death-cell almoner, the doctor claims he has come to alleviate. Like Meursault, Pablo responds by wondering why the doctor fails to see that he too is mortal. The doctor has in fact come for medical research (the sly pulse-taking) on the physical rather than the psychological effects of impending death. "Il était venu regarder nos corps, des corps qui agonisaient tout vivants." The psychological resurfaces in the eye-battle (and I-battle), the exchange of stares between him and Pablo. This ocular confrontation foreshadows the psychological warfare at the climax between Pablo and the interrogating officers. Pablo returns the gaze, outstares the doctor for a time, but is then surprised to find himself drenched in sweat,—a sign that his body is starting independent life no longer controlled by his mind. Pablo loathes the idea of being objectified by this Other as a physiological case of funk, yet cannot stop oscillating between aggressiveness and limpness. Not humourless, however (as we will see again in the partly comic finale), Pablo notes sardonically that, when the doctor kindly reassures Juan that dying is rapid, he talks like a private quack mollifying a paying patient. All three men look at the man who will survive them, and whose body still obeys him. The doctor still has a future, whereas theirs is end-stopped. Death cuts off the future, a crucial dimension for the forward-orientated Sartre. When the doctor mentions the time, Pablo and Tom are jolted. "Nous ne nous étions pas encore aperqus que le temps s'écoulait." Pablo had been adrift in timelessness, between a now meaningless past and an unimaginable future. "Nous le regardions et nous sucions sa vie comme des vampires." Juan goes further. In an animal urge, he tries not to suck but to bite the doctor's hand, like a madman. This act underlines their status: they belong to a different, and inferior, species. They are guinea-pigs. At the end, Pablo will try to reverse this position to one of extra or supra-humanity.

The doctor is a human alien presence, but objects too intrude. For Sartre, when we are passive in the face of objects, and do not include them in a project which might give us the sense of making the world more ours and less foreign, they make themselves felt menacingly. In "Le Mur," the objects surrounding the budding corpses are *mortified*. To Pablo, they seem to have retreated from him, like his former life and loves (Concha who had been everything to him and now means nothing; even her gaze would no longer travel towards him, but would stay locked in her eyes). Objects hold back, "discrètement, comme des gens qui parlent bas au chevet d'un mourant." Like the doctor, they will survive him. This awareness of the change in his relationship to objects is a proliferating phenomenon. If he thinks he can quarantine himself against contamination by the fear of the other two men, he can do little about this threatening inhuman spread. The colour of nausea is grey. Ramon Gris; the obsessive stress on *gris* or *terreux* throughout, applied to Juan's pincer-like hands; Tom's ashen face; Pablo's own body; the cellar that confines them all. Like mauve in *La Nausée*, grey denotes an intermediate colour, a drained one, almost a non-colour. Finally, it is the hue of dead flesh and, before that, of lifeless fear.

Because of the multiple effects of impending death, which he believes has evacuated virtually everything of meaning, Pablo can tell himself that, even if he were inexplicably released, nothing would be salvageable from the general wreckage. Indeed, his release at the end will bring him no relief, for he is too far gone. Not only objects but also his own body seem to recede from him. "Mon corps, je voyais avec mes yeux, j'entendais avec mes oreilles, mais ça n'était plus moi; il suait et tremblait tout seul et je ne le reconnaissais plus [. . .] le corps d'un autre." In a telling image, Sartre nuances this stark dualism, this schizophrenia: "Par moments je le sentais encore, je sentais des glissements, des espèces de dégringolades, comme lorsqu'on est dans un avion qui pique du nez." There are, then, still signs of life, still life: "Il se tenait coi." Like that Sartrian nightmare state, *le visqueux*, Pablo's own flesh appears to him "louche": "Une présence immonde contre moi; j'avais l'impression d'être lié à une vermine énorme." Twenty years on, Sartre would define torture as the attempt to turn human beings into vermin while still alive. Pablo confesses he would talk if tortured. Despite his cult of being "un dur," he wants to be no hero, for heroes (Cf. Malraux) require an audience, and Pablo poses mainly before himself.

Unlike those who resist and morally outface torture by asserting their humanity, Pablo, refusing compassion for others or even for himself, feels "inhumain." It seems a question of style, of an aristocratic urge: "Je veux mourir proprement," though he has the normal shock-reaction when he hears salvoes outside. It is to keep face, and to keep faith with a pigheadedness he admits he does not understand, that he conducts psychological warfare, a war of attrition, with his interrogators. As with the doctor, it is a battle of eyes and egos. In preparation for his final, lethal joke, Pablo feels amused, despite his inferior position. He knows more acutely than they that, mortal too, their behaviour is mere posturing, not true action but only gestures. He transfers to them his conclusions about the futility of his own life. All lives are interchangeable, equally valid, or rather invalid. Death, as Meursault informs the chaplain, flattens everything in its path like a Juggernaut. "Leurs petites activités me paraissaient choquantes et burlesques." He sees through their petty games. His macho, childish pride in outfoxing them leads him to the potentially crazy idea that he is the only one in the right.

His own obstinacy foxes him. He has only a residual admiration for Ramon Gris as "un dur." If he cannot understand himself, how can he hope to understand others, or death itself? Pablo's mulishness is comic: "Une drôle de gaieté m'envahit." *Galgenhumor*, precisely, reacting against the "esprit de sérieux" of his persecutors. As with the idiosyncrasies of Juan or Tom, he fixes on the moustache of a Falangist. His amusement enables him to switch round the earlier mention of vermin, and to look at the officers "avec curiosité comme des insectes d'une espèce très rare." In effect, by adopting a superhuman perspective, he renders them infra-human. All this hilarity and contempt help him to decide to play a practical joke on his captors ("leur faire une farce"), to send them on a wild-goose chase. A clear tip that he is acting suspectly follows the decision: "Je me sentais abruti et malicieux." Even more reprehensibly in Sartre's scheme of things, Pablo is alienating himself: "Je me représentais la situation comme si j'avais été un autre." When it is so hard to coincide with oneself, how can he authentically be another? Note that he is part of the comedy. "Ce prisonnier obstiné à faire le héros, ces graves phalangistes avec leurs moustaches et ces hommes en uniforme qui couraient entre les tombes; c'était d'un comique irrésistible." This situation, unlike death, is visualisable, hence its attraction for Pablo, who here contradicts his earlier distaste for heroics.

Pablo's political commitment had been to the Anarchists. Opposite to the trajectory of the "fascist" Lucien Fleurier in "L'Enfance d'un chef," he moves from *engagé* to *dégagé*. Sartre himself clearly had not developed his celebrated theory of *engagement* in the 1930s. It is the later Sartre who commented on Pablo: "Il n'est pas suffisamment dévoué à une cause pour que sa mort ne lui paraisse pas absurde." Further in the same interview, Sartre clarifies this peremptory statement:

> C'est dans la mesure qu'il veut jouer avec des forces qu'il ne comprend pas qu'il dévie contre lui les forces de l'absurde. Cela ne vient pas d'un 'destin' absurde qui entraînerait les hommes. Cela je n'y ai jamais cru; Camus, lui, y croyait [. . .] En ce sens il n'est pas totalement innocent parce qu'il n'a pas su jouer le rôle qu'il avait à jouer; il est d'ailleurs bien excusable, parce qu'il n'est pas formé complètement comme un révolutionnaire.

In other words, Pablo had largely played at politics, and so his end-game is in keeping. Absurdity is not a given state of play: we create it by our attitudes, and especially by evasion of responsibility. Presumably for Sartre, if Pablo had been a communist, he might have been sustained by his sense of group-membership, whereas, as an Anarchist, he acts individualistically, in aleatory fashion.

Believing in an absurd universe, a world drained of sense, Pablo should echo Roquentin's refrain that anything might happen. Thus the fatal coincidence at the end of "Le Mur" is just as likely as any other eventuality.

"Objectively," Pablo has grassed on Ramon Gris's whereabouts. Well before *Critique de la raison dialectique*, Sartre was magnetized to acts that escape our control, to "contre-finalité," Murphy's Law. Pablo's random naming of a location becomes blackly, and doubly, a shot in the dark. We should remember, however, that if Ramon had not been in the cemetery, Pablo would have been summarliy executed for false information; Pablo thinks he is signing his own death-warrant by playing his game, which could thus be an indirect suicide. Pablo is no more ready to survive than he was to die. The French term for Freudian slip, *acte manqué*, seems apposite here: Pablo's act fails in its desired effect (to frustrate and pull the leg of the enemy). Praxis, this could be the lesson, beats parapraxis. His ludic act has lethal consequences. In refusing "l'esprit de sérieux," he swings to the opposite extreme: "le jeu." Against Sartre's own cutting rejection of Camus's belief in the Absurd, quoted above, Pablo has in effect acted like Camus's ambiguous hero, Caligula. He has played diamond-cut-diamond, retaliated absurdly, giff-gaff, against absurdity, instead of combating or transcending it.

Rybalka adduces Kant on the imperative of never lying, even when the truth is harmful to oneself or others. "Celul qui *ment*, si généreuse puisse être son intention en mentant, doit répondre des conséquences de son mensonge [. . .] si imprévues qu'elles puissent être." Even before his repeated efforts to write an *Ethics*, Sartre seems always to have felt this Kantian desire to be a moral being, despite everything. When he developed his existentialist credo, he made it clear that one person's exercising of freedom must not annul another's, as Pablo does, "accidentally." There is a clear moral divide between taking risks with one's own life and with that of another. All that remains for Pablo is to laugh, bitterly, the wrong side of his face. At the end, he is in as farcical an impasse as he had tried to land the enemy soldiers in. As Kadish puts it: "Whereas Lucien Fleurier becomes object, totally exposed to and defined by the view of society, Pablo Ibietta [sic] at the end of "Le Mur" is nothing but a shadowy subject, invisible to anyone but himself." All this as a result of disassociating himself from the others, and from his own body and previous life. Of course, if the alternative was to become a Lucien Fleurier and join the oppressors, this comically anguished end-state would seem preferable, but are these the only alternatives? Perhaps the true prison is Sartre's either/or thinking.

Has Sartre achieved what Christopher Ricks, with splendid wordplay put to telling work, demands: "The insistence that your own death is inconceivable is only worth something if a writer will at the same time utter his utmost, his uttermost; do his blessedest or damnedest to conceive it"? Pablo's mistake, his existential error, is to try to live his death in advance, to be one of the living dead. This has its valuable side. Montaigne in his wisdom wanted to experience, like a modern mother choosing to be fully conscious during childbirth, "une mort agie." Sartre, and Pablo, are closer to the spirit of Montaigne than to that of Pascal, who enjoins us to live in constant apprehension of dying. Yet, if a human subject, for Sartre, is above all a questioning animal, does Pablo ask the right questions? Or is he too sweeping, too all-or-nothing? Pablo is an absolutist. Anglo-Saxons need to work on themselves in order to appreciate how intense is the anti-empiricist bent in the French tradition represented by Sartre.

Three of the stories of *Le Mur* (the other two being "Intimité" and "Erostrate") are narrated in the first person. In "Le Mur," Sartre has no desire to make his narrator unambiguous, even though Pablo is somewhat nearer the angels than Lulu or Paul Hilbert. The fact that on occasion Pablo annexes the confident penetration of an omniscient author (e.g. when he "knows" that Tom has located death in a bench) is a sign that Sartre allows for the appropriating tendencies of narration, the urge for the author to play God. This may, of course, be a further reason for punishing his hero's presumption, because soon after the writing of this story Sartre was to chastise Mauriac on precisely this score. How can Pablo *know* that Juan is, protected by his fever, less affected by imminent death than himself or Tom, unless it is on some snobbish, prejudiced level of assumption? The most blatant nemesis, of course, is that apparently bloody-minded fate which directs the searchers to the exact spot where Ramon Gris is hiding. This Maupassant-type "twist of fate," this surprise, could make "Le Mur" unreadable or less profitably readable a second time round. It could, but for the fruitful ambiguities Sartre has imaginatively built into the rest of the story. His authorial praxis controls the parapraxes inherent in living and making decisions in the dark.

MARIE McGINN

The Writer and Society:
An Interpretation of Nausea

Interpretations of Sartre's novel, *Nausea*, have focused largely on its metaphysical themes: the contingency of existence, the contrast between contingent existence and the being of abstract and aesthetic objects, the nature of bad faith, and the possibility of an authentic consciousness. All of these themes are clearly present, yet they do not on their own provide a satisfying reading of the work as a whole. The novel remains a collection of striking illustrations of philosophical ideas, but never gels into a unified work of art in which all the parts are motivated by an overriding aesthetic aim. In this paper I want to offer an interpretation of *Nausea* that connects it not with Sartre's metaphysical views, but with his psychological interest in the question of how someone becomes a writer, and in particular, with his unresolved anxieties concerning the problem of the relation between the alienated bourgeois writer and the bourgeois society that produces him.

One of the most problematic elements of *Nausea* lies in its final passages. In the closing pages of the diary that constitutes the bulk of the work, the fictional author, Antoine Roquentin, appears to put an end to his metaphysical unease by resolving to write a novel. In general, philosophers have felt perplexed by this ending, and uncertain of Sartre's purpose in choosing to put aside the philosophical revelations of contingency that have plagued its hero and restore him to apparently purposeful existence.

From *The British Journal of Aesthetics* 37, no. 2 (April 1997): 118–29. © 1997 by Oxford University Press.

159

Interpreters are undecided as to whether we are to take Roquentin's decision to try to justify his existence by writing a novel as an expression of Sartre's belief that human existence may be redeemed by art, or whether it is to be taken ironically. There is an unclarity as to whether Roquentin is simply taking refuge in an illusion which, in combination with the uncertainty over whether he ever produces the projected work of art, lends the ending of the novel a degree of ambiguity. In reading the secondary literature, there is a sense that the novel rather fizzles out, and that all the real work, and all the real philosophical interest, lies in the metaphysical reflections that Roquentin records prior to this final entry in his diary.

Anthony Manser, for example, sees the ambiguity of the ending as a reflection of Sartre's own failure, at the time of writing *Nausea*, to come up with any solution to the problem of human existence. He interprets Roquentin's final intention to write a novel not as a genuine escape from the nausea that existence inspires in him, but as a form of distraction from the terrible truths that his philosophical reflections have revealed. He compares the ending of *Nausea* with Hume's remedy, at the end of Book IV of the *Treatise*, for the sceptical crisis into which he is led by his attempt to provide a philosophical account of our belief in the existence of external body:

> In many ways Roquentin is an up-to-date Hume, an existentialist version of the Scottish philosopher. Roquentin's novel is likely to be as important (or as unimportant) as Hume's game of backgammon. The solutions are alike in that they seek a way out of a philosophical impasse by giving up philosophizing.

Iris Murdoch is also inclined to see the end of the work as incidental rather than central to the novel's philosophical purpose: 'The interest of *La Nausée* does not lie in its conclusion, which is merely sketched in; Sartre has not developed it sufficiently for it even to pose as a solution to the problem'. The interest of the novel lies, Murdoch believes, entirely in the description of the metaphysical unease that Roquentin feels as his vision penetrates the veil of domesticated order and perceives the senseless, oozing, terrifying existence underneath. Danto, too, downplays the conclusion of the work and locates the central preoccupations of the novel in Roquentin's reflections 'on the relationships and ultimate discrepancies between the world and our ways of representing it'. Danto finds it difficult to see how Roquentin's 'hyperaesthetic, precious view of art and artistic creativity', expressed in the closing pages of the diary, fits into Sartre's philosophy at all, and he is perplexed by the obvious contrast that it presents to Sartre's later commitment to engaged literature.

None of these interpreters sees Roquentin's decision to become a writer as central to the novel. Yet it is the case that what Roquentin's diary records is precisely his evolution from a man of action to someone who, in the closing pages, identifies himself as a writer: 'The fact is that I can't put down my pen: I think I'm going to have the Nausea and I have the impression that I put it off by writing'. Furthermore, they all see the uncertainty of the ending as a defect of the work, even though the ambiguity that characterizes it is no more than a continuation of an equivocal note which forms a major strand of the novel as a whole. For while it is true that Roquentin is a model of existential clear-sightedness in his acknowledgement of the contingency of existence and in his exposure of the bad faith of the bourgeois citizens of Bouville, it is also the case that he is himself a bourgeois who is led by his rejection of the bourgeoisie into a state of complete withdrawal and impassivity. Throughout the diary, Roquentin reveals himself as an exile from the human world, unable to act or to connect with other human beings, whose overwhelming sense of boredom—of having 'outlived' himself—often proclaims itself as a state of debilitation or weakness. For Roquentin's rejection of the values of the bourgeoisie is linked not with practical rebellion or political action, but with a growing inertia that culminates in an almost total obliteration of the self. 'Now when I say "I", it seems hollow to me. I can no longer manage to feel myself, I am so forgotten . . . [S]uddenly the I pales, pales and finally goes out'. It is this negative element in Sartre's portrait of Roquentin that is the source of an underlying ambivalence in the novel, which I suggest reflects Sartre's own deep anxieties about the motives of the bourgeois turned writer. The whole development of the novel, from Roquentin's first posing of the problem of his existence to his final identification of himself as a writer, can thus be read as Sartre's exploration of a single problematic: the evolution of the anti-bourgeois writer who seeks refuge from his bourgeois origins in the aesthetic and the imaginary. On this interpretation, *Nausea* is primarily a psychological study of a particular form of bourgeois alienation. Roquentin represents not only some of Sartre's deepest misgivings about his own historical choice of himself as a writer, but the dangers and illusions that are connected with the choice of a life of the imagination as a means to escape from a profound sense of exile from the human world. This sense of Roquentin as a focus for Sartre's own anxieties is clearly expressed in *Words*: '*I* was Roquentin; in him I exposed without self-satisfaction, the web of my life.'

The clear element of autobiography in Sartre's portrait of Roquentin leads George Bauer to interpret *Nausea* as Sartre's attempt to place before the public his own ideas about the false uses of art, and his attitude towards the art object and the project of artistic creation. Bauer sees Roquentin as expressing Sartre's own self-consciousness as a writer who understands both the illusory nature of art and the essential antithesis between art and action. Similarly, Frank Kermode sees Roquentin as echoing the young Sartre's understanding of the distinction between life and art and of the dangers of confounding the two. The problem with these interpretations, however, is that they focus exclusively on Roquentin's philosophical deliberations, which they take to be an expression of Sartre's own beliefs about the relationship between art and life, and overlook the decidedly negative aspects that are present in Sartre's portrait of Roquentin's psychological development. They are thus led to neglect the fact that *Nausea* describes the history of someone who becomes increasingly isolated and impassive, and whose final decision to become a writer is the culmination of a prolonged psychological crisis which at times amounts to a terror of the everyday world. This leads them, in turn, to underestimate the extent to which Sartre is exploring not a positive image of the anti-bourgeois writer, but the fatal psychological temptation to take refuge against a hatred of one's own class in a form of aestheticism where the decision to write expresses the writer's desire to 'dehumanize' himself and approach the being of a mere abstraction. What we see in Roquentin's diary is the evolution of someone whose choice of himself as a writer denotes a more fundamental desire to slip the bonds of human praxis and relate to the world and to others purely through the imagination. Sartre's study of Roquentin is as much a psychological exploration of these temptations as it is a vehicle for the expression of metaphysical truths.

Roquentin's first significant encounter with a work of art occurs early in the novel, when he recalls how he came to return to France from Indo-China. The decision to give up his travels and return to France is made whilst he is looking at a little Khmer statuette that is standing on the desk of a French official who is trying to persuade Roquentin to join an archaeological expedition. It is while he is looking at the statuette that Roquentin first becomes aware of the growing sense of boredom and unease—the nausea—that he feels in relation to the abundance and pointlessness of existence. George Bauer identifies this as the true beginning of the novel, and he sees in it the origin of its metaphysical preoccupation with the relation between life and art:

> [F]or Sartre, the relation of the artist to society is as crucial as the artist's own relationship to the work of art. Roquentin's first crisis . . . is the contemplation of the Khmer figure. His withdrawal from active participation in life stems from that moment. Roquentin['s] . . . initial reaction is withdrawal from what he thought was a life of adventure and a return to a project which would be his creative life.

However, this does not capture the real significance of the crisis that the Khmer statuette provokes. First of all, it ignores important events in Roquentin's life (described later in the diary) that provide the psychological prologue to the crisis in Indo-China. Secondly, it overlooks the fact that Roquentin's evolution into a writer still lies ahead and is only completed in the final pages of the novel. Finally, it fails to acknowledge that the episode with the statue is characterized not merely by the rejection of an illusion, but by a rejection of the real and positive world of action, and by Roquentin's first movement towards the abstracted, deathlike state that he reaches just prior to his decision to write a novel.

Before the final decision to write is made, Roquentin undergoes an extended crisis which Sartre uses to explore many of the themes that are central both to his autobiography and to his later studies of Flaubert and the Goncourts. These latter writers, as Sartre sees them, share with Roquentin not only his rejection of bourgeois values, but also his inability to identify with the working class or to translate his alienation into action; writing is for them a way of 'forever escaping the necessity of acting'. As a result, Sartre believes, they remain fundamentally attached to, and dependent upon, the bourgeois class that they ostensibly reject. Their escape from their own class is purely symbolic, for it is confined to their attitude of mind. They use the art of writing to turn away from life and flee from their own distaste for human existence. These writers do not aim at communication but seek their salvation in a symbolic society of artists; they think of the consequences of writing purely in terms of posterity. Such writers, Sartre believes, are under the illusion that they may cease to be bourgeois simply by withdrawing from life and absorbing themselves in a world of the imagination. What Sartre wants to show us is the essential barrenness of the aesthetic isolationism into which they are led; these writers are solitary and ineffectual, and their writing is doomed to retain an 'aspect of pure negativity'. He describes the plight of these writers as follows:

> It is no longer a matter of escaping from the bourgeois class; one must leap out of the human condition. It is the family patrimony that these sons want to squander, it is the world. They have come back to parasitism as to a lesser evil, abandoning everything, studies and professions, by common consent; but they have never been satisfied with being parasites on the bourgeoisie; their ambition has been to be parasites on the human race. Metaphysical as it may be, it is clear that they have been unclassed from above and that their preoccupations have strictly forbidden them from 'finding a public in the working class'.

Reading *Nausea* from this perspective allows us not only to acknowledge the negative elements in Sartre's portrait of Roquentin, but also to draw together the many episodic and apparently incidental aspects of the book into a coherent whole. By writing the novel in the form of a diary, Sartre is able to catch Roquentin before he has succeeded in transmuting his experience into art, when his capacity to produce a work of art is still in question. The diary itself is something less than a work of art, for it merely records Roquentin's own experiences in his own words. The focus of our interest is not, therefore, on Roquentin's art, nor even on him as an artist, but on the moment of his psychological history when he is led to choose himself as a writer, and when he serves as an exemplar of a particular stage of bourgeois evolution. Roquentin's bourgeois status is revealed in a number of details. We know that he has travelled the world, that he lives on a private income (Roquentin's brand of radicalism would be impossible without independent means), and that he is writing a historical study of Monsieur Rollebon (a member of the Court of Queen Marie Antoinette). It is also the case that even while he is offering his critique of the bourgeoisie he is taking part—bodily at least—in many of their traditional pursuits: he walks in the rue Tournebride and on the jetty on Sunday, he eats in the Brasserie Vezelize with the stockbrokers, doctors, and Naval Commissioners, he works in the library, visits the town museums, and so on. When Doctor Roge comes into the cafe and teases the down-and-out, M. Achille, he looks at Roquentin conspiratorially, as one who is like him. Roquentin's only divergence from the bourgeoisie amongst whom he lives lies purely in his attitude: in his loathing of their smugness and seriousness, in his rejection of their utilitarian ethic, in his aestheticized view of the world, in his inertia and his desire to live as little as possible. It is not the art that such a writer might produce that Sartre is interested in, but the psychological phenomenon itself.

Roquentin's critique of the bourgeois value of moral seriousness reaches its climax in his visit to the Bouville museum to look at the portrait of a merchant and politician, Olivier Blevigne. Interpretations of these passages generally focus on Roquentin's rejection of the bourgeoisie's use of art to justify and reinforce the power of the ruling class. This is clearly a theme to which Sartre is, and always remains, completely sympathetic. The art that Roquentin sees in the museum is supported, paid for, and largely consumed by the bourgeoisie, and the role of the artist is restricted to one of reflecting back to the bourgeois his own conception of himself and his relation to society. These artists have used their art to give authority to bourgeois values, to flatter and idealize the important citizens of Bouville, and to warn and intimidate those who would rebel against them. At the entrance to the gallery there is a picture entitled The Bachelor's Death—

'a gift from the state'—in which a dead man lies on a bed of tangled sheets, while his servants rob him and others stand by indifferent both to his death agony and to his death. The painting serves as a warning to those who would live only for themselves. The picture does not appeal to the freedom of the viewer, but attempts through terror to force him into acceptance of the ideology that is expressed in the one-hundred and fifty portraits of the men who made Bouville. These portraits offer the viewer the promise of a well-ordered life, a well-ordered death, and a right to immortality. There is no room within this bourgeois institution for the free operation of artistic talent; everything is made to serve the interest of the bourgeois elite, every painting repeats the same refrain: the bourgeois elite has a right to its privileges. However, underneath this sympathetic element in Sartre's description of Roquentin's response to the portraits, a more equivocal and anxious voice can be heard.

When we turn from the discussion of the portraits to a comparison between Roquentin and the citizens who are portrayed, we begin to discern a more fretful and negative note. For the men whose portraits hang in the gallery have one and all been moved by a utilitarian ethic to lead lives of active, practical philanthropy. They have not only 'made Bouville the best equipped port in France', but they have stopped 'at no sacrifice to help the rise of the best elements in the working class'; they have created nurseries, schools, technical colleges, and churches, they have founded scholarships, fought for their country, and worked to restore it to prosperity and order. Roquentin despises them, but what he hates in them is not what they have achieved but simply the fact that they take themselves so seriously, that they have never doubted their purposes or questioned the value of their enterprise. It is not their actions but their spirit of seriousness that he rejects.

Once again, therefore, we find that Roquentin's opposition to this central bourgeois value is defined by his repudiation of the utilitarianism and practical energy of these worthy citizens. Yet all that this produces is someone who is committed to not acting, to inertia and impassivity, whose life grows 'in a haphazard way', who can sometimes feel nothing 'but an inconsequential buzzing'. Even Roquentin himself is aware that beside these powerful and impressive men he is weak and ineffectual:

> I was neither a grandfather, nor a father, nor even a husband. I didn't vote, I scarcely paid taxes; I couldn't lay claim to the rights of a tax-payer, nor to those of an elector, nor even to the humble right to honour which twenty years of obedience confer on an employee. My existence was beginning to cause me serious concern. Was a mere figment of the imagination?

The final decision to write is one that grows directly out of this state of weakness and inertia, for the decision presents itself as a way of escaping still further from the demands of practical life; it is a means of living without living, of acting without acting. For writing a novel not only avoids all taint of the useful, it draws Roquentin even more closely into the world of abstractions and lets him live entirely among the products of his own imagination.

It is this draining away of Roquentin's practical substance—which Sartre describes in his study of Flaubert as 'death by thought'—that marks his evolution as a writer and forms the heart of his apparent radicalism. It is connected both with Roquentin's sense of becoming something thin and unreal—'an abstraction'—and with the derealization of his surroundings, and it is the essential prologue to his final decision to write a novel that is 'beautiful and hard as steel'. It is not only that, during this process of development, Roquentin's own existence comes closer and closer to that of a work of art, but the world too becomes, through his act of withdrawal, aestheticized and abstract. This sense that the world has ceased to be a setting for human action and become a quasi-aesthetic object is expressed in a number of ways: in Roquentin's love of desolate, dark surroundings, where nothing is alive and existence approaches the purity of a triangle; in his sensitivity to the beauty of the sky; and in his fascination with the agony of the charwoman, whom he sees purely as a curiosity, as someone 'transfigured, beside herself suffering with an insane generosity'.

Before his present crisis began, Roquentin had longed for the moments of his life to take on the order and necessity of a work of art; the crisis itself is provoked in part by the realization that life is merely endless, monotonous addition. In the state of passivity and withdrawal that the crisis produces, Roquentin is able, at certain moments, to empty the world of some of its substance and experience it as if it were itself something almost unreal, as a pure spectacle from which he is completely detached. But this experience is unpredictable and necessarily brief. This contrasts with his experience of the jazz tune 'Some of These Days', which is a reliable source of relief from the nausea and terror that the human world of existence induces in him. It is the tune, therefore, that eventually reveals to Roquentin the possibility of permanent escape from the teeming, practical world and which triggers his final decision to become a writer.

The decision to write a novel is made, therefore, not as an expression of a return to the world of human action, but as a means to preserve the abstracted point of view on life that is the full extent of Roquentin's rebellion against the moral seriousness of the bourgeoisie. The outcome of his rejection of the bourgeois commitment to a utilitarian ethic is an apathetic aestheticism which, if it aims at anything, aims, as Sartre believes Flaubert aims, 'to infect the reader with his own pessimism'. Roquentin wants his novel '[to] make people ashamed of their existence'. However, the final decision to write is made above all as a means to achieve permanently the state of ataraxia that he experiences only in moments of pure aesthetic contemplation. The process of evolution that unfolds through the diary is one that leads Roquentin to a condition of absolute detachment from life, in which his existence is, as far as is possible, reduced to a pure abstraction. In the same way, Sartre sees Flaubert's profound passivity as 'a vain effort of his body to transform itself into an idea'.

However, all this invites the question: Why does Roquentin's rebellion take the form that it does? If there is something in the thought that the work is a psychological study of bourgeois alienation, then we should not look for the answer to this question in metaphysical truths; the answer must lie, as Sartre believes it lies for Flaubert, in the writer's own psychological history. The aspect of the novel that is relevant here concerns what Roquentin reveals of his relationship with his ex-mistress, Anny. Roquentin's relation to Anny is, on the surface, one of equality. Yet there are a number of remarks that betray the infantile nature of his need for her and the relative strength and independence of Anny. While every other human being disgusts him and fills him with loathing, Roquentin feels a unique and unqualified tenderness for Anny. At moments when he is afraid, he calls out for her like a child: 'I wish Anny were here', 'if she lived here for only a few hours . . . I couldn't feel frightened any more', I know very well what I am secretly hoping: I am hoping that she will never leave me again . . . I am weak and lonely, I need her'. It was Anny who sustained his being while he was with her, and it is her abandonment of him that gives rise to the feeling of emptiness which is the psychological prologue to his decision to abandon his travels and return to France. It is this experience of abandonment, rather than the bare intuition of a harsh metaphysical truth about the relation between life and art, that is the real root of Roquentin's crisis. These themes of infantile need and abandonment are central to Sartre's study of Flaubert and his contemporaries, in which he repeatedly suggests that the desire to write is never a pure aim to communicate, but is essentially linked with an infantile urge to recreate and entrap the world within the power of one's own words.

It is, moreover, in Anny's own desire to give her life the beauty of a work of art—'to enjoy "perfect moments'—that we can find the origins of Roquentin's desire to shed his existence and approach the realm of being. Anny embodies the aesthetic; her whole life has been dominated by her desire to create situations that have the formal grace and grandeur of the pictures in her childhood picture book. Her view of the world is—as Roquentin's has now become—aestheticized and abstract. She sees her father's death, for example, purely in terms of the opportunity it provides for striking poses, and she deplores the human reactions of her aunt and mother, which reveal their inability to appreciate the aesthetic possibilities of the situation:

> When my father died, they took me up to his room to see him for the last time. Going upstairs, I was very unhappy, but I was also as it were drunk with a sort of religious ecstasy; I was at last going to enter a privileged situation. I leaned against the wall, I tried to make the proper gestures. But my aunt and my mother were there, kneeling by the bed, and they spoiled everything with their sobs.

Roquentin's development as a writer can be traced directly to his loss of Anny. Anny had been his only real possession, his only point of connection with the world and even with his own past: 'As long as we were in love with each other we didn't allow the tiniest of our moments, the smallest of our sorrows to be detached from us and left behind . . . Three years present at one and the same time'. Now Anny had gone, and the world and his past have both slipped away from him:

> And then, when Anny left me, all at once, all together, the three years collapsed into the past. I didn't even suffer, I felt empty. The time started to flow again and the emptiness grew larger. Then, in Saigon, when I decided to come back to France, all that was left—foreign faces, squares, quays beside long rivers—all that was wiped out, and now my past is nothing but a huge hole.

It is this loss of a female mother-figure who is the embodiment of the aesthetic that is the real beginning of Roquentin's evolution as a writer. Before Anny left him he was a man of action whose practicality was a source of irritation to her: 'you annoyed me with your down-to-earth look, you seemed to be saying: I'm normal; and you set out to breathe health through every pore, you positively oozed moral well-being'. His desire to write emerges only in the crisis provoked by Anny's leaving him, and can be seen as a sublimation of his continuing desire for her. In his desperate need to recapture their former love for one another his whole being strains towards the art-object that has always been the meaning of Anny's existence.

Roquentin's desire to achieve a unity with aesthetic objects is, at bottom, a desire to reinstate the unity that he once shared with Anny; by reducing himself as far as possible to a mere abstraction, by concerning himself purely with what is not useful, he attempts to give his own life the condition of the only objects that Anny seems to care for. The ground of Roquentin's rejection of the seriousness and the utilitarianism of the bourgeois is thus seen to be psychological rather than political or philosophical. It is an expression of his nostalgic desire for a maternal love, which is inextricably linked for him with the beautiful and the aesthetic, that leads him into a life of imagination which defines itself in opposition to the practical values of the bourgeoisie.

When we view it in the context of the psychological history leading up to it, we can understand why Roquentin's decision to write has no connection with a desire to communicate. Roquentin does not want to write in order to be read; writing is the means that his own past history suggests as the way to escape the terror that life without Anny induces in him. Sartre's autobiographical account of his evolution as a writer confronts the same negative themes in his own development. Thus he connects his own urge to write, as he connects Flaubert's, with a refusal to live:

> I was intoxicated with death because I did not like life . . . [I]f I probe into the origins [of my decision to write], I can see in them a flight forward and a suicide a la Gribouille [a character of folklore who jumped into the river in order to avoid getting wet in the rain] . . . I discovered that the Giver, in Belles-Lettres, can change himself into his own Gift; that is to say, into a pure object.

This original decision is not an expression of a desire to communicate—'It never occurred to me that a man might write in order to communicate'—but of a wish to take on the being of an aesthetic object. His audience, like Roquentin's, is conceived only as a means to ground his immortality: 'I wanted debtors, not readers'.

Sartre sees this unhappy stage in his own development as a direct reflection of the influence that Flaubert has on him:

> [T]he ancient bile of Flaubert and of the Goncourts poisoned me; their abstract hatred of man, introduced into me under the disguise of love, infected me with fresh pretensions . . . It all seemed very simple: to write was to add another pearl to the Muses' chain, to leave to posterity the remembrance of an exemplary life.

It is an influence which he clearly feels must be struggled against: 'a knot was tied in my heart: the knot of vipers which it took thirty years to untie'. It is this knot, I suggest, that Sartre lays before us through the figure of Roquentin. Roquentin represents the past, something from which we must escape. Writing in *What Is Literature?*, Sartre contrasts the decadence of writers like Roquentin with the ideal of a committed writer, who writes as a matter of urgency to disclose the world to his reader:

> [T]he writer should commit himself completely in his works, and not in an abjectly passive role by putting forward his vices, his misfortunes, and his weaknesses, but as a resolute will and as a choice, as this total enterprise of living that each one of us is . . .

This later conception of the self-conscious, actively committed writer is to be seen, therefore, as Sartre's solution to the problematic that *Nausea* presents.

ROBERT PICKERING

Témoignage *and* Engagement *in Sartre's War-Time Writings*

The link, crucial for an understanding of post-Liberation France in its relationship to the war years, between the spirit of Resistance during the German Occupation of France and the advocacy by Sartre, as the mouthpiece of post-war French Existentialism, of personal commitment as the primary means of living authentically, has not before been given the attention it deserves. The aim of this article is to introduce briefly some of the most prominent aspects of this complex subject, and to demonstrate the extent to which Sartre's relationship with the Resistance concept of *témoignage*, far from constituting merely the circumstantial background on which his thought materializes and assumes the intellectual specificity of commitment, is in fact embedded in an empathetic and conceptual identification with the nexus of Resistance values. In exploring this field, I am concerned less with the corpus of Resistance texts than with the writing of Sartre, composed both during the war and immediately after it, although analysis of this writing needs necessarily to be based on an understanding of the concept of *témoignage* and on the forms the latter can take in its associated literature. On this basis, I explore some of the primary reflections of the concept in Sartre's writing of this period, and outline a tentative appraisal of the relative status and influence of each in respect to the other.

From *Modern Language Review* 92 (special issue, April 1997): 308–323. © 1997 by the Modern Humanities Research Association.

The most cogent recent research in this context can be found in the analysis of the concept of *témoignage* in Chapter I of Margaret Atack's important study, the main elements of which need briefly to be summarized. Atack begins by engaging with the inadequacies of both understanding and interpretation that all too frequently invest the criticism levelled at Resistance literature as writing based on documentation and hence on 'circumstance', limited in its literary scope, since too closely bound to the events it reflects and transposes. It must be said that there are certain grounds that serve to explain, if not to justify, this tendency to consider writing of circumstance as a poor man's literature. The principle of authenticity, rooted in subjectivity of perception, in the irreducible presence of experience and in an immediacy of response (the 'I', the 'here' and the 'now' that are the basic narrative ingredients of any literary elaboration) has proved slippery in its application to this particular context, since the claim to truth in the very criterion of testimony is based precisely on immersion in the event, and on an inability to disengage, to achieve that degree of extrapolation and global understanding that the view of a great tradition in writing tends to promote as one of the guarantors of literary value. As Ian Higgins has also stated in relation to the poetry of the Resistance, a widely held view of such texts sees in their circumstantial nature both the source of their recognition as a highly particularized moment of creative writing and the very factor that would appear to limit their value as the products of a critical, organizing consciousness, capable of mediating the sharper and less coherent aspects of experience by a higher degree of aesthetic and human understanding.

In the notion of the writer as witness, the imperative of immediacy has thus tended to be regarded as something of a disadvantage in any claim to permanent status in the literary canon, rather than as an essential pointer to the truth of a given social, political, or experiential nexus. But as Atack affirms in her treatment of *témoignage*, literary values alone were never conceived to be the fundamental grounding of Resistance writing, attuned as it is to a complex intermeshing of political and ideological preoccupations, and to their relationships with cultural dissemination and advancement. '[The literature of the Resistance] cannot be judged in isolation from the conditions of its existence; it has a mission, a purpose not grounded in literary values alone. The notion of committed literature had its theoretical apogee after the war with *Qu'est-ce que la littérature?*, but the refusal of purely literary values, the awareness of the political context of the struggle against the Army of Occupation, the ideology of Nazism, of Vichy, awareness of the political use of culture, are inherent in all Resistance writing'. While agreeing with the essence of these remarks, I find it interesting that the principle of commitment is tacitly posited as the common denominator binding post-war Sartrean existentialism and its political ramifications to Resistance writing. This view is significant, in that it typifies the rather uncritical acceptance as a homogeneous unity of the sometimes parallel, but also sometimes divergent directions that underlie the two approaches (testimony and commitment) to the status of writing, and thus invites much closer scrutiny of the entire relationship between both than has hitherto been the case.

Political and ideological preoccupations were, of course, more than sufficient in war-time France to drive Resistance writers into concealment. But the presence of such preoccupations is not necessarily restricted to clandestine publications alone, thereby opening the bitter and sometimes very ambiguous divide between legality and illegality. The authorized first performance of Sartre's *Les Mouches* on 3 June 1943 and that of *Huis Clos* in May 1944, to restrict myself here to just two works immediately associated with my topic, has been the subject of occasionally heated discussion from very different ideological standpoints. If *Les Mouches*, in particular, could with difficulty be viewed as indifferent to, or critical of, the Resistance, the conclusion of the play would nevertheless appear to be linked to complexities in Sartre's thought that make for a degree of imprecision in interpretation.

Although this specific case questions, in its own way, any simplistic equation of legalized publication and a form of betrayal during the Occupation, the fact remains that the clandestine circulation of non-authorized writing at the time is perceived by the Resistance as a quantifiable act, and thus reorientates the potentially passive connotations of testimony towards a peculiarly active dimension. To circulate writing judged by the occupying power to be illegal is itself, from the Resistance viewpoint, the clearest possible affirmation of the status of literature, as fundamentally set against the grain, in opposition to officially promulgated doctrines. To this extent, the importance of such texts surpasses from the outset the specific historical circumstances of the German Occupation, since the writing reaffirms contact with a subversive current which, whatever may be its ideological foundation, seeks to cleanse language and to view reality afresh, unfettered by the particular oppressive power that might attempt to order it at any given point in time.

For writers of Resistance persuasion, the regeneration of language and the 'reviewing' of reality are therefore necessarily linked to the immediacy of the event, but not in any restricted or evanescent sense. For in that very immediacy there lies dormant, proscribed by the full weight of the occupying authorities, a perception of things not just as they are but as they might and could be. It is only when this multilayered potential of perception is recognized by the reader that the hidden richness of a great deal of Resistance writing can effectively be measured. The suspicion of a kind of journalistic superficiality to which such texts, and beyond them, the entire concept of testimony, are subject founders on this deepening polyvalence as the primary dynamic in putting pen to paper. It is not by sheer coincidence that a number of the most powerful Resistance texts are generated from an all-penetrating vision, a roving gaze that is given priority even over the act. of spoken communication. Vercors's *Le Silence de la mer* is only the most obvious instance where a rejection of things as they are takes as its starting-point a visual recording, and subsequent reordering, of the world. In many other texts animated with the spirit of Resistance, an emphasis on dream, or on the strangeness of the world, provides an equally potent thematic focus as the self relates differently to its surroundings, stripping away tendentious layers of ideological prescription and relocating the hidden essence, the unviolable authenticity, of its experiential situation.

The final resonance in the notion of *témoignage* would appear to be related to the others, but is, in important respects, quite different. Just as the deepening perception of a moment in time gives onto an appreciation of the world which is marked by its relativity or its transformability, so too does testimony arrive at a sense of continuity with the past, and stimulate a will to perpetuate values, principles and ways of living considered to be under threat. What could be called a humanistic aspiration, centred on the present difficulties of the human condition, differentiates this direction from the desire to cleanse events of their links with all past ideological resonance, viewing them afresh. Atack quotes Jean Lescure who, in a special number of *Messages* devoted to writing in France in 1943, sees in such works 'the obscure passion which links us to the duration of a civilization', and presents the special number as an 'historical work of witness'. Testimony here assumes its broadest connotation as the exemplary affirmation of incontrovertible human and national values. To write is to re-establish contact with a certain unchanging essence, to relativize the despair of the moment in the march of History, and, as *Les Lettres françaises* would have it, in a review published in October 1943 of Malraux's *Les Noyers de l'Altenburg*, 'to recognize suddenly the great voice which, across the centuries, ensures our action and our duration'.

It is tempting to view *témoignage* and *engagement* as coterminous, and the essence of my argument in relation to Sartre's perception of the war is that his attitude exists in tension with, but also in close proximity to, the values of the Resistance as outlined above. There is in Sartre's philosophical and political project a potential difficulty of transfer between the instinctive respect for individual conscience and freedom, and the no less imperative desire to weld that freedom onto a collective awareness. A letter written in the immediate post-war period significantly views the Occupation as a time less of forthright idealistic affirmation than of searching, from which French Existentialism was eventually to be born: 'La guerre et l'occupation, en nous révélant la pression de l'histoire et en nous faisant sentir profondément notre historicité, nous ont mis dans l'obligation de chercher une attitude philosophique qui rendrait compte de notre caractère historique et social tout en sauvegardant la valeur de la personne. Ce qu'on appelle l'existentialisme français est né de cette double influence.' In Sartre's view, the relationship between the individual and society is less self-evident than latent, requiring to be formulated and expressed: the clearer perspectives afforded by the Liberation permit retrospective appraisal, with the implication that the period of searching is terminated.

It is in many respects this sense of instability, of active quest and continuing discovery of the full implications of events as they unfold, which marks most deeply Sartre's writing during the war. *Les Carnets de la drôle de guerre* and the *Lettres au Castor* (the war correspondence with Simone de Beauvoir) both bear eloquent testimony to the pressure of events on certain fundamental ideas, which are not perceived as set in stone but on the contrary as being subject to constant revision, as the unpredictability and strangeness of the war context bear in on them. The abundant correspondence with de Beauvoir during the phoney war is marked by the awareness of radical disruption, which filters through to all levels of consciousness and becomes more and more pronounced as the threat clarifies, assuming tangible form. The format of the letter allows of the almost daily notation, until 10 June 1940, of evolving ideas and attitudes in which much of the resonance of what the Resistance will encapsulate in the notion of *témoignage* is already present.

A leitmotif of the text, until Sartre's capture by the Germans on 21 June 1940, can be located in a deep-seated sense of impermanence, in the shifts and dislocations of experience that mobilization in Alsace inevitably provoked. From an early stage in the correspondence, this presence of discontinuity lodges essentially in a temporal dimension, embracing the absurdity engendered by the vagaries of postal communication (Sartre's aunt, Marie Hirsch, informed by telegram of the death of her son in Shanghai, and a month later receiving a letter from him 'où il expliquait comme il était heureux'), or the peculiar division of the 'future' into autonomous units which prevent one from thinking ahead ('j'attends le lendemain *pour lui-même*') (Sartre's italics throughout). The paradoxically immediate, yet still translucid, nature that the future thereby acquires ('donner une *réalité* à l'avenir tout en gardant à la conscience sa translucidité') is characterized both by the certainty of its coming and by its total emptiness ('[raconter l'histoire d'un procès] Demain peut-être, car en somme, demain il ne m'arrivera rien'). The awareness of changes in the very waging of war, an awareness that exacerbates the growing sense of a time before, irrevocably distances the here and now of living and writing (in the confusion surrounding the notion of desertion, 'les anciens concepts de guerre ne collent plus'). The future in any case poses acutely the problem of how to live, of the mode of existence which one might have to assume ('le futur très lointain—comment vivre *après*—et ça me donnait des sueurs froides'), prompting the compensatory recourse to the present ('Je ne [. . .] vois toujours pas d'avenir [au roman, *L'Age de raison*]. Je m'y intéresse au présent. Penser qu'il sera publié on toute chose analogue, que des gens le liront, c'est à cent lieues de mon esprit'). In these varied ways, the fact of living according to the dictates of a mode of permanent uncertainty permeates all registers in the awareness of time, including that of literary creativity, and hence undermines the validity of the very act of writing: 'On vit tenement coupé d'un avenir—surtout d'un avenir littéraire—en ce moment, ça fait si vain, des petits carnets'.

Coupled with this questioning of the future, and running in parallel with one of the dominant modes associated with the Resistance notion of *témoignage*, is a sense of the strangeness engendered by the entire context: of two armies in confrontation, but in a situation of stalemate and of inactivity, of expectancy and of hope, constantly kindled and no less constantly denied. The letters and the *carnets* are fraught with this fundamental tension, but at no stage does it become a source of total disorientation or of incipient nihilism. There exists in the writing a kind of reflex dynamic, triggered precisely when perspectives seem to be the most threatening or the most problematical. The writing can of course become very dark with the accumulated weight of doubt, unverifiable rumour, and lack of information, but there is a natural tendency to search for the saving graces of a given situation, and paradoxically to see in them a possible refuge. If, as Sartre writes in the third *carnet* (November–December 1939), 'je vis flottant entre le passé et l'avenir', this force for disorientation must be read in its context, giving it an entirely different resonance:

> Cette crise passionelle c'est tout simplement le dévoilement [. . .] de toute une dimension de mon univers et de mon avenir [. . .], le dévoilement de la terrible *simultanéité* qui, par bonheur, nous demeure cachée la plupart du temps. J'imagine que si on la vivait *ici* dans toutes ses dimensions, la simultanéité, on passerait ses journées à saigner comme un sacré-coeur, mais bien des choses nous la couvrent. Par exemple les lettres que je reçois mettent trois jours à me parvenir, celles que j'envoie mettent trois jours à

> arriver. En sorte que je vis flottant entre le passé et l'avenir. Les lettres que je reçois sont des bouts de présent entourés d'avenir mais c'est un présent passé entouré d'un avenir mort. Moi-même, quand j'écris, j'hésite toujours entre deux temps: celui où je suis en traçant les lignes pour le destinataire, celui où sera le destinataire quand il me lira.

Sartre concludes: 'Cela ne rend pas cet "entourage" irréel, mais plutôt intemporel. De ce fait il s'émousse, il perd de sa nocivité.' The salutary overlapping of temporal perspectives designated here is one of the effective constituents in that reflex action which comes into operation when despair threatens to gain the upper hand, and is a powerful constituent of Sartre's peculiarly animated and thrusting style. The unthinking submission to time is scrutinized and reformulated, to positive analytical ends. An entry dated Sunday 10 March 1940 in the last *carnet* rounds typically on the temporal discontinuity that overshadows the correspondence, and makes of it a justification retrospectively legitimizing its existence, a source of strength and not of weakness: 'Pour nous, où irons-nous? Si c'est à Tours [. . .] je m'en réjouis [. . .]. Mais je me demande si je tiendrai encore ce carnet. Sa signification principals était d'accentuer cet isolement où j'étais et la rupture entre ma vie passée et ma vie présente'.

Even when the present seems to be the only plane of experience possible, totally oppressive in the sheer weight of its absurdity, the self reacts in a way that can only reduce that opacity: 'Quand les types crèvent comme des mouches dans le Nord et quand le destin de toute l'Europe est en jeu, [. . .] c'est *mon* destin, mon étroit destin individuel et aucun grand épouvantail collectif ne doit me faire renoncer à mon destin'. The claim for the freedom to make that destiny one's own, moreover, prompts clarification of the status of the very act of writing, which is no longer what it was:

> Je n'ai plus ces petites vanités et ces petits espoirs d'auteur dont je ne pouvais me défendre l'an dernier. Je suis aussi pur que lorsque j'écrivais *La Nausée* ou les premières nouvelles du *Mur* [. . .]. Mais c'est encore autre chose, ça fait plus "existential" et plus sombre, et c'est tout de même *contre* la faillite de la démocratie et de la liberté, contre la défaite des Alliés—symboliquement—que je fais l'acte d'écrire. Faisant jusqu'au bout "comme si" tout devait être rétabli.

To write 'against', to act 'as if', are not here simply compensatory or illusory, but have all the force and conviction of a personal calling: the experience of dislocation and discontinuity brings with it a sharpening of focus and a qualitatively different sense of worth. The same is true of the perception of strangeness, which can invade observation and reflection. At no stage does it become a force of disruption or of cessation, being bent in the Sartrean scale of values towards the general task of existential clarification and the pursuit of philosophical or experiential goals that surpass it. The war may seem irremediably strange in the new context of human relationships it fosters: a moving letter written on Sunday 12th May 1940, speaks of the 'rapports neufs entre les gens qui sont des rapports de guerre, une autre manière de se voir, de penser les uns aux autres [. . .] ces rapports-là, maintenant j'y suis tellement habitué que je vois le monde à travers eux', yet prefaces this observation with the crucial remark, 'Entendez-moi, je n'ai oublié *personne* des gens à qui je tenais'.

An immense distance separates this perception from the pre-war Sartre, notably from the perception of pure contingency in a Roquentin, for example, transfixed by the worm-like or crab-like movements of his hand. Now that contingency is presented differently, as a harrying intelligence tries insistently to see what it might camouflage: 'J'ai déjà dit que la guerre pouvait servir de justification: elle allège, elle excuse "d'être là". A présent je vois que la mort aussi. Tant il est difficile de vivre seulement, sans être *aucunement* justifié'. Subjected to the extreme pressure of locating authenticity in attitude and act, the strangeness attendant upon a disintegrating system and an increasingly hollow ideological defence cannot but give way to the irreducible realization of standing alone. But it is a realization totally devoid of panic or despair; absent from it also is any tone of resignation or of exacerbated personalism, and to this effect Sartre would seem to me, in this particular instance, to be well in advance of Camus's *L'Étranger*, which was not published in Paris until 1942. In effect, Sartre writes to Simone, on Saturday 8 June 1940, when the turn of events is already abundantly clear:

> Ce que vous m'écrivez sur cette étrangeté qu'il y aurait à ce que le pire se réalise, je l'ai senti bien vivement [. . .]. J'ai vraiment vécu le pire, je m'y suis *préparé*. [. . .] Tous nos barrages idéologiques qui nous servaient à penser les Allemands comme totalement fous et abjects ne pouvaient avoir aucun poids contre cette nécessité historique qui les remiserait au rang des vieilles lunes si les Allemands étaient vainqueurs [. . .]. Aussi [nos idéologies] me lâchaient-elles un peu et je n'avais pour me raccrocher que l'authenticité pure et simple. [. . .] j'étais blindé, c'est-à-dire que le pire avait perdu son caractére étrange, il était devenu un possible normal, comme la mort, intégré parmi *mes* possibilités.

The previous day, Sartre significantly borrowed an image from Lautréamont to express the arbitrariness of uncoordinated and increasingly desperate action 'De loin ça faisait beaucoup plus surréaliste qu'un parapluie et une machine à coudre sur une table de dissection, ces trois chaises coquettes au soleil, au fond d'un camion avachi et poussiéreux'. But the reflex towards the positive (in this case, the humour that can be generated from the ridiculous) is still forcefully present ('Et j'imagine que quand nous étions dessus, ça devait faire plutôt comique').

To witness for Sartre is therefore to be acutely and positively present, to be totally isolated from the comforting illusions of connection and of meaningful insertion in the progress of events, but in no way to submit or to refuse to relate the events of the moment to the imperative of personal responsibility for shaping our existence into what it is. Quite apart from any conceptual justification inherent in a growing philosophical system, it is for this reason that Sartre can speak so regularly in the correspondence of freedom, even in a letter written in captivity on 10 December 1940 from Stalag XII: 'Je lis Heidegger et je ne me suis jamais senti aussi libre'. The active connotation the Resistance comes to see as being embedded in the notion of *témoignage* is also strongly visible in Sartre's writing from the declaration of war onwards, as both the *carnets* and the correspondence amply show. The themes of waiting, of hesitancy and expectancy which more often than not prove to be completely unfounded, do not, in the *carnets*, lead on to sterility, but on to continuing reflection devoted to what the future might be in the absence of justifying principles—notably the central philosophical tenets of lack and of nothingness, as the structure of *L'Etre et le Néant* begins to crystallize and condense.

Viewed in this light, the many pages where the stifling inactivity at the front is analysed are deeply imbued with a sense of becoming, of expectations that are nurtured and partially fulfilled but do not create feelings of disillusionment, leaving room for future developments, normally centred on the possibility of social and political betterment. The active formation of self will be refined during the war as one of the cornerstones of an emerging philosophical stance. But it is clearly being adumbrated at a very early stage in the growing preoccupation with authenticity, and will become one of the indispensable measures whereby other writers are judged. An article on Bataille praises the latter's elevation of 'la condition d'homme' at the expense of 'la nature humaine', and continues, 'M. Bataille, qui fut chrétien dévot, a gardé du christianisme le sens profond de l'historicité. [. . .] l'homme n'est pas une nature, c'est un drame; ses caractères sont des actes: projet, supplice, agonie, rire, autant de mots qui désignent des processus temporels de réalisation, non des qualités données passivement et passivement reçues'.

It is against this set of emerging intellectual attitudes and their extensions in terms of act that the specificity of Sartre's ideas and their relationship to the Resistance ethic can best be judged. In 1938 *La Nausée* had demonstrated the full virulence of Sartre's animosity to any form of humanism situated outside the parameters of an existentialist ontology ('L'humaniste radical [. . .] l'ami des fonctionnaires. L'humaniste dit "de gauche" [. . .] c'est aux humbles qu'il consacre sa belle culture classique. [. . .] Il aime aussi le chat, le chien, tous les mammifères supérieurs. L'écrivain communiste aime les hommes depuis le deuxième plan quinquennal [. . .]. L'humaniste catholique [. . .] a choisi l'humanisme des anges'.

It would be erroneous to suggest that this ironic rejection of humanistic values, such as Sartre sees them to be cunningly transmitted for ideological ends, undergoes any primary transformation as a result of his experience during the Second World War: the major literary and philosophical shift in Camus, between *L'Étranger* (1942) and *La Peste* (1946), is absent. But it is impossible to read the correspondence, or indeed the *carnets*, without becoming aware of a widening of focus, which can encompass the identity of the individual and also consider the latter in relation to a collective entity, including on occasion consideration of the Germans themselves.

This may not be humanism in any traditional sense, and it avoids in particular any reference to that 'recognition of the great voice' defining the deepest attachment to duration and worthwhile actions, an attachment that circumscribed for the Resistance one of its most stable points of reference. The permanent role in Sartre's thought of historicity, of the Heideggerian being-in-the-world, calling for the acceptance and incorporation of 'the' war as 'my' war, brings to the self's situation an awareness of its relative social and historical status, in which any kind of constant or absolute that is not engendered in the self's problematical freedom has little place. This condition of freedom is an essential one, and explains why Sartre can write to Simone, 'n'est-il pas possible [. . .] qu'en s'assumant comme Juif on reconnaisse une valeur culturelle et humaine au Judaïsme', or state the obligation of 's'assumer comme Français (sans rapport a priori avec le patriotisme naturellement)'. The entities thereby created are valid ones in Sartre's view, since 'toute assomption est dépassement vers l'homme': man becomes the central focus of an experience of the world which is both distinct from, and strangely similar to, what the Resistance will define as a fundamental aspect of its operational ethic.

It would seem, therefore, that Resistance intellectuals recognized, over and above Sartre's highly distinctive philosophical views, a kindred spirit, welcoming his unequivocal moral credentials and his active participation in intellectual resistance during the Occupation (symbolized by his important role in the Comité National des Écrivains from 1943 onwards). More important, however, there would appear to be evidence of the recognition by Resistance intellectuals of common ground, shared with elements of the humanistic and libertarian strain in Sartre's thought, with that importance of being oneself and of being French, but without being so in any traditional patriotic sense, as he puts it in his correspondence. When viewed from this perspective, the possibility of certain links with the kind of writing Sartre practised during the war years, despite obvious differences with the Resistance ethos, calls for much closer study than has hitherto been devoted to this crucial aspect of his intellectual development.

To an extent, this important dovetailing with the Resistance ethic is a perfectly logical and expected one, despite the fact that in the composition of the Comité National des Écrivains, Sartre's voice is, in theory, a very distinctive one. It is true of course that his pre-war reputation for uncompromising and incisive writing, enhanced during the Occupation by its public reception in the theatrical productions of *Les Mouches* and *Huis Clos*, and coupled with what was already known of his strident anti-conventionalism, was probably well sufficient to qualify him for the inner circle of Resistance orthodoxy. His articles for *Les Lettres Françaises*, *Combat*, and *La France libre* confirm the importance conferred on his role as 'witness', embodying *témoignage* in the most immediately journalistic sense. It is true also that both the correspondence and the *carnets* written at this time are by definition areas of private observation and recording, of which the circle of intellectuals associated with the Resistance cannot have been aware.

But these important literary sources suggest from time to time a widening of perspective that must have been given expression in contexts of discussion and exchange, a willingness to note the actions and attitudes of others without necessarily referring them to an all-embracing conceptual system for validation or judgement. In the correspondence, for example, one is struck by the breadth of Sartre's reading, in the original, of German literature, a source sometimes of scandal or contempt for his fellow soldiers, and which cannot be imputed only to his pre-war experience of Berlin or to his general knowledge of German language and culture. Glaeser's *Classe 22*, Kafka, Goethe, Schiller ('Je lis Goethe ou Schiller pour me mettre en train, en allemande, [. . .] et j'ai l'impression sous-cutanée d'être au XVIIIe siècle dans quelque halle jésuitique'), various books by Ludwig on Goethe, Guillaume II, and the outbreak of war in 1914, bespeak a willingness to venture beyond the otherwise overpowering conventions of friend and foe.

Other elements as well enrich this growing awareness of the other, in a sense that is different from that which it would have in Sartre's systematization of the self's identity and its relationship with 'pour-autrui'. Reflection on the plight of a soldier under charge of desertion solicits the remark, 'Il faut un effort pour penser qu'il a une *condition humaine*': the writing is redolent with a feeling for the 'human condition', understood of course, in the Sartrean sense of self-assumption, of 'une fatalité reprise et assumée par une volonté'—'dire c'est *ma* guerre et [. . .] essayer de la vivre', but permeated also with a constant degree of empathy for the personal circumstances of his fellows-in-arms.

There exists even, at certain times, a willingness to try to reconnect, to attempt to recapture the happiness and the equilibrium of the inter-war years, in radical opposition to Drieu la Rochelle's or Montherlant's apocalyptic dismissal of their degeneracy and despair: a natural movement towards positive appraisal which on other occasions seeks a form of historical continuity between 1939, 1914, 1870 and as far back as Napoleon. The opening of self to 'un temps d'été, tout calme et beau, tout chargé de souvenirs' reinstates a pregnant simplicity and directness, far removed from more sombre thoughts and theorizing. The affirmation of life invests the theoretical substratum of the *carnets* with an urgency which is sometimes lost in more arid contexts: 'Je pense à présent qu'on ne perd jamais sa vie, je pense que rien ne vaut une vie. Et pourtant j'ai conservé toutes mes idées; je sais qu'une vie est molle et pâteuse, injustifiable et contingente. Mais c'est sans importance, je sais aussi que tout peut m'arriver mais c'est *à moi* que cela arrivera; tout événement est *mon* événement'. In the stress laid here on 'life' and on its 'worth', the prefiguring of the famous conclusion to *Les Mots* situates consciousness '*sur fond de vie*', using a mode of self-discovery that is less an interiorization than an integration with the events and the fellow beings defining its situation.

If, in the third *carnet* of November–December 1939, Sartre can write of the 'témoignage' his writing will bring, it is again because of the way in which he feels it to be instinctively attuned to what he calls 'generality', and to the 'mediocre', simple stuff of living. To this extent, the radical alienation created in the war experience, inviting a literature of extreme situations, needs to be measured carefully against these other perceptions of an individual's situation in the world, where the sharp asperities of existential dilemma or crisis come necessarily to be attenuated by the comradeship established with other 'mediocre' beings. Even what he calls the 'valeur historique de mon témoignage' does not have to it the ring of thrusting intellectual enquiry that the notion of historicity elsewhere confers on the text. In a central paragraph, he brings together most of the crucial constituents of témoignage, differentiating them from the diary of Gide: 'Le témoignage d'un bourgeois de 1939 mobilisé, sur la guerre qu'on lui fait faire. [. . .] j'écris n'importe quoi sur mon carnet, mais c'est avec l'impression que la valeur historique de mon témoignage me justifie à le faire. [. . .] mon journal est un témoignage qui vaut pour des millions d'hommes. C'est un témoignage *médiocre* et par là même *général*.

In addition, the testimony proposed is, like that of the Resistance, a fundamentally active one: 'Ce journal est une remise en question de moi-même. [. . .] cette remise en question, je ne la fais pas en gémissant et dans l'humilité, mais froidement et afin de progresser'. The importance of bearing witness, of stilling the clamouring claims and counter-claims of a viscous and impenetrable present, the better to capture the truth of a given situation of duress, or of violence, or of oppression, but also to progress, can be forcefully expressed. The writing gives voice to the gathering certainty that active involvement is the only form of testimony that can legitimately be envisaged: 'pour atteindre l'authenticité, il faut que quelque chose craque'.

The impulse to activity, to participation in multiple fields of personal commitment, finds visible literary expression in the oscillation between very different genres and forms. The correspondence with Simone is pursued with the seriousness of a daily responsibility; the *carnet* is viewed, with the customary admixture of lucidity and deflation, as the ideal format for the shaping and honing both of ideas and of personal convictions or precepts for action. At the same time, in what is to become the first volume of *Les Chemins de la liberté*, Sartre is rethinking and reformulating the role of the novel in presenting the turns and twists of consciousness, as it struggles to come to terms with, or to shirk, the responsibilities bearing down on it. As Atack has noted, the articulation of characterization across ignorance and knowledge in the war novel generally, but with particular pertinence in the case of the trilogy, is a crucial feature of literary *témoignage*, as the means by which the writer encourages the reader to apprehend the full impact of the 'historical real' against which the fictional construct functions. The importance of progress noted above finds here an ideal outlet in the characters' faltering moves towards knowledge, which for Sartre is the assumption of the predicaments marking their existence. The attenuated presence of an extra-diegetic narrator conforms fully with one of the principles of testimony, as the fictional participants struggle in isolation through the dilemmas with which they are faced.

The novel is thus a privileged medium, since it both expresses the crux of testimony and advances the search for freedom, rendering all the more probable a complete existential and political commitment to changing the face of society as Sartre sees it. But the range of genres in which he works during the Occupation extends even further: theatrical production, as he comes to realize its potential in communicating ideas to a wider audience;

literary reviews and particularly newspaper articles, as the imperative in the notion of *témoignage* to inform and to persuade takes shape with greater precision. Camus's commissioning from Sartre, on 22 August 1944, of a highly prestigious series of seven articles for the Resistance newspaper *Combat*, under the general title of 'Un Promeneur dans Paris insurgé', is in many respects one of the clearest expressions of the dovetailing between commitment and *témoignage*: the momentous event of an entire city, and beyond it, a nation, awakening to their real identity and to the necessity of self-commitment, rendered all the more emphatic since it equates in this specific case to self-liberation, is expressed through the 'promenade', which both emerges in its originality as the roving gaze of a non-mediated perception of experience, central to *témoignage*, and claims its legitimacy in certain consecrated models of French literature (Rousseau, *Les Rêveries d'un promeneur solitaire*).

In its inspiration as in its substance, the text thus acts as vehicle for the immediacy of visual observation and a deeply rooted sense of continuity. It is not difficult to appreciate its close articulation in accordance with all the primary criteria defining the role of the 'witness' in the Resistance pantheon. One encounters the sense of patient expectancy ('[les civils] attendaient, patiemment, sans colère'), or of limited knowledge that activity alone can dispel ('Garages qui brûlent? Immeubles en feu? Personne ne le sait. On ne sait rien'; 'pour les habitants du quartier, les visages de leurs défenseurs sont encore inconnus. Les forces de la Résistance sont presque un mythe: on y croit de toutes ses forces mais on ne les connaît pas'; *'la liberté ça ne se donne pas, ça se prend'*). The difficult assumption of its own destiny by the crowd as a collective, unitary phenomenon is stressed ('c'est la première fois [. . .] que [la foule] prend conscience d'elle-même. [. . .] les gens sont transformés. [. . .] Ils ont pris parti'), as too, are the glimpses of a possible linking-up with the past ('Les drapeaux aux fenêtres, la foule dans la rue rappelaient les anciens 14 juillet'). The 'human' is thereby rediscovered, sweeping aside the 'strange' ('Pendant quatre ans, la guerre avait tourné vers nous une face inhumaine; [. . .] les soldats que nous croisions semblaient marqués par un impitoyable destin; ils appartenaient à un monde étranger, un monde fantastique et désolé. Et voilà que [les soldats français de Leclerc] sont des hommes'). Sartre concludes by emphasizing the need to redeploy military activity, now almost stilled with victory, towards a continuing struggle to assure the future: '[La foule] comprenait obscurément le double caractère de ce défilé patriotique et révolutionnaire; elle sentait [. . .] qu'il ne s'agissait pas seulement de chasser les Allemands de France, mais de commencer un combat plus dur et plus patient pour conquérir un ordre neuf'.

The commentary here is an example of highly sophisticated journalism, not to say a little disingenuous, since in the one sentence Sartre manages first to associate patriotism (dismissed in the correspondence for being too tendentiously loaded) with revolution, and then to bend this revolutionary patriotism towards the establishment of a 'new order', calling upon 'combat', which happens to be the name of the newspaper in which he is writing. The subtle intrusion of certain political considerations in the final article also distinguishes surprisingly between the Forces Françaises de l'Intérieur, 'ces sinistres voitures des gangsters de Chicago, qui conduisent des tueurs dévaliser une banque', and the 'autos puissantes et silencieuses [. . .]: l'ordre, le pouvoir' of the regular troops. The rather unflattering comparison is hastily rectified in the following paragraph ('Jamais, de mémoire d'homme, l'insurrection n'a ainsi voisiné, fraternisé avec l'armée'); but the impression of elements of possible discordance persists, heightened by the replacement of the hitherto regularly used 'insurrectionnel' with 'révolutionnaire', in the climactic stage of the report.

The extent to which the Resistance saw its programme, and its ethical duty, as one of revolution is, of course, a moot point, and one that falls outside the present discussion. But I can see no tangible or consciously formulated hint of it in the concept of *témoignage*, since the imperatives of persuasion and of action, whether the latter be envisaged in terms of 'revolt', 'insurrection' or the more generalizing 'resistance', are not given any uniform definition in ideologically or politically motivated terms. Sartre's post-war stance on commitment remains as morally trenchant as ever it was, and the essays collected under the title 'Lendemains de guerre' in *Situations* III offer many an acute insight into the experience of occupation, the nature of resistance, and also the motivations in collaboration. But the context of composition here is in the process of change: if the war is still very present in its lived immediacy, the mode of presentation is necessarily one of retrospective appraisal, with a consequent sense of historical distance from the experience, of measured summary and judgement.

This paradoxical combination of simultaneity and retrospection is confirmed by the fact that three of the essays either were written during the war or are contemporaneous with the end of it (the capitulation of Japan on 15 August 1945). Sartre lessens the impression of the war as historical past by conventional stylistic techniques, such as the use of the historic present, of the imperfect with its undefined continuity of past action, or of the present perfect, as in the opening sentence of 'La République du silence' ('Jamais nous n'avons été plus libres que sous l'occupation allemande'), where distance between the present and the past is modulated and weakened by the compound verbal structure. The tone, however, changes in significant ways, even if there are the same fundamental insights and approaches as those which, during the war, anchor his writing solidly in the most important aspects of *témoignage* (the strangeness of objects and of experience; the rupture with the past, necessitating the creation of a new relationship with history and with a continuity of human aspiration, the whole expressed via a progressing but limited knowledge which the present can now clarify; the process of depersonalization and dehumanization, from which the Resistance alone offered refuge).

As the war closes and ushers in its equally sinister nuclear aftermath, such sentiments are written with a sharper and more incisive edge than before. The indeterminacy in notions of friend and foe, which in the correspondence is far from being reprehensible, is cited both as an explanation of the plight of France and as an implicit accusation. A much more precise conception of commitment can now round on the war years, and pinpoint the full ambiguity or defects in attitude and response as devolving as much from 'impotence', with its connotations of equally personal responsibility, as from duress. In a very valid sense, the stakes are now perceived as being far higher: the last essay, 'La fin de la guerre', written after the atomic bombs on Hiroshima and Nagasaki, is finely attuned to a new sense of urgency. A lapidary, condensed style outlines the inescapability of the new issues facing all, in which the word 'commitment' changes its status from the essentially demonstrable, persuasive value it had during the war to a performative necessity: 'Ses ultimes moments [cette guerre-ci] ont été pour nous avertir de la fragilité humaine. [. . .] cette petite bombe [. . .] nous met tout à coup en face de nos responsabilités'. The absurd now has a presence, and a finality, 'purifying' personal freedom and the obligation to choose from any vestige of obscurity or of uncertainty that the pervasive ambiguity of the Occupation experience might have bequeathed to it, raising it to an awesome degree of isolation ('Désormais ma liberté est plus pure [. . .]. Il faut que je sois, en ce jour même et dans l'éternité, mon propre témoin'.

Much of the writing, particularly in the last essay, is invested with a pervading sense of the end of an era, of the beginning of a period of peace that poses acutely the question of life and death, now more pressing than ever in the face of weapons of mass destruction and the not so hypothetical or fantastic vision of total annihilation. At the same time, there is still a proximity to the real experience of the war that brings it alive in the text, giving it tangible substance, and effectively counterbalancing the desire for measured withdrawal and global appraisal. This equilibrium of complementary directions had already become attenuated by 1947, with the publication of *Qu'est-ce que la littérature?*, the essay which, most strongly among Sartre's works, argues the responsibility and the commitment with which the writer is faced. By 1947, with the Cold War fully in progress, and with Sartre deeply embroiled in his conflictual relationship with the Communist Party, the war is more easily apprehensible in its shifting ambiguities, with the result that active participation in Resistance in the past is perceived less as immanent to the human dilemma than as a fixed value, transmuted subtly in its substance by the objectification effected by the word 'engagement' itself, which is far from being systematically used by Sartre during the period of the war itself.

'Si nous parions pour la vie, pour nos amis, pour notre personne, nous parions pour la France, nous prenons l'engagement de chercher à l'intégrer dans ce monde rude et fort, dans cette humanité en péril de mort': the words, with their peculiarly Pascalian resonance, could well figure in *Qu'est-ce que la littérature?* (1948). But the comment here engages with a difficulty which, in the one remark, still significantly embraces considerations bearing on 'humanity' at large and the one personalized necessity of commitment, thereby opening perspectives the more trenchant post-war attitudes do not satisfactorily accommodate. In effect, the dovetailing of *témoignage* and of *engagement*, the latter invested with the particular existential connotations it will assume in Sartre's system of values after the war, raises certain important questions regarding the nature of both, and hence of their interdependence and interaction. When Atack states 'However much he is anticipating the well known arguments of *Qu'est-ce que la littérature?*, Sartre is merely expressing a typical Resistance view when he writes in a clandestine (and anonymous) article: "Literature is not a song of innocence and facility which can adjust to any kind of régime. By its nature it poses the question of politics: to write is to demand freedom for all men"', she sketches in a whole range of concomitant issues, which modify significantly our view of the intellectual and experiential bases in which his post-war reflection is deeply embedded. Thus she rightly emphasizes the discrepancy between the clarity of his pronouncements in *Les Temps modernes* in 1952 regarding political choice during the war and the far more nuanced view of his actual stance with regard to the latter given by Simone de Beauvoir in *La Force de l'âge*. She further identifies the 'predominantly polemical rather than analytical' nature of Sartre's articles in *Les Lettres françaises*, even when they are discussing the role of literature: an emotive adherence to the events inspires a tone which is very different from the kind of ironic distance which, in *Qu'est-ce que la littérature?*, can judge and generalize.

There is no doubt, on the basis of his writing, private and public, that *témoignage* and the values it represents are considered by Sartre for a substantial period of the war to be the most appropriate response to the particular circumstances pertaining. All the more, since the conceptualization of his notion of individual commitment is still in the process of refinement and definition of application: comments figuring in *Situations* II in 1948, which, for example, identify 'novels of *situation*, without internal narrators or omnipotent witnesses', benefit from the clarity of hindsight, by means of which the precise scale of the crisis posed by the Occupation can be measured. As Sartre himself implies in *Quest-ce que la littérature?*, designating context and efficacy as opposed to verisimilitude as the essential parameters of the war-time response to Vercors's *Le Silence de la mer*, a *theory* of committed literature and hence of the act of writing as commitment is not the kind of consideration that is most pressing when draconian constraints and extreme repression are the stuff of everyday living. His extraordinary post-war dismissal, in *Qu'est-ce que la littérature?*, of Resistance poetry, arguably the finest literary achievement of clandestine writing during the Occupation, can perhaps best be imputed, over and above his natural antipathy for poetry, to a changed mode of scrutiny, one that is necessarily less the product of that context of speaking and writing as the very act of Resistance, whereby 'chaque parole devenait précieuse comme une déclaration de principe [. . .], chacun de nos gestes avait le poids d'un engagement' ('La République du silence', *Situations* III).

It would in effect be wrong, to my mind, to see Sartre's relationship with the Resistance, and through it, with the concept of *témoignage*, as merely a kind of foil or formative catalyst in the elaboration of theories and attitudes whose intellectual influence tended subsequently to overshadow the Resistance's integral role in their elaboration. There are, in that role, elements of complexity and of empathetic identification that distance it from any easy reduction to the preparatory grounding of the theories of literary production and status for which Sartre is now remembered. His role as one of the primary moral spokesmen for the conscience of post Liberation France calls for reappraisal in the light of this rich, sometimes conflictual but consistently illuminating encounter with the Resistance ethic.

SHARON GHAMARI-TABRIZI

Feminine Substance in Being and Nothingness

In the seeming exhaustiveness of *Being and Nothingness* (1966), Sartre anxiously but incompletely expressed approach and recoil from the feminine as Other. While he described the phenomenology of love in terms of engagement with the free subjectivity of the beloved, he addressed the (masculine) subject's relation to female *embodiment* as the movement of the *for-itself*'s encounter with the facticity, in which one attempts aggressively to appropriate the autonomy of the Other, then, in recoil, one flies from the obscenely intimate entanglements of other-being. In this essay, I will examine the unstable relation of the *for-itself* (man) to the *in-itself* (woman as an objective structure) in the brief, but suggestive chapter, "Quality as a Revelation of Being," in the section preceding the conclusion of *Being and Nothingness.*

In this chapter, Sartre attempted to anatomize the existential symbolism of things by locating his discussion in two qualities of *being*: the externality of facticity and the subjectively infused *situation*. Within this framework, he established another binary field within which he laid out his meandering fretwork of world-in-situation. He divided *being* along the archaic cleft between the feminine as the continuous, and the masculine as the discontinuous, separate, and apart. Given the importance of his anxiety concerning the annihilation of the *for-itself*'s composure by too-intimate

From *American Imago* 56, no. 2 (Summer 1999): 133–44. © 1999 by The Johns Hopkins University Press.

contact with facticity, the potentiality of the engulfment of the masculine self by a yielding, plastic femininity must be construed as a permanent danger. For Sartre, desire describes the experience of the body-in-situation, " . . . [is] a passion by which I am engaged in the world and in danger in the world." The danger in the case of feminine *being* is the experience of "being swallowed up in the body."

Although Sartre declared that he would pursue a psychoanalysis of "presexual structures," in order to examine the way the subject appropriates the world in the "manner in which *being* springs forth from [an object's] surface," the text gives evidence to an intensely sexualized rumination about the intricate adjustments of ascendancy between the sexes in the arena of ordinary presence. While at this point in his book, he has already elaborated the notion of desire at great length in the section on being-for-others, one cannot help but be piqued by an argument in which the *for-itself* at the axis of his phenomenology is masculine, and is revolted by feminine embodiment.

Sartre considered his ontological analytic to be closer to the truth in having the boldness to address erotic verities, in contrast to Heidegger, who " . . . does not make the slightest allusion to it (sex) in his existential analytic, with the result that his *Dasein* appears to us as asexual." Thus, Sartre declared that " . . . the *for-itself* is sexual in its very upsurge in the face of the Other, and that through it, sexuality comes into the world." Following this assertion, he conceded that not all relations to the Other can be reduced to the sexual, yet it is nevertheless fundamental. By a variety of strategies, Sartre repeatedly disregarded the acknowledged subjectivity of the Other as a phenomenological incarnation, and instead, plotted the female role as a species of conniving, disreputable facticity, as the slimy and the hole. He asked, "To what fundamental project of myself am I referred if I want to explain this love of an ambiguous, sucking-in-itself?" In such a formulation, he disclosed his uneasiness by casting the Other as obscenely feminine, a slimy devouring hole irremediably fixed as an ontological category.

His thoughts about the female Other as an unsettling structure of ontology are presented in the context of an anti-empirical, existential psychoanalytic. For Sartre, the notion of feeling as self-originated mood is unacceptable. Emotion corresponds to an actual structure in the world; it is an "objective transcending relation." This does not imply that the feeling-experience confirms, or is the conventional response to the objective features of one's situation. He wants neither a documentary catalogue of psychic symbolism, something akin to Freud's lists of correspondences in *The Interpretation of Dreams*, nor the claim that "feeling a feeling" is the draw of fortuitous whimsy. Rather, ontology issues from the constituting *for-itself*.

Sartre identifies the world as the ontological structure within the *for-itself* as an internal map of one's situation. Thus, "It is impossible to distinguish facticity from the project which constitutes it in situation." Ontology is the objective world, yet suffused with the emotive and perceptual predisposition of the *for-itself* which assigns, delimits, and is the author of each *in-itself*'s discerned particularity. This, then, is Sartre's psychic matrix of feeling.

Hence, in the "psychoanalysis of things," he attempts to determine the meaning of the process by which the individual chooses the world. "World" designates the interplay of given objects and qualities, some manipulable such as trees which can be hewn, along with manufactured and social quantities, and some not, such as alpine ridges. "A psychoanalysis of things and of their matter ought above all to be concerned with establishing the way in which each thing is the objective symbol of *being* and of the relation of human reality to this *being*." For Sartre, each object is installed in a constellation of *being*, in the discernment of which the perceiving subject manifests an idiomatic style, whose texture traces the eruption of his fundamental choices. So, for example, whether or not Sartre chooses to bend to pick up and sniff a stray bit of filthy paper uncovers an important note about his way of attempting "to be what he is not, yet."

Here, in the opening of his discussion of quality as a revelation of being, Sartre comes to trouble, for he begins with the notion of the unique object. "Each thing is chosen for its ability to render *being* in a particular fashion or mode." He carries this formulation, the importance of the individual chosen object, to the end of the chapter on quality where he discusses the quality of a pink cake *as* the cake. Yet, in the context of a psychoanalysis of the symbolic meaning of the qualities of particular things and the emotions they arouse, Sartre chooses to study the slimy and the hole, which are fundamental, not particular, structures. Specifically, he appears to study obliquely the sexual characteristic of women as a sort of generally repugnant appeal, rather than the specific qualities of a particular woman or erotic encounter.

We begin with *quality*, " . . . the presence of its (*being*'s) absolute contingency; its . . . irreducibility." He argues the predicate in support of the existential character of the substance. "The meaning of quality indicates something as a reinforcement of 'there is' since we take it as our support in order to surpass the 'there is' toward *being* as it is absolutely. . . ." He also describes quality as an arc which ". . . transcends the opposition of the psychic and the physical." Feeling, ignited by the qualities of a thing, approximates and comes closest to non-thetically grasping the *in-itself*. "In every apprehension of quality, there is in this sense a metaphysical effort to escape from our condition so as to pierce through the shell of nothingness about the 'there is' and to penetrate to the pure *in-itself.*" Following Hegel's dialectic of social recognition, Sartre characterizes the being-in-the-world of the *for-itself* as an aggressive cognition propelled by the libidinal energy of the human project.

He is after an elusive thought here. He argues against understanding qualities as objective correlatives for inner states. Ontology is not a symbolism of *being*. The apperception of quality does not give rise to a poetics of *being* where, for example, the individual slimy thing would be altered by cognitive knowledge of the class of sliminess. If this were the case, Sartre would ". . . then have enriched the slimy by projecting upon it my knowledge with respect to that human category of behavior." In other words, the psychology of projection would amount to idealism. He is not after this at all. Rather, Sartre expresses an erotics of *being*, the surface of which alone is caught up in the nominative (ostensive) texture of language. One can never appropriate the *in-itself*, one apprehends quality ". . . as a symbol of a *being* which totally escapes us even though it is totally there."

Sartre's discussion of the slimy and the hole can be read as a series of oblique narratives pertaining to coitus. It gives expression to his theory of primary aggressive (libidinal) conflict between the *for-itself* and the *in-itself.* In this reading, his subtexts insist on oppressively ruinous encounters between men and women. (One can easily confirm this by perusing his novels, short fiction, and plays.) Whereas genital physiology is merely complementary, Sartre distinguishes gender as ontological poles, one of which is essentially ascendant over the other.

Recurrent figures in this chain of narratives are: desire as an entrapment of the consciousness by the body and by the world; the erotic look at the other as a radical negation of her *being* in situation, "in order to dissolve the situation and to corrode the Other's relations in the world" so that she appears as brute facticity. Sartre's fantasy of engulfment by the world translates into anxiety of over-identifying with the feminine, thereby relinquishing masculine autonomy, a danger of being dissolved into sliminess by means of the negating caress of the female Other.

In both the sections on Being-for-others and Quality as a revelation of Being, in multiple instances in which he either catalogues genital physiology or lists the effects of sexual response, Sartre generally avoids articulating the locus of his anxiety—the vagina. Amid his many composed references to the breast, the anus, and the penis, the equally primary vagina is not to be found. Instead, Sartre diverts the subject into a discussion of the "presexual" object, "the hole" of the anus, and the feminine quality of *being*, "sliminess." He further qualifies his discussion of the slimy by alluding to the situation in which coitus is given meaning: the machinations of bourgeois romance. His reflection on the feminine role introduces the quality of "feminine sweetness" as "sugariness."

Conditions that are irreducibly complex, liminal, and hard to classify ordinarily illicit the greatest anxiety. In one respect, a discussion of the slimy is appropriate to a psychoanalysis of the feelings accompanying states of things. The slimy, as Sartre puts it, has an "ambiguous character as a 'substance in between two states,'" that is, liquidity and solidity. He characterizes the slimy as the odious facticity against which the *for-itself* has little capacity to resist. He draws down the archaic threat of cataclysm and engulfment which slime connotes. It is "the revenge of the *in-itself*." The crux of the awful potentiality of the engulfment of the separate self in flowing vertiginous being—his celebrated experience of nausea in the face of the world—is an image of unreason. The categories shatter, the particulars melt and blend, and meaning itself dissolves. The *for-itself* is choked in the runny maelstrom of substance which lies in wait behind the comforting density of solids, and the instantaneous flight of water. Slime, being neither one nor the other, in this view, prefigures the deluge. Sartre assigns to this dread potentiality a feminine nature.

The movements of his description of the slimy are strongly reminiscent of fin-de-siècle ideas of feminine malevolence: "a sickly sweet feminine revenge," the "leech-like" clinging, the "soft-yielding action, a moist and feminine sucking," "softness like a retarded annihilation." He describes the encounter between subjectivity and slimy *beings* the deceptive appeal that the *in-itself* has for the *for-itself*. The world is always in the process of being transposed into a qualitatively distinct situation by the "assimilating and creative power" of subjectivity. However, the slimy is a peculiar species of *being*, for in its encounter with subjectivity, *being* absorbs the subject into its own facticity.

The *in-itself* supinely presents itself to the inquiring, appropriating *for-self*. Menace underlies its mild appeal, its compressibility, the apparent docility inherent in its softness. "The slimy when perceived is a slimy to be possessed." However, once having grasped it, the subject cannot withdraw from intimate contact. Slimy substance clings and conforms to the subject. Any kind of slime, including human secretions, is a negative mold that outlines the fusion of the world with the subject's body. Thus, for Sartre, the quality of slime as *being* is revealed: ". . . there is a possibility that the *in-itself* might absorb the *for-itself* . . . into its contingency, into its indifferent exteriority, into its foundationless existence." Touching the slimy, the *for-itself* is mantled in a casket of soft, imprisoning substance. In the (masked) conquest of (feminine) *being* over against free subjectivity, "a sugary sliminess is the ideal of the slimy; it symbolizes the sugary death of the for-itself . . ."

Slime dissolves meaning as well as the subject's freedom. Consciousness itself can become slimy. Sartre moves from describing a disgusting feeling of stickiness and ooze, to the feeling of being caught by innumerable "parasites" of the past such that the freedom of action is lost. Slimy consciousness cannot move forward, it is stuck.

> . . . we are haunted by the image of a consciousness which would like to launch forth into the future, toward a projection of self, and which at the very moment when it was conscious of arriving there would be slyly held back by the invisible suction of the past and which would have to assist in its own dissolution in this past which it was fleeing, would have to aid in the invasion of its project by a thousand parasites until finally it completely lost itself.

Sartre describes the relation between the slimy and the self as a representation of the "anti-value" or "foundationlessness" of facticity prevailing over anxious subjectivity. Sliminess therefore represents the threat of the nothingness of the world, a "constant danger which [consciousness] is fleeing." In the ontological encounter with slimy substance, the *for-itself*'s usual cognitive and libidinal act of appropriation has in this case turned into a "project of flight." Sartre concludes that "henceforth," the *for-itself* will be alert to the ever-present danger of sliminess, "a threatening mode of being which must be avoided, a concrete category which it will discover everywhere." If slimy substance is primordial, and its quality of being presents "an objective structure in the world," it follows that female sexual response can only be construed as danger.

Rather than pursuing this idea, at this point in the argument Sartre abruptly introduces a new and uncharacteristic consideration of infantile anal sexuality. Nowhere else in his book does he appear concerned with establishing a theory of developmental psychology and phenomenology. Insofar as Sartre formally addressed immature consciousness at all in his *oeuvre*, it was in laying the grounds of his existential biographies. Rarely, if at all, does Sartre mention the formative role the Mother plays in establishing the conscious autonomy of her infant. Neither does he mention the important functions that a Sister-as-Other (or male sibling, for that matter) may have in the dialectics of social aggression, cooperation, and ambivalence. How can one, then, account for the following statement in which he deflects the course of his argument away from the mature female Other? "What we say concerning the slimy is valid for all the objects which surround the child."

Sartre devotes the next several pages of his text to the infant's exploration of objective structures in the world, and his subsequent discovery that his anus is a hole.

> The gluey, the sticky, the hazy, etc., holes in the sand and earth, caves, the light, the night, etc.—all reveal to him modes of pre-psychic and pre-sexual being which he will spend the rest of his life explaining. It seems to us that this matter and these forms (in the child's environment) are apprehended in themselves, and they reveal to the child the *for-itself*'s mode of being and relations to being which will illuminate and shape his sexuality.

Sartre accomplishes two things in this section which throws light on his final discussion of mature female sexuality. As in his section on Being-for-Others, one requires the mediation of the Other in order to grasp one's facticity. Hence, the negative parts of the child's body must be identified and so construed by an Other. Prior to that, lie merely exists in them. Yet, importantly, Sartre posits this needed mediation in its infantile character. The child needs his nurse to delimit this cavity requisite to any further psychological development. "It is only to another person that the anus appears as an orifice. The child himself can never have experienced it as such. . . ." There is the sense that in the same way that ". . . the hole is originally presented as a nothingness 'to be filled' with my own flesh," the infant's inchoate sexuality is also a nothingness to be filled with the informing knowledge of the precise form of his facticity.

The symbolic appeal of the hole is that it requires a sacrifice ". . . in order that the plenitude of being may exist." The sacrifice alluded to is the sacrifice of some body part in order to plug the whole, thereby establishing a plenitude. Still referring to infantile sexuality, Sartre discloses his core idea: the obscene. "The hole, before all sexual specification, is an obscene expectation, an appeal to the flesh." The obscene here conveys not just the sense of brute facticity. It is not merely an imploring nothingness. The obscene insists on the arousal (the troubling) of the serene consciousness. The *for-itself* attends the obscene with a distinctly moral revulsion before the mutiny of its own responding (yet undesiring) flesh. This may appear to muddy the distinction he sets out between sexual desire on the one hand, and the obscene on the other. Yet one cannot understand him otherwise, for it is not merely the erotic display of a particular woman, or even a particular sort of woman that is obscene for Sartre, but he declares an obscenity fused to the heterosexual erotic.

After characterizing the appeal of the hole as infantile in origin, retaining traces of its origin in its consequent established nature thereafter, he writes,

> The obscenity of the feminine sex is that of everything which "gapes open." It is an appeal to being as all holes are. In herself woman appeals to a strange flesh which is to transform her into a fullness of being by penetration and dissolution. Conversely woman senses her condition as an appeal precisely because she is "in the form of a hole."

Sartre has inverted the aspect of the feminine from exhibiting secret ensnaring power into infantile incompletion. Furthermore, the female requires a sacrifice as the anus requires the sacrifice of flesh from the child. Yet coming as it does after a section on the origin and nature of infantile sexuality, one feels that the feminine mouth is contiguously associated with the infantile, blind, pressing, sucking mouth. "Beyond any doubt her sex is a mouth and a voracious mouth which devours the penis—a fact which can easily lead to the idea of castration."

Sartre is uncompromisingly provocative. Perhaps he may have been employing a misogynist rhetoric ironically. Throughout this section, indeed throughout the book, traces of irony are to be found. Two points on this must be made in order to respond fairly to this objection. His tone is alternately disingenuous and forthright; his argument is too erratic and disjointed to give evidence of the kind of sure patina literary irony usually lends to the surface texture of an argument. It seems to me that Sartre's prose is more exploratory than duplicitous. Moreover, insofar as he equates the feminine with facticity, his allegedly profound aversion to the looming presence of the *in-itself* is consistently represented. One must take his tone, therefore, to be straightforward on this point, as it appears he means to be when referring to his nausea in the face of the world in general.

In the section on desire, he wrote, "Her flesh is a flesh which is no longer anything but the property of an Other-as-Object and not the incarnation of an Other-as-consciousness." How can one regard feminine as substance with the context of desire laid out in the more important section on Being-for-Others? In that, the vagina annihilates the autonomy of the man by causing a part of his body to disappear, hence by achieving a sacrifice, the feminine achieves ascendancy. Insofar as the *for-itself* must surpass and annihilate its own facticity when lodged in female substance towards pleasure, Sartre regards the female Other instrumentally. Yet this does not explain, finally, why he has characterized the female Other as a species of facticity. In his section on Being-for-Others, he represents desire as a sort of equitable though failing negotiation of facticity, laid out in a dialectical movement between being-for-others and being-for-itself. There are no satisfactory answers for this. Sartre's discussion of desire offers multiple readings, all of them suggestive, some contradictory.

Desire is narcotizing and profoundly bemusing. "Let any man consult his own experience, he knows his consciousness is clogged by sexual desire; it seems that one is invaded by facticity, that one ceases to flee it and that one slides towards a passive consent to desire." As a mechanism for carrying out the dialectics of pleasure, he introduces a liminal substance, flesh, which corresponds to the slimy. Flesh is charged facticity. It is saturated with corporal awareness; it is the incarnation of the Other-as-consciousness. So, in effect, in this paradigm, Sartre has written the *for-itself* into the structure of the *in-itself*. His description of arousal, however, describes the constitution of flesh through the "troubling" of consciousness, perfectly presaging his account of the slimy. "Suddenly the man who desires becomes a heavy tranquillity, which is frightening, his eyes are fixed and appear half-closed, his movements are stamped with a heavy and sticky sweetness." He underscores the identification of flesh and the slimy by asserting the dual character of desire: ". . . desire is not only the clogging of a consciousness by its facticity; it is correlatively the ensnarement of a body by the world."

The female is posited as a passivity to be acted upon and appropriated. "To take hold of the Other reveals to her inertia and her passivity as a transcendence-transcended." He argues that even in regarding the female Other as an in-itself, a transcendence-transcended, one still distinguishes the Other's facticity as a sign of "the pure contingency of presence." Sartre insists on the shifting ontological grounds upon which desire is pursued, solicited, negotiated, and surpassed.

> . . . all the patterns of conduct toward the Other-as-Object include within themselves an implicit and veiled reference to an Other-as-subject. Upon the death of a particular conduct toward the Other-as-object arises a new attitude which aims at getting hold of the Other-as-subject, and this in turn reveals its instability and collapses to give way to the opposite conduct.

In another place, Sartre explicitly justifies his ambivalence regarding the status of the female Other.

> It is necessary that I drag him onto the level of pure facticity; he must be reduced from himself to being only flesh. Thus I shall be reassured as to the permanent possibilities of a transcendence which can at any instant transcend me on all sides. This transcendence will be no more than this: it will remain enclosed within the limits of an object.

In his most extreme position, Sartre escapes into paradox to convey the enigmatic quality, finally, of the female Other. "I try to use the Object-Other so as to make her deliver her transcendence, and precisely because she is all object she escapes me with all her transcendence." This last dialectic captures his relation to women adroitly.

Chronology

1905   Jean-Paul-Charles-Aymard Sartre born in Paris on June 21.

1907   Father dies; mother, Anne-Marie (née Schweitzer) and son reside with her parents in Meudon. He will be raised as a Catholic by his mother and grandmother.

1909   Suffers from leucoma in right eye; leaves him, as he later describes, "half-blind and wall-eyed."

1911   Family leaves Meudon and lives in Paris. Sartre teaches himself to read in grandfather's extensive library.

1914   Grandfather, disappointed with Sartre's progress in school, engages private tutors.

1916   Anne-Marie remarries and family moves to La Rochelle.

1917–19   Studies at the Lycée de la Rochelle.

1920   Moves to Paris; passes first part of baccalaureate exam.

1922   Passes second part of baccalaureate exam.

1924–28   Studies at the Ecole Normale Superieur.

1927   Writes thesis but fails exam.

1929   Places first in exam score; receives aggregation in Philosophy. Meets Simone de Beauvoir, who places second.

1931   Appointed Professor of Philosophy at the Lycée of Le Havre, where he remains for two years.

1932–34   With stipend from the Institut Français, studies in Berlin the philosophies of Edmund Husserl and Martin Heidegger.

1934–36   Professor of Philosophy at the Lycée de Le Havre; *L'Imagination* published.

1936–37   Professor of Philosophy at the Lycée de Laon; publishes "La Transcendance de l'Ego."

1937–39   Professor of Philosophy at the Lycée Pasteur. *Le Mur* published: contains "La Chambre," "L'Enfance d'un chef," "Erostrate," "Intimite," and "Le Mur." *La Nausée* published and becomes an unlikely bestseller.

1938   Hitler invades Sudetenland; Sartre torn between commitment to pacificism and anti-Nazi feelings.

1939   Drafted into the army; *Esquisse d'une théorie des émotions* published. Sartre and Albert Camus edit underground newspaper *Combat.*

1940–41   Germans invade France; Sartre taken prisoner of war June 21. Escapes March 1941; starts "Socialism and Liberty" resistance group in April. Begins teaching at the Lycée Condorcet in October and dissolves "Socialism and Liberty." Writes a play, *Bariona,* and publishes *L'Imaginaire, psychologie phénomenologique de l'imagination.*

1941–44   Professor of Philosophy at the Lycée Condorcet.

1943   *L'Etre et le Néant* and *Les Mouches* published. With Albert Camus, founds new philosophy of Existentialism.

1944   Gives up teaching to devote his time to writing. *Huis-clos* premieres in May. With de Beauvoir, escapes from Paris in July; begins publication of *Les Temps modernes.*

1945   *Huis-clos* published.

1945–49   *Les Chemins de la liberté* published: includes *L'Age de raison* (1945), *Le Sursis* (1945), *La Mort dans l'âme* (1949), and "Drôle d'amitié" (1949).

1949   *L'Imaginaire, psychologie phénomenologique de l'imagination* translated by Bernard Frechtman and published in London as *The Psychology of the Imagination.*

1946   *L'Existentialisme est un humanisme; La Putain respectueuse*; and
        Descartes 1596–1650 published. *Huis-clos* translated into English
        by Stuart Gilbert and published in London as *In Camera*.
        Lectures with de Beauvoir in Switzerland, Italy, and the
        Netherlands.

1947   *L'Homme et les choses* published. *Huis-clos* translated by Stuart
        Gilbert and published in New York as *No Exit*. *Les Jeux sont faits*
        published and produced for film; translated by Louise Varese and
        published in New York as *The Chips Are Down*. *Morts sans
        sépulture; Reflexions sur la question juive; Situations I*; and his study
        on Baudelaire published. *Le Sursis* translated by Eric Sutton and
        published in New York as *Reprieve*. *Théâtre* published, includes
        Les Mouches, Huis-clos, Morts sans sépulture, and *La Putain
        respectueuse*. Visits Sweden with de Beauvoir.

1948   *L'Engrenage; Esquisse d'une théorie des émotions; Les Mains sales*
        and *Entretiens sur la politique*, with David Rousset and Gerard
        Rosenthal, published. *Le Mur* translated by Lloyd Alexander
        and published in the United States as *The Wall and Other Stories*.
        Reflexions sur la question juive translated by George J. Becker and
        published in New York as *Anti-Semite and Jew*; translated by
        Eric de Mauny and published in London as *Portrait of the Anti-
        Semite*. *Situations II* and *Jean-Paul Sartre repond a ses detracteurs*
        published. Travels to the United States, South America, and
        Algeria with de Beauvoir.

1949   *La Mort dans l'âme* (Volume 2 of *Les Chemins de la liberté*) and
        Situations III published. *La Nausée* translated by Lloyd Alexander
        and published in London as *The Diary of Antoine Roquentin*.
        Translated by Lionel Abel, *La Putain respecteuese*, as *The Respectful
        Prostitute; Morts sans sépulture*, as *Victors; Les Mains sales*, as *Dirty
        Hands*, published in New York.

1950   Denounces Soviet labor camps. Translated by Kitty Black, *La
        Putain respecteuese* and *Morts sans sépulture*, as *Men without
        Shadows*, published in London. *La Nausée* published in the United
        States as *Nausea*. Travels to Africa and throughout Europe with
        de Beauvoir.

1951   *Le Diable et le Bon Dieu* premieres and is published. *La Mort dans
        l'âme* translated by Gerard Hopkins and published in New York
        as *Troubled Sleep*.

1952   *Les Mains sales* produced for film, directed by Fernand Rivers. *La Putain respectueuse* produced for film, directed by Charles Brabant and Marcello Pagliera. *Saint-Genêt, comédien et martyr* (Volume 1 of the *Oeuvres completes* of Jean Genêt) published. *Le Diable et le Bon Dieu* translated by Kitty Black and published in London as *Lucifer and the Lord*.

1954   *Huis-clos* produced for film in France. *Kean*, an adaptation by Sartre of the play by Alexandre Dumas, published; translated by Kitty Black and published in London.

1955   *Nekrassov* published. Travels to China with de Beauvoir.

1956   *L'Etre et le Néant* translated by Hazel Barnes and published in New York as *Being and Nothingness*. *Nekrassov* translated by Sylvia and George Leeson and published in London.

1957   *Kean* produced for film, directed by Vittorio Gassman.

1958   Participates in protest against Algerian War and holds press conference on human rights.

1960   *Critique de la raison dialectique* published; translated by Hazel Barnes and published in New York as *Search for a Method: The Sartrean Approach to the Sociology and Philosophy of History*. *Les Séquestrés d'Altona* published; translated by Sylvia and George Leeson and published in London as *Loser Wins*. Leeson translations of *Nekrassov* and *Le Diable et le Bon Dieu*, as *The Devil and the Good Lord*, published in New York. Visits Cuba with de Beauvoir, where they meet Fidel Castro and Che Guevara. Albert Camus dies in car crash January 3.

1961   *Sartre on Cuba* published in New York, a collection of articles which appeared in *France-Soir* from June 28 to July 15, 1960. Leeson translation of *Les Séquestrés d'Altona* published in New York as *The Condemned of Altona*.

1962   *Huis-clos* produced in Argentina for film, *No Exit*. *Marxisme et Existentialisme: Controverse sur la dialectique*, written with Roger Garaudy, Jean-Pierre Vigier, and J. Orcel, published. *Les Séquestrés d'Altona* produced for film, screenplay by Abby Mann, directed by Vittoria De Sica. *L'Imagination* translated by Forrest Williams and published in the United States as *The Imagination*. Invited with de Beauvoir to Moscow. Adopts Arlette Elkaim, a gifted musician.

1963   *Les Mots* published; *Saint-Genêt, comédien et martyr* translated by
        Bernard Frechtman and published in New York as *Saint Genet.*
        Critique de la raison dialectique translated by Hazel Barnes and
        published in New York as *Search for a Method: The Sartrean
        Approach to the Sociology and Philosophy of History*.

1964   Refuses Nobel Prize for Literature, declaring that it would
        undermine his influence as a writer, and to protest it being
        awarded only to Western writers and Soviet dissidents. *Situations
        IV, Portraits; Situations V, Colonialisme et neo-colonialisme;* and
        Situations VI, Problemes du Marxisme 1 published. *Les Mots*
        translated by Bernard Frechtman and published in New York as
        The Words.

1965   *Situations VII, Problemes du Marxisme 2* and *Les Troyennes*
        published. *Search for a Method: The Sartrean Approach to the
        Sociology and Philosophy of History*, edited with an introduction by
        Robert Denoon Cummings, published in New York in 1965 as
        The Philosophy of Jean-Paul Sartre.

1966   Travels to USSR and Japan with de Beauvoir.

1967   *Le Mur* produced for film, directed by Serge Roullet. Travels to
        Egypt, Israel, and Sweden with de Beauvoir.

1968   *Textes choisis*, edited by Marc Beigbeder and Gerard Deledalle,
        published in Paris. Sartre briefly arrested during Paris students'
        revolt.

1970   Sartre and de Beauvoir edit "La Cause du peuple."

1976   Awarded and accepts honorary doctorate from Hebrew
        University.

1980   Dies in Paris on April 15 after visiting Israel with his adopted
        daughter.

Contributors

HAROLD BLOOM is Sterling Professor of the Humanities at Yale University and Henry W. and Albert A. Berg Professor of English at the New York University Graduate School. He is the author of over 20 books, including *Shelley's Mythmaking* (1959), *The Visionary Company* (1961), *Blake's Apocalypse* (1963), *Yeats* (1970), *A Map of Misreading* (1975), *Kabbalah and Criticism* (1975), *Agon: Toward a Theory of Revisionism* (1982), *The American Religion* (1992), *The Western Canon* (1994), and *Omens of Millennium: The Gnosis of Angels, Dreams, and Resurrection* (1996). *The Anxiety of Influence* (1973) sets forth Professor Bloom's provocative theory of the literary relationships between the great writers and their predecessors. His most recent books include *Shakespeare: The Invention of the Human*, a 1998 National Book Award finalist, and *How to Read and Why*, which was published in 2000. In 1999, Professor Bloom received the prestigious American Academy of Arts and Letters Gold Medal for Criticism.

ROBERT CHAMPIGNY is a French critic, philosopher, and poet who taught at the University of Indiana and has written studies of both Albert Camus (*A Pagan Hero: An Interpretation of Meursault in Camus's* The Stranger, 1969) and Jean-Paul Sartre (*Stages on Sartre's Way*, 1938–52, 1959).

FREDRIC JAMESON is an influential Marxist theorist and professor at Duke University. He is the author of *Marxism and Form: Twentieth Century Dialectical Theories of Literature* (1971); *The Prison-House of Language* (1974); *Fables of Aggression: Wyndham Lewis, The Modernist as Fascist* (1979); *The Political Unconscious: Narrative as a Socially Symbolic Act* (1981); *Sartre: The Origins of a Style* (1984); *The Geopolitical Aesthetic* (1992); *The Seeds of Time* (1994); and *The Cultural Turn: Selected Writings on the Postmodern, 1983–1998* (1998).

GARY WOODLE's essays have appeared in numerous journals, including *Review of Existential Psychology and Psychiatry.*

DOMINICK LaCAPRA has served as Goldwin Smith Professor of European Intellectual History at Cornell University. He is the author of *A Preface to Sartre, Emil Durkheim: Sociologist and Philosopher, History and Criticism,* Madame Bovary *on Trial,* and *Rethinking Intellectual History: Texts, Contexts, Language.* He is co-editor, with Steven L. Kaplan, of *Modern European Intellectual History: Reappraisals and New Perspectives.*

HAZEL E. BARNES has translated many of Sartre's writings and has written extensively on the subject of existentialism. Her works include *Sartre, Sartre and Flaubert, The Literature of Possibility: A Study in Humanistic Existentialism,* and *An Existentialist Ethics.* She has served as Professor of Classics at the University of Colorado and has contributed many articles to scholarly periodicals. Her most recent book is *The Story I Tell Myself: A Venture in Existentialist Autobiography.*

S. BEYNON JOHN is the author of several books of French literary criticism, including *Saint-Exupery, Vol de Nuit and Terre des Hommes* and *Anouilh, L'Alouette and Pauvre Bitos.*

CATHERINE SAVAGE BROSMAN is a poet and literary critic. Among her works are several guides to French novelists; two collections of poems, *Passages* and *Watering* (1972); *Jean-Paul Sartre* (1983); *The Shimmering Maya and Other Essays* (1994); and *Visions of War in France: Fiction, Art, Ideology* (1999).

THOMAS B. SPADEMAN has been published in several journals, including *Philosophy Today.*

BRIAN SEITZ is the author of *The Trace of Political Representation* (1995) and co-editor of *Eating Culture* (1998).

WALTER REDFERN is the author of *Sartre, Les Séquestrés d'Altona; Feet First: Jules Valles; Michel Tournier, Le Coq de Bruyère;* and, most recently, *Jean Giono, Le Hussard sur le Toit.*

MARIE McGINN teaches in the Department of Philosophy, University of York, UK. Her critical works include *Sense and Certainty: A Dissolution of Scepticism* and *Routledge Philosophy Guidebook to Wittgenstein and the Philosophical Investigations* (1997).

ROBERT PICKERING is the author of several books of criticism on Paul Valéry and *Lautréamont/Ducasse: Image, Theme and Self-Identity*.

SHARON GHAMARI-TABRIZI teaches at Wesleyan University in Connecticut.

Bibliography

Alberes, René Marill. *Jean-Paul Sartre: Philosopher without Faith*. Translated by Wade Baskin. New York: Philosophical Library, 1961.

Arnold, A. James. "*La Nausée* Revisited," *French Review* 39, no. 2 (1965): 199–213.

Aronson, Ronald. *Sartre's Second Critique*. Chicago: University of Chicago Press, 1987.

———. *Jean-Paul Sartre: Philosophy in the World*. London: New Left Books, 1980.

Barnes, Hazel E. Introduction to *Being and Nothingness* by Jean-Paul Sartre. New York: Philosophical Library, 1956.

Bauer, George H. *Sartre and the Artist*. Chicago: University of Chicago Press, 1969.

Beauvoir, Simone de. *The Ethics of Ambiguity*. Translated by Bernard Frechtman. New York: Philosophical Library, 1948.

Bentley, Eric. *The Playwright as Thinker*. New York: Noonday Press, 1955.

Blackham, H. J. *Six Existentialist Thinkers*. New York: The Macmillan Company, 1952.

Brombert, Victor. *The Intellectual Hero: Studies in the French Novel, 1880–1955*. Philadelphia: Lippincott, 1961.

Catalano, Joseph S. *A Commentary on Jean-Paul Sartre's Being and Nothingness*. Chicago: University of Chicago Press, 1980.

———. *A Commentary on Jean-Paul Sartre's Critique of Dialectical Reason*. Chicago: University of Chicago Press, 1987.

Collins, Douglas. *Sartre as Biographer*. Cambridge, Mass.: Harvard University Press, 1980.

Collins, James. *The Existentialists: A Critical Study*. Chicago: Regnery, 1952.

Contat, Michel and Michel Rybalka. *The Writings of Jean-Paul Sartre*. Translated by Richard C. McCleary. Evanston, Ill.: Northwestern University Press, 1973.

Danto, Arthur. *Sartre*. Glasgow: Fontana, 1975.

Davies, Howard. *Sartre and "Les Temps Modernes."* Cambridge: Cambridge University Press, 1987.

Desan, Wilfrid. *The Tragic Finale: An Essay on the Philosophy of Jean-Paul Sartre*. Cambridge, Mass.: Harvard University Press, 1954.

———. *The Marxism of Jean-Paul Sartre*. Gloucester, Mass.: Peter Smith, 1974.

Douglas, Kenneth. "Sartre and the Self-Inflicted Wound," *Yale French Studies* 9 (Spring 1952): 123–31.

Fells, Joseph P. *Emotion in the Thought of Sartre.* New York: Columbia University Press, 1965.

Flynn, Thomas. *Sartre and Marxist Existentialism: The Test Case of Collective Responsibility.* Chicago: University of Chicago Press, 1984.

Frohock, W. "The Prolapsed World of Jean-Paul Sartre," *Accent* 7 (Autumn 1946): 3–13.

Goldthorpe, Rhiannon. *Sartre: Literature and Theory.* Cambridge: Cambridge University Press, 1984.

Grene, Marjorie. *Existentialism.* Chicago: University of Chicago Press, 1960.

Howells, C. "Sartre and Freud," *French Studies* 33 (1979): 152–74.

Jarrett-Kerr, Martin. "The Dramatic Philosophy of Jean-Paul Sartre," *Tulane Drama Review* 1, no. 3 (1957): 41–48.

Laing, R. D., and D. Cooper. *Reason and Violence: A Decade of Sartre's Philosophy 1950–1960.* London: Tavistock, 1964.

LaPointe, Francois H., and Claire Lapointe. *Jean-Paul Sartre and His Critics: An International Bibliography (1938–1980)*, second edition. Bowling Green, Ohio: Bowling Green University Press, 1981.

Lavers, A. "Sartre and Freud," *French Studies* 41 (1987): 298–317.

Mansur, Anthony R. *Sartre: A Philosophic Study.* London: Athlone Press, 1966.

McCall, Dorothy. *The Theater of Jean-Paul Sartre.* New York: Columbia University Press, 1969.

Mehlman, J. *A Structural Study of Autobiography: Proust, Leiris, Sartre, Levi-Strauss.* Ithaca: Cornell University Press, 1974.

Murdoch, Iris. *Sartre, Romantic Rationalist.* New Haven: Yale University Press, 1953.

Nelson, Robert J. *The Play Within a Play. The Dramatist's Conception of His Art.* New Haven: Yale University Press, 1958.

Peyre, Henri. *The Contemporary French Novel.* New York: Oxford University Press, 1955.

——. *Jean-Paul Sartre.* New York: Columbia University Press, 1968.

Rau, Catherine. "Aesthetic Views of Sartre," *Journal of Aesthetics and Art Criticism* 10 (1950): 139–47.

Salvan, Jacques Leon. *To Be or Not to Be. An Analysis of Jean-Paul Sartre's Ontology.* Detroit: Wayne State University Press, 1962.

Scriven, M. *Sartre's Existential Biographies.* London: Macmillan, 1984.

Slochower, H. "The Function of Myth in Existentialism," *Yale French Studies* 1 (Spring-Summer 1948): 42–52.

Suhl, Benjamin. *Jean-Paul Sartre: The Philosopher as Literary Critic.* New York: Columbia University Press, 1970.

Thody, Philip. *Jean-Paul Sartre: A Literary and Political Study.* New York: Macmillan, 1960.

Wahl, Jean. *A Short History of Existentialism.* Translated by F. Williams and S. Maron. New York: Philosophical Library, 1949.

Warnock, Mary. *The Philosophy of Sartre.* Paris: Presses Universitaires, 1965.

Wilcocks, Robert. *Jean-Paul Sartre: A Bibliography of International Criticism.* Edmonton: University of Alberta Press, 1975.

Wild, John D. *The Challenge of Existentialism.* Bloomington: Indiana University Press, 1959.

Acknowledgments

"Comedian and Martyr: *Le Diable et le bon Dieu*" by Robert Champigny. From *Stages on Sartre's Way, 1938–52*. © 1959 by the Indiana University Press. Reprinted by permission.

"The Rhythm of Time" by Fredric Jameson. From *Sartre: The Origins of a Style*. © 1961 by Yale University Press. Reprinted by permission.

"*Erostrate*: Sartre's Paranoid" by Gary Woodle. From *Review of Existential Psychology and Psychiatry* 13, no. 1 (1974): 30–41. © 1974 by Humanities Press, Inc. Reprinted by permission.

"Early Theoretical Studies: Art Is an Unreality" by Dominick LaCapra. From *A Preface to Sartre: A Critical Introduction to Sartre's Literary and Philosophical Writings*. © 1978 by Cornell University Press. Reprinted by permission.

"Sartre's Concept of the Self" by Hazel E. Barnes. From *Review of Existential Psychology and Psychiatry* 17, no. 1 (1980–81): 41–65. © 1981 by Humanities Press, Inc. Reprinted by permission.

"Politics and the Private Self in Sartre's *Les Chemins de la liberté*" by S. Beynon John. From *Australian Journal of French Studies* 19, no. 2 (May–August 1982): 185–203. © 1982 by Monash University. Reprinted by permission.

"Sartre's *Kean* and Self-Portrait" by Catherine Savage Brosman. From *French Review* 55, no. 7 (special issue, Summer 1982): 109–22. © 1982 by the American Association of Teachers of French. Reprinted by permission.

"Rights and the Gift in Sartre's *Notebooks for an Ethics*" by Thomas B. Spademan. From *Philosophy Today* 39, no. 4 (Winter 1995): 421–430. © 1995 by DePaul University. Reprinted by permission.

"Power and the Constitution of Sartre's Identity" by Brian Seitz. From *Philosophy Today* 40, nos. 3–4 (Fall 1996): 381–87. © 1996 by DePaul University. Reprinted by permission.

"Praxis and Parapraxis: Sartre's 'Le Mur'" by Walter Redfern. From *Romantic Review* 88, no. 1 (January 1997): 163–72. © 1997 by the Trustees of Columbia University in the City of New York. Reprinted by permission.

"The Writer and Society: An Interpretation of *Nausea*" by Marie McGinn. From *The British Journal of Aesthetics* 37, no. 2 (April 1997): 118–29. © 1997 by Oxford University Press. Reprinted by permission.

"*Témoignage* and *Engagement* in Sartre's War-Time Writings" by Robert Pickering. From *Modern Language Review* 92 (special issue, April 1997): 308–323. © 1997 by the Modern Humanities Research Association. Reprinted by permission.

"Feminine Substance in *Being and Nothingness*" by Sharon Ghamari-Tabrizi. From *American Imago* 56, no. 2 (Summer 1999): 133–44. © 1999 by The Johns Hopkins University Press. Reprinted by permission.

Index